THE GEOGRAPHY OF INTERWAR BRITAIN: THE STATE AND UNEVEN DEVELOPMENT

HISTORICAL GEOGRAPHY SERIES

Edited by R.A. Butlin, University of Loughborough

The Development of the Irish Town
Edited by R.A. Butlin

The Making of Urban Scotland
I.H. Adams

The Fur Trade of the American West, 1807–1840
David J. Wishart

The Making of the Scottish Countryside
Edited by M.L.Parry and T.R. Slater

Agriculture in France on the Eve of the Railway Age
Hugh Clout

Lord and Peasant in Nineteenth-Century Britain
Dennis R. Mills

The Origins of Open-Field Agriculture
Edited by Trevor Rowley

English Country Houses and Landed Estates
Heather A. Clemenson

The Medieval English Landscape
Edited by C.M. Cantor

An Atlas of Rural Protest in Britain 1548–1900
Edited by A. Charlesworth

Glasgow: the Making of a City
Andrew Gibb

The Shaping of Colonial Africa
A.J. Christopher

Social Formation and Symbolic Landscape
Denis E. Cosgrove

The Evolution of Middle Eastern Landscapes
J.M. Wagstaff

Gaelic Scotland: Transformation of a Culture Region
Charles W.O. Withers

THE GEOGRAPHY OF INTERWAR BRITAIN:

THE STATE AND UNEVEN DEVELOPMENT

STEPHEN V. WARD

ROUTLEDGE
LONDON AND NEW YORK

First published in 1988 by
Routledge
a division of Routledge, Chapman and Hall
11 New Fetter Lane, London EC4P 4EE

Published in the USA by
Routledge
a division of Routledge, Chapman and Hall, Inc.
29 West 35th Street, New York NY 10001

Printed in Great Britain by Billing & Sons Ltd, Worcester

British Library Cataloguing in Publication Data

Ward, Stephen V. (Stephen Victor), *1948–*
The geography of interwar : the state
and uneven development.
1. Great Britain. Regional economic
development. Policies of government,
1918–1985
I. Title
330.941'082

ISBN 0-415-00460-8

Library of Congress Cataloging-in-Publication Data

ISBN 0-415-00460-8

Typeset at Oxford University Computing Service

Contents

LIST OF TABLES

LIST OF FIGURES

LIST OF MAPS

For Maggie

PREFACE

The origins of this book go back many years. I first started researching the interwar period in 1970-1 and developed my interest in a more systematic and sustained way from about 1977 when I began a PhD thesis on interwar local government completed in 1983. Since then I have been broadening my understanding of the period, latterly with the specific objective of producing this book. In many ways though the motivations for these research interests go back much further to the experiences of my early years on the Yorkshire coalfield. Thus, although I was a product of the postwar 'baby boom', the transmitted folk memories and experiences of the interwar period made a powerful and lasting impression. This was not the trite sentimental glow of nostalgia manufactured by modern advertising to promote sales of brown bread, pale ale and malted milk. It was more an acute awareness of tensions between the energies and hopes of the period and its black disappointments.

This long predated my intellectual awareness of the academic debate between 'optimistic' and 'pessimistic' interpretations. It was rooted in family and community recollections and perceptions of the period. These showed that great social expectations had been raised during those years. Some had been fulfilled, but many had not, giving rise to a sense of disappointment and even betrayal. Later I understood that a collective desire to fulfil the unfulfilled hopes and avoid the mistakes of the interwar years was a powerful and, in many ways, a dominating social and political goal in the late 1940s and 1950s. At the time, however, it was something that I was aware of only at a personal and emotional level, expressed as parental and wider family hopes for my own life, but couched in terms that referred back to their own experiences in the 1920s and 1930s. The interwar years thus became an implicit yardstick against which my own life chances were measured.

Fundamentally then this book and the research which underpins it develop from these inherited values. It represents an attempt to explore and seek greater understanding of them and of the period which indirectly has played such an important part in my own life. However, in writing the book I have tried to relate these personal concerns to wider themes of relevance in contemporary Britain. My intention has been both to inform and stimulate. I have offered explanation and interpretations that I hope will be questioned and debated. The period has not yet received the attention it deserves, especially from geographers, and I hope this book encourages or provokes further work.

There are many debts to be acknowledged in writing this book. Some of these are implicit in what I have already said. The role of my parents and older relatives, many of them now dead, was obviously fundamental. My research interests and skills in relation to the period were greatly encouraged and developed by Gordon Cherry, who supervised both my early research attempts and my doctoral thesis. The staff of many libraries and record offices have assisted the collection of material for this work. Most important have been the Public Record Office, Kew, the Bodleian Library, Oxford, Senate House Library, London, and local libraries in Croydon, Burnley, Gateshead, Merthyr Tydfil, Wakefield, South Shields, Norwich, Liverpool and Birmingham. Oxford Polytechnic library has also yielded unexpected riches of contemporary interwar material and its inter-library loan service has produced obscure material very rapidly. There are too the personal debts. Many colleagues at Oxford and elsewhere have encouraged and assisted this endeavour with suggestions and ideas for reading. Joy Dalton has wordprocessed the whole book from my manuscript and prepared it for Lasercomp typesetting, a process that was entirely beyond me. An added bonus was her genuine interest in the content of the book which boosted my flagging enthusiasm while preparing the final draft. Rob Woodward prepared the maps and diagrams with his customary skill and efficiency. Finally of course there is the debt to my own family. My children, Thomas, Rosamund and Alice, have shown remarkable restraint on account of 'Daddy's book' (though a personal stereo has certainly helped). My wife, Maggie, has coped with the consequences of my working on it and still found it possible to encourage me. Despite other important debts this is the greatest and, in recognition of this, I dedicate the book to her.

I

Uneven Development

Introduction: The Major Themes of the Book

Essentially the story of interwar Britain is of an incomplete transition from the Victorian to the modern economy. All the pillars that had supported the pre-1914 international dominance of British capitalism experienced more or less serious erosion. Some, like the postwar attempts to restore free trade and the associated international monetary system based on the gold standard, simply collapsed in the acute world depression of the 1930s. By contrast the Empire, enlarged by the 1919 peace settlements, retained and in some ways increased its importance as an outlet for British investment and trade, even though its constituent parts were increasingly less willing to be the passive servants of British capitalism that they had once been. More generally British export performance was very poor, particularly during the 1930s. The traditional export industries (coal, cotton, iron and steel, and shipbuilding) and dependent sectors were depressed in varying degrees after the postwar boom faded in 1920. Acute unemployment was manifest in the north, Wales and Scotland (outer Britain) where these industries were concentrated. However, new sources of growth appeared (such as building, motor vehicles, electrical goods and retailing) based more on domestic consumption and contributed to a surprisingly high interwar growth rate, rather better than during the first two decades of the century. Spatially though these growth sectors were heavily concentrated in the midlands and south (inner Britain) adding considerably to the social costs of economic transition.

These variations in the performance of different sectors of a highly industrialised and geographically concentrated capitalist economy became a potent new source of unevenness between localities and regions in interwar Britain. Less dramatic in immediate effects, but of equal significance in the longer term, were the organisational shifts towards large scale firms or combinations of firms. This was associated with a shift in economic power to the south as firms sought (or were forced) into closer links with the London banking world and with government. Major decisions about the future of provincial localities were increasingly made in or around London and there were some clear signs of a parallel concentration of research and development activity developing in the south. The longer term impacts of these insidious processes were the transformation of outer Britain to a periphery dependent on decisions made either in the core area of inner Britain or, in the case of foreign companies, somewhere else entirely. By the late 1930s it is possible, though only with hindsight, to detect the beginnings of a dependent and externally controlled 'branch plant economy' in depressed outer Britain. However this element of transition was far from complete by 1939 so that branch plants did not begin to substantially fill the void left by declining industries in outer Britain until the 1960s.

These two distinct but interrelated processes of uneven development, the one dramatic and immediate in its impact, the other insidious and long term, together form one of the two major themes of this book. The other is state intervention. Another facet of the incomplete transition of the British economy was the growth of the various agencies of government. We will show how this reflected a combination of the perceived functional requirements of a capitalist system under stress, working class pressures, and in some important respects the managerial practice of a relatively autonomous state system. These forces, which varied in importance between the different areas of government activity and over time, were sufficient to project state intervention further and wider than it had previously gone in peacetime conditions. However there was no long term view of the state's role behind these expansions. Rather the growth was empirical and piecemeal. A mixed economy and semi-welfare state existed by 1939, but there was no sense of coherent management. The predominant ideologies animating state actions in the interwar period held that economic salvation would come only through market processes and that the state's role was to lubricate or at least not add to the friction within these processes and stand back. While such ideologies were rather at odds with the realities which were pressing new functions on the state, they served to inhibit the development of more positive and coherent approaches to state policy making such as developed after 1939. However, this did not prevent state intervention before 1939 having real impacts on the space economy in ways that were imperfectly foreseen and understood at the time.

Essentially we will argue that the state's actions, at least in many fields, substantially exaggerated the unevenness that arose from the varying performance of different sectors of the economy and the longer term processes that were concentrating economic power in the south. The remainder of this chapter examines key features of uneven development and dimensions of spatial unevenness while the next chapter does the same for state intervention. Chapter 3 then sketches out some alternative conceptual and interpretative frameworks within which these phenomena can be examined. Chapters 4 - 9 examine the spatial impacts of specific central and local state interventions in the fields of defence, industry, the labour market, a cross section of local government services and the embryonic field of regional policy. Finally Chapter 10 draws together the major arguments of the book as conclusions.

The pre-existing sources of spatial unevenness

The processes of uneven development in interwar Britain superimposed themselves on pre-existing patterns of spatial unevenness. Thus the face of Britain in 1919 bore the imprint of three major processes of uneven development:

1. Concentrations of capital and labour in urban areas (urban-rural unevenness).
2. Social and functional segregation processes within cities (intra-urban unevenness).
3. Local and regional economic specialisation (inter-urban and inter-regional unevenness).

These sources of spatial unevenness did not disappear, but were overlain and incorporated into the newer processes of uneven development during the interwar period. Our particular concern in this work is with the way the last of these was incorporated into the dominant spatial problem of the interwar period between the depressed and buoyant areas. Accordingly it is useful here to consider the earlier development of this dimension in some detail.

Essentially it was a manifestation of the highly concentrated nature of the 19th century space economy. Individual towns and cities became highly specialised in particular sectors of the economy, often in specific processes or markets within a wider regional specialisation (P. Hall 1976, pp395-436). This pattern of economic development has been subjected to quantitative analysis by C.H. Lee (1981), who undertook cross-sectional and intercensal factor analysis of counties over the period 1841-1911. By this means he identified four basic types of regional economy in Victorian Britain:

1. Textile oriented
2. Mining and metal-working oriented
3. Metropolitan
4. Peripheral rural

The first three were buoyant economies, while the last was the rapidly shrinking residual of a pre-industrial agrarian economy, acting principally as a labour reserve for the developing urban industrial economies of the other regions. By the interwar period the economic distinctiveness of rural areas had greatly diminished (though it left a social and cultural legacy of great potency) and the regional pattern was formulated primarily in terms of the first three of Lee's categories.

The first two were 'export' economies in the sense that they depended for growth on meeting demands outside the region. In many cases this would involve them being literally export oriented by dependence on selling to markets outside the national economy. Both, but especially the mining and metal regions, were associated with a relatively low development of service employment. In complete contrast the growth of the metropolitan economy was primarily service-related, dependent for its growth on a demand for goods and services that was generated internally by the high incomes of a proportionately large middle class population. This pattern gave particular encouragement to new industrial and service developments like motor vehicles, electrical engineering and retailing that were to be of long term significance in the British economy. As Lee observes, the south east was 'the world's first large scale consumer society' (p451).

Unfortunately there are some gaps in the analysis. Thus he takes little account of 'invisibles' or investment income. It seems virtually certain that the export of financial and other services and capital to other regions and overseas via the City of London accounted for a large part of these higher incomes in the metropolitan region. During the later nineteenth century London-based banking had achieved near-complete dominance of financial activities as large scale joint stock banks operating on a branch system became typical (J. Sykes 1926; S. Pollard 1962, pp14-18). Former provincial banks disappeared by amalgamations or saw their local connections eroded as they were drawn into the London banking system. Although Scotland retained a more independent financial sector, provincial centres accounted for only 5.2% of total bank clearings in England and Wales in 1913, though war temporarily checked this long term centralisation and in 1919 it was 7.4% (Statistical Abstract). All other indicators reinforce this picture of increasing financial centralisation in the last decades before 1914 (F. Capie and G. Rodrik Bali 1982).

In such circumstances therefore most of the huge overseas export of capital that was characteristic of the pre-1914 economy inevitably went through London at some stage. Foreign importers of British products were obliged to buy sterling in London to pay for them. Within Britain too this metropolitan concentration of banking activity was also an early stage in a wider concentration of economic power that has become more prominent since world war I. As Lee points out, the importance of the metropolitan economy, the largest subnational economy in Victorian Britain, has been rather neglected in conventional accounts which have focussed on the spectacular developments in mining and manufacturing. This is unfortunate since the expanding metropolitan economy of the nineteenth century appears to presage a pattern that became rather more important in the interwar period. Thus inner Britain was an economy based largely on internally generated consumption underpinned by overseas income that, in effect, had spread out from London. Economic power also became increasingly concentrated in or around the capital. Meanwhile, the other two types of growing regional economy of the nineteenth century declined relatively or absolutely.

The most highly developed of these more familiar types of Victorian economic regions was the cotton textile economy of Lancashire and the north west. By the early 20th century this area had a near monopoly of UK cotton textile production and exported nearly 90% of its cloth production (W. Smith 1949, pp462-99; J.A. Farnie 1979). This access to a wide market underpinned the regional specialisation itself and the remarkable degree of local, subregional divisions of production processes and related services within the industry. Thus there were geographical divisions of spinning and weaving and further subdivisions of the coarser and finer sides of each section. The capital requirements and technologies of the different sections varied, and the system of local wage 'lists' reflected and reinforced local patterns of work practice, and skill and gender differences in labour force composition (W. Lazonick 1986, pp24-7). It all added up to a regional and inter-urban geography of great complexity, spatially divided between different localities yet highly integrated within a wider region.

The major integrating elements in the region were found in the merchandising and associated financial functions of Manchester and, for raw cotton, Liverpool. These in effect welded the disparate elements of the spinning and weaving towns into a functionally cohesive and truly regional economy. A critical element in this was the high degree of regional control. This was in turn linked to the remarkable tenacity of provincial banking and associated financial activity in the north west. Nowhere in England and Wales was the spate of London based bank amalgamations of the 1890s and early twentieth century resisted more fiercely (Pollard 1962, p15). The result was that even the larger firms of the region could secure comprehensive financial services at the regional level and recruit regional financiers on to their boards without recourse to London. Scott and Griff (1984, p90) demonstrate this clearly in their study of interlocking directorships amongst the top 250 companies in 1904. Of these firms registered in the north west, 43% of interlock lines were internal to the region, the highest figure in England and Wales. Many were directly related to cotton. Clearly if this were true of the largest firms, which were most reliant on money markets for the raising of finance, it would be much more certainly the case for the far more numerous and, at that time, collectively more important smaller firms, many of them still private, often family, but essentially local businesses.

Implicit in what has already been said is that the north west was not typical. With one important exception the coal and metal regions showed a higher degree of external control of capital, principally from London, by the early twentieth century. Their internal geographies showed many features similar to the north west. On the north east coast, for example, the regional capital and mercantile centre of Newcastle presided over interrelated systems of coal production and shipment, iron and steel and shipbuilding in a spatially differentiated but apparently highly integrated regional economy (N. McCord 1979, pp111-57). However the regionally controlled banking sector was rather less developed than in Manchester or Liverpool and the main Newcastle banks were incorporated into the emergent national clearing banks around the turn of the century (Benwell CDP 1978, p32; McCord, pp147-8). By 1904 only 16% of the interlock lines of directorships of large north east registered firms were internal to the region. Significantly a very large apparently regional firm like the North Eastern Railway was registered in London.

Though Scott and Griff did not consider south Wales, its regional pattern of industrialisation was from the first more externally controlled. Cardiff was a 'coal metropolis', the hub of a network of coal and iron towns in the valleys and increasingly on the coastal plain, but it lacked the strong mercantile traditions of other provincial capitals and its banking sector was very weak (M. Daunton 1977, pp15-71).

This was in complete contrast to Scotland (which Lee would identify as several distinct regional economies), where a strong regional banking and financial sector was present from the earliest days of industrialisation (B. Lenman 1977, pp189-91). These regional banks, based increasingly on Edinburgh, were more closely interrelated with Scottish industry than their English counterparts, and although peripheralised by nineteenth century banking legislation, avoided actually being swallowed up in London-based banks. Accordingly 53% of the directorship interlock lines of large Scottish registered firms in 1904 were internal, making it the most distinctive British region measured in terms of economic control (Scott and Griff, pp87- 8).

Overall therefore the pre-1919 British space economy exhibited a high degree of intra- and inter-regional unevenness in economic specialisation. Most of the industrial regions consisted of an array of production centres more or less specialised in particular products or processes and one or more regional centres that supplied common merchandising and other producer services. Such economic functions of these regional capitals, together with their wider cultural and political roles were important in expressing the economic coherence of the region. The nature of these major urban centres was an important indicator of the extent of regional rather than external control of the regional economy. Of increasing importance during the later nineteenth century was the metropolitan economy, which was becoming the major financial centre of the national economy (and indeed of the world) and the hub of a network of national financial relationships that were visibly eroding and replacing the internal financial control of the other regional economies. The high incomes of the south east, which we have suggested were generated essentially by the exports of capital and services to other regions and overseas, underpinned a substantial internally generated service and consumer good industry within the metropolitan area, providing the visible manifestation of its growth.

However, unlike rural problems or the disposition of space within the city, these spatial manifestations of regional specialisation and spatial concentrations were not regarded as problems in the pre-1919 period. In that sense the distinctive feature of the interwar period in the historical development of the British space economy was the recognition of this larger scale spatial problem.

Major sectoral trends 1919-1939: a dual economy?

Table 1.1 indicates the major sectoral characteristics of the changing framework of production between the wars.

TABLE 1.1: GROSS DOMESTIC PRODUCT BY SECTOR 1920-37: % CONTRIBUTION

	1920	1929	1937
Agriculture etc.	6.2	3.9	3.5
Mining and Quarrying	6.6	3.6	3.5
Manufacturing	30.1	28.2	30.3
Building and Contracting	4.3	4.5	4.9
Services	45.0	55.4	57.0

Source: Feinstein, cited from Buxton and Aldcroft (eds), p15

It shows the declining importance of the primary sectors, the stagnating position of manufacturing and the very marked expansion of the tertiary sector. However these are relative shifts. The GDP growth background was an average compound growth rate of 1.8% per capita over the 1920-38 period, but with marked cyclical fluctuations (C.H. Feinstein, cited from S. Glynn and J. Oxborrow 1976, p23). This absolute growth was not sufficient to disguise the decline in the primary sector, but it did mean that manufacturing experienced absolute if not relative growth. Figures for sectoral employment trends broadly parallel the GDP figures (Glynn and Oxborrow, p92).

Historians however have tended to concentrate on the mining and manufacturing sectors. This reflects the priorities of contemporary thinking (such as the Balfour and Barlow Reports), and the related focus of statistical information (e.g. the Board of Trade's Census of Production and the insured worker data of the Ministry of Labour). Furthermore economic and social historians have traditionally tended to be more interested in mining and manufacturing industries, and there is a more considered and carefully argued view that such sectors continued to be the mainsprings of economic change measured in such ways as technical progress and productivity (Buxton, pp15-16). Thus services, despite being throughout the main sector and by 1937 bigger than all other sectors combined, have been implicitly or explicitly represented as a dependent element. Though this is changing, service activities have not in general been examined with the seriousness and depth that has been accorded to mining and manufacturing. Moreover it is the services most closely related to manufacturing, such as railways, building and public works and electricity supply, that have received most attention (D.H. Aldcroft 1968; H.W. Richardson and D.H. Aldcroft 1967; L. Hannah 1979). Accordingly the traditional mining and manufacturing focus has acquired a degree of depth that gives it great credibility in seeking to interpret the changing interwar economy, spatially and otherwise. In this brief review however we cannot readily break free of such traditional emphases, despite an awareness that current thinking in geography and economics now points towards a reassessment of the role of at least some services.

In essence the conventional wisdom about the sources of unevenness in the interwar space economy is that promulgated most comprehensively in the Barlow Report of 1940. As indicated in Table

TABLE 1.2: REGIONAL EMPLOYMENT STRUCTURES AND CHANGE 1923-37

	Employment Change		Employment Structure % Insured Workforce in:					
	Actual % Change	Predicted % Change *	16 Expanding Industries 1923	16 Expanding Industries 1937	5 Declining Industries 1923	5 Declining Industries 1937	7 Local Industries 1923	7 Local Industries 1937
London and Home Counties	+43	+40	21	25	1	1	35	38
Midlands	+28	+29	26	30	12	7	16	20
West Riding, Notts and Derbys	+15	+ 9	9	14	43	32	14	21
Mid-Scotland	+10	+18	10	13	24	15	25	33
Lancashire	+ 8	+11	9	16	36	24	19	26
Northumberland and Durham	+ 5	+ 4	6	9	49	33	16	25
Glamorgan and Monmouth	- 4	+ 1	4	6	59	41	13	22
Great Britain	+22	+22	14	19	23	14	24	30

* On basis of 1923 structure

Source: Barlow Report, p276

1.2, this argued that the primary source of unevenness was the pre-existing specialisation of particular areas in particular mining or manufacturing industries that declined or expanded in the interwar period. Thus the technical appendix from which the table is taken argued that:

> 'The divergence in the rates of growth in the various areas may be largely explained by the varying patterns of industry in 1923.' (p274)

In other words they attached only secondary importance to the varying rates of growth in the same groups of industries between areas or to actual movements of industries from one area to another. On the whole the evidence on the latter, though sketchy, supports this view (C.M. Law 1981, pp180-3). However the issue of spatial variations in rates of growth within the same industries needs further examination.

The Barlow analysis also shows that in the 'local industries' (principally services such as distribution, building, road transport and laundries), the rate of insured worker growth in London was not outstanding and was exceeded in some areas that otherwise did rather badly. However there are some important weaknesses in such a view. Thus it is at least arguable that the scale of growth is more significant than the rate and London retained a much higher proportion of jobs in such activities despite a lower growth rate. Less obviously the exclusion of a large number of services from the insured worker scheme or at least from parts of it that could be analysed on a subnational basis (notably banking and insurance) had the effect of distorting the data and, almost certainly, underestimating interregional differences (p279).

Additionally the actual data presented for the expanding and declining industrial groups do in fact suggest some significant distinctions were apparent in their growth/decline performance between areas. Thus the growing industries (which included cycles, vehicles, aircraft, brick manufacture, etc.) exhibited particularly low growth rates in south Wales and mid-Scotland, while in Lancashire they did rather well, without achieving the scale of growth apparent in London or the Midlands. Conversely the declining industries (coal, cotton, wool, iron and steel, and shipbuilding) declined rather less rapidly in the West Riding and the east midlands, where they were very important in the pre-existing industrial structure, than in south Wales, Scotland or the north east coast.

Thus while the pre-existing industrial structure seems to be important in distinguishing London and the home counties and, to a lesser extent, the midlands from the rest, there were more subtle distinctions apparent elsewhere, suggesting that other factors were also involved. In part local and regional multiplier effects operated, limiting the scale (if not always the rate) of expansion in 'local' and probably other industries in areas that were performing badly overall.

There were also some spatial variations in the productivity improvements apparent in some older declining industries that particularly affected the demand for labour in some areas. The Scottish and Northumberland coal industries, for example, displayed relatively high mechanisation and productivity (Buxton 1979b, pp66-7). However, perhaps the most potent factor, widely acknowledged both during the period and subsequently, was the extent of export dependence (see e.g. W. Smith, pp689-92).

Export dependence was a factor that immediately separated the declining from the major expanding industries. Thus the cotton industry was exporting over 80% of total cloth output in the early 1920s, when it accounted for about a quarter of the total value of British exports. At the same time about 50% of woollen and worsted cloth was exported, representing over 7% of total exports (M.P. Fogarty 1945, p217,p249; Glynn and Oxborrow, p77). Conversely 10% of vehicle output was exported, representing with aircraft less than 2% of total exports in the same period (M. Miller and R.A. Church 1979, p195). Other rapidly expanding industries such as building materials were not significant exporters, while all the declining industries had relied on exporting a substantial proportion of output.

Export dependence was also important in explaining spatial variations in the performance of the same declining industries. In coal particularly there was a clear distinction between the export fields of south Wales, coastal Scotland, the north east coast and Cumberland, and the remaining home coalfields of Yorkshire, the Midlands, Lancashire and various small southern fields. Thus in 1913 the export fields had exported some 56% of output (61% in south Wales), which had fallen to 38% in 1937. Conversely the home fields had exported 13% in 1913 and only 7% in 1937. This was directly linked to the extent of their decline so that whereas the export fields produced 25% less in 1937 compared with 1913, the fall was only 9% in the home fields (W. Smith, p304). There were similar if less marked variations in the performance of the iron and steel industry with a greater decline in the coastal more export oriented areas compared to those in the most domestic market oriented east midlands (see Chapter 5). Shipbuilding also showed a rather less severe decline in the south where naval shipbuilding and repairing in the Royal Dockyards dominated compared to the north and Scotland (see Chapter 4).

Elaborating on this distinction between the export or non-export dependence of the basic industries in different parts of the country,

Glynn and Booth (1983) have advanced the notion of a two sector dual economy. This comprised two separate parts each showing different dynamics and needing different macro-economic strategies to function effectively. Spatially it was reproduced in the divide between a declining export dependent outer Britain in the north, Scotland and Wales and an expanding domestic consumption dependent inner Britain in the south and midlands.

Despite differences in the use of the term export, this suggested model of the interwar space economy has clear links with Lee's analysis referred to above, though Glynn and Booth do not refer directly to it. However on the basis of the two it is possible to suggest a simple scheme of transformation in the British space economy. Thus it can be argued that inner Britain represented the continued expansion of the already rapidly growing pre-1914 metropolitan mass consumption economy, embracing those mining and manufacturing regions that were least export (in the sense of ex- national export) dependent, and the surrounding peripheral rural areas of east Anglia and the south west. Conversely outer Britain represented those mining and manufacturing regions that were national export dependent, together with the peripheral rural areas of the north, Wales and Scotland.

Such a simple model of the interwar space economy has much to commend it and certainly captures some of the key elements producing change. In general the interpretation is consistent with analysis based on most statistical sources, such as the Board of Trade's Census of Production, focussing on output (see especially PEP 1939, p44), census data (see Law, pp83-95) and Ministry of Labour insured worker data. Thus an analysis of change 1923-37 based on comprehensive regional divisions, rather than the narrow industrial districts used by the Barlow Commission shows a clear distinction in growth performance that corresponds closely with the postulated inner-outer Britain divide.

TABLE 1.3: % INCREASE IN INSURED WORKERS BY REGION 1923-37

	Insured Workers	Insured Workers in employment
London	39	45
South East	54	59
South West	34	40
Midlands	27	32
North East	18	14
North West	9	12
North	3	2
Scotland	12	12
Wales	2	-14
Great Britain	22	24

Source: Fogarty 1945, p13

Regional coverage is shown on Map 1.3

However there is a problem in drawing a clear distinction and most of these analyses suggest slightly different areas. The east midlands and Yorkshire are areas of particular ambiguity. Thus Table 1.2 puts Nottingham and Derby with Yorkshire, while Table 1.3, based on standard Ministry of Labour regional divisions, separates them, but puts Yorkshire with Lincolnshire in the north eastern division. The pre- 1935 Census of Production (and therefore all trend series) includes the east midlands with Humberside, east Anglia, the south west, much of the outer south east, the rural west midlands and Cumbria in a rather unhelpful 'rest of England' category.

Nor are such problems merely statistical. A literal 'dual economy' demarcation based on basic sector export dependence would probably have to draw a distinction between the export dependent west Yorkshire woollen area and its declining coal industry and the somewhat less export dependent south Yorkshire coal and metal district. However on many indicators, notably unemployment, south Yorkshire was weaker than west Yorkshire. At the local level the pattern becomes even more complex. Thus although it continued to speak for the cotton industry, Manchester's important service functions and engineering industries gave it a more favourable balance of activity that meant its economy had more in common with parts of inner Britain than most of the rest of the north west (Fogarty, pp229-32). Edinburgh and east central Scotland also avoided many of the problems that afflicted the Glasgow region (pp142-65). To a lesser extent this was true of other big regional cities like Leeds, Newcastle and Cardiff. And a few smaller districts in outer Britain that had local balances of employment particularly favourable for growth, notably Blackpool, seemed in many ways more like inner Britain.

Overall though these are qualifications rather than fundamental criticisms of the two sector dual space economy model. It remains a powerful simplifying device for making sense of the interwar period. However we have not yet considered its most serious weakness, which is the implicit idea of a mutual sectoral and spatial autonomy in responding to changing markets that underpins the idea of two distinct or separate subnational economies. Put more simply, it is a model that contains no sense of economic power.

Major organisational trends: a core-periphery model?

The organisational shifts in the interwar economy were less immediately obvious but in several ways were more important than sectoral developments. The period was characterised by the growing significance of large-scale firms, combines and trade organisations of all kinds. In 1924 J.M. Keynes wrote of 'the end of laissez-faire' as more such firms or combinations appeared in all sectors of the economy, in many cases occupying semi-monopolistic positions (cited from Pollard 1962, p163). Hannah has attempted to show the importance of this for manufacturing, and estimates that the share of the 100 largest firms in net output rose from 15% in 1907 to 17% in 1919, 26% in 1930 and then declined slightly to 23% before resuming an upward course again from the 1950s (1983, p180). Such trends were even more apparent for railways when just four main companies replaced the 120 pre-existing in a government encouraged regrouping in 1923 (Aldcroft 1968, pp39-47). Banking also continued its already rather dramatic concentration, and by 1938 the 'big five' banks accounted for over 78% of UK deposits, capital and reserves (Pollard 1962, p231). Retailing too showed the same basic trends though small enterprises remained typical. However the market share of small scale retailing (i.e. not co-operative societies, department stores or multiples with less than ten outlets) declined from about four fifths in 1920 to just under two thirds by 1939 (J.B. Jeffreys 1954, p73; midpoints of estimates).

The concentration of a bigger share of output into a decreasing number of firms had some important spatial characteristics. It increasingly tended to involve multi-locational operations, particularly as firms grew by incorporating other firms. However a tendency for large firms to spawn entirely new branch establishments was already well developed within banking and retailing during the 1920s (e.g. G. Rees 1969, pp55-88) and became more apparent for manufacturing during the later 1930s, especially for firms involved in rearmament (see Chapter 4). Inevitably too some form of hierarchical division would tend to appear in the activities of large multi-locational firms. We should not exaggerate this, and the experience of rearmament showed that the largest firms in the country still had much to learn about the management of a spatially divided production process.

More common though was a growing centralisation of top management activity at one site. Increasingly the headquarters of larger firms were becoming concentrated in London and the south east. In 1919 one third of the 50 largest manufacturing firms had their headquarters there; by 1930 this had risen to over a half (Law, p159). One of the most visible symbols of this concentration of capital was the appearance of impressive new headquarters offices of the new giants such as ICI, Unilever, Shell-Mex and Vickers Armstrong in central London. However, many other firms' headquarters, particularly those of the buoyant consumer industries, were still attached to factories in the expanding suburbs of the metropolis (G. Weightman and S. Humphries 1984, pp38-69).

In the consumer industries, the attractiveness of London as a headquarters location for large scale multi-locational firms derived partly from its importance as by far the largest domestic market. However more generally important to all large firms was its position as a national and international communications centre; the associated access to information of all kinds; and the proximity to government and major financial services (Law, pp159-61). The exact importance of each of these would vary. Thus access to government would be particularly important for large firms like Vickers-Armstrong who were heavily dependent on government contracts. Conversely proximity to commodity markets and international business information would be more important to companies like Imperial

Tobacco or Unilever. However access to major banking and financial services seems to have been important for all large firms. Thus while smaller firms could rely on private finance, local bank managers and flotations on provincial stock markets (PEP 1939, pp75-6), larger firms were inevitably drawn into close and continuing relationships with the main money markets of the capital. In that sense the centralisation of banking and related activity on London was itself a spur to the parallel centralisation of business headquarters.

As we noted earlier, banking was already heavily concentrated in London by 1914, with Scotland and south Lancashire the two areas where some regional autonomy remained. The 1920s and 1930s witnessed further erosion of the latter's position as mergers created just two Lancashire banks (Martin's and the District) that, despite their regional base, were part of the London Banks Clearing House, perhaps the most critical element of London's banking supremacy (Pollard, p231; Sykes). North of the border the independence of banking was also compromised as English clearing banks secured participations in or controls of several Scottish banks (Scott and Griff, p88).

These trends were directly associated with a decline of regional control of large scale capital. Thus by 1938 there were only 18 of the top 250 firms registered in Scotland compared to 27 in 1904, and the percentage of internal Scottish directorship interlocks within these was only 20%, compared to 53% in 1904 (Scott and Griff, p89). The number of north west company registrations declined less from 24 to 19 over the same period, but only 14% of interlock lines were now internal (compared to 43% in 1904). On the north east coast, where regionalisation of large firm control was already low by 1904, it fell still further so that by 1938 just 6% of the interlock lines within the five regionally registered large firms were internal to the region.

How far though were these trends counteracted by the activities of the still important small-medium sized firms sector? Performance of large firms has rather dominated historical discussion, and while the trend to concentration in output is unquestionable, it is capable of bearing several interpretations about the role of smaller firms. Thus they could be seen simply as a large residual whose operations were increasingly dependent on the big battalions of large scale capital. Alternatively they could be seen as the basis of future development. In a pioneering study, Foreman-Peck (1985) has tried to interpret the patterns and assess the significance of new (predominantly small) firm formation in the interwar economy. On the basis of a sample investigation of the register of business names, he found (pp412-6) that

London and the south east accounted for a wholly disproportionate amount of all new firms formed (over 55% of his sample) particularly in the service sector (over 60%), within which most new firms were formed. The worst regional performances were in Wales and the north, though there were no clear differences between the 'outer' part of inner Britain and the 'inner' part of outer Britain. Generally he interprets the geography of new firm formation primarily in terms of consumer demand, arguing that it was a dependent rather than a causal element of uneven development between the wars, and made little contribution to the alleviation of unemployment. Overall he finds little evidence that new firm formation was providing the 'seedcorn' for future development and concludes rather that it represented the 'chaff' of an economy operating suboptimally. On the whole therefore his interpretation does not challenge the big firm concentration perspective.

However, viewed from an international standpoint, one of the most striking features of the interwar British economy was the relatively slow growth of the very large firm compared particularly to the USA and Germany. Accordingly the structure of British capital remained rather old fashioned and fragmented, perpetuating the separateness of banking and industrial capital rather than integrating into a large scale finance capital meso-sector. Spatially this point has been developed by Heim (1983) who links the underdevelopment of large scale enterprise especially in the newer manufacturing industries to the regional economic problem. Thus she argues that if large scale firms had been more advanced they would have spawned rather more new branch plants than they did and would have located these in outer Britain to take advantage of their labour reserves. Such a view is obviously open to some criticism in that there is no real evidence of problems of labour shortages in the buoyant industries of inner Britain until the rearmament-fuelled boom of the late 1930s, when some outer Britain branch plant developments were beginning to be evident, especially in war production (see Chapter 4). But she does recognise that ultimately the gap left by the declining industries of outer Britain was filled by the branch activities of large scale firms, and raises important questions about why this did not occur earlier.

This general framework of discussion has implicitly rested on a developing core-periphery model of the interwar economy. The general model is well known and has been much utilised as an explanatory device for the postwar geography of Britain. It rests on the notion of London and the south east as a core area within which economic power is concentrated, generating a relatively favoured regional economy. This core is gradually transformed through an outer core in the south west and the midlands to a periphery in outer Britain dependent on external decision making and control, this reproducing itself in the various characteristics of a less favoured region. Much of this discussion has rested on the spatial clustering of company headquarters and research and development operations - the power to initiate and originate - and of government within the core area around London, while the peripheral regions are characterised by lower level branch or dependent activities controlled by decisions made in the core area.

Such a 'mature' core-periphery patterning is largely a post-1945 and more especially a post-1960 phenomenon. In the interwar period we can clearly identify some of the preconditions of this pattern in financial concentration, the appearance of a significant large scale firm sector headquartered increasingly in London and growth in central state powers and responsibilities. As we will see in Chapter 4, the organisation of a spatially divided war production process in the late 1930s gave the first glimpses of a core-peripheral pattern that was later to become familiar. But, following Heim, we might consider the spatial transformation of the interwar period largely in terms of a decline of the highly regionalised Victorian space economy, and its incomplete transition to a nationally based twentieth century economy in which the fundamental distinctions were based not on sector but on power and control. In the longer term the two-sector dual economy that was apparent in the interwar period was changing into a single core-periphery economy. This incomplete transition reproduced itself across a wide range of economic and social indicators, some of which have become synonymous with the spatial problems of the interwar period.

Dimensions of unevenness

One of the main criteria used to delineate interwar unevenness was spatial variation in the incidence of unemployment. This was measured monthly from 1923 by reference to the unemployment insurance scheme introduced in 1920. At the outset this excluded nearly 40% of workers and, although subsequently extended, still excluded large numbers of workers by 1939, particularly in service and higher paid employment (Glynn and Oxborrow, p147). Since uninsured groups were less susceptible to unemployment than insured workers, these unemployment data persistently overestimated the rate of unemployment while underestimating its absolute proportions.

A much more accurate figure is available for the 1931 Census, which suggests a persistent exaggeration of the national unemployment rate by insured worker data of about 30% (C.H. Feinstein, cited from A.E. Booth and S. Glynn 1975, p632). However the correction of regional and local insured unemployment figures is much more difficult because of spatial variations in the proportions of insured to uninsured workers. Generally the buoyant regions had more of the latter so that paradoxically insured worker data probably underestimates the relative difference between inner and outer Britain. But despite these problems, insured worker data is available consistently from 1923, unlike Census data which is only available for a single day. For this reason we use insured worker data to prepare Maps 1.1 to 1.3.

Regional Boundaries As Defined By Ministry of Labour
1. 1923-1936 Adminstrative Divisions

South-Eastern Bedfordshire, Buckinghamshire, Cambridgeshire, Essex, Hertfordshire, London, Kent, Middlesex, Norfolk, Suffolk, Surrey and Sussex. For certain purposes, Greater London statistics were extracted separately. This area was defined as *London Division* and corresponded closely with the City and Metropolitan Police District.

South-Western Berkshire, Cornwall, Devon, Dorset, Gloucestershire, Hampshire, Oxfordshire, Somerset and Wiltshire.

Midlands Derbyshire (except Glossop and New Mills), Herefordshire, Huntingdonshire, Leicestershire, Northamptonshire, Nottinghamshire, Rutland, Shropshire, Staffordshire, Warwickshire, Worcestershire, Soke of Peterborough, Stamford district of Lincolnshire.

North-Eastern Durham, Lincolnshire (except the Stamford district), Northumberland (except the Berwick district) and Yorkshire.

North-Western Cheshire, Cumberland, Lancashire, Westmoreland, and the Glossop and New Mills districts of Derbyshire.

Scotland Scotland and the Berwick district.

Wales Wales and Monmouthshire.

2. Changes 1936-7

A new *Northern Division* was formed consisting of Northumberland (except Berwick), Durham and the Cleveland district of Yorkshire (previously part of the North-Eastern division) and Cumberland and Westmoreland (previously part of the North-Western division).

London became a separate division, and Buxton was added to the North-Western division.

South-Eastern division was enlarged by the addition of most of Berkshire (previously in South-Western division), the Soke of Peterborough and Huntingdonshire (previously in the Midlands division). The Stamford district of Lincolnshire was transferred from the Midlands to the North-Eastern division.

MAP 1.1

UNEMPLOYMENT 1923, 1927 AND 1932 : BY ADMINISTRATIVE DIVISION

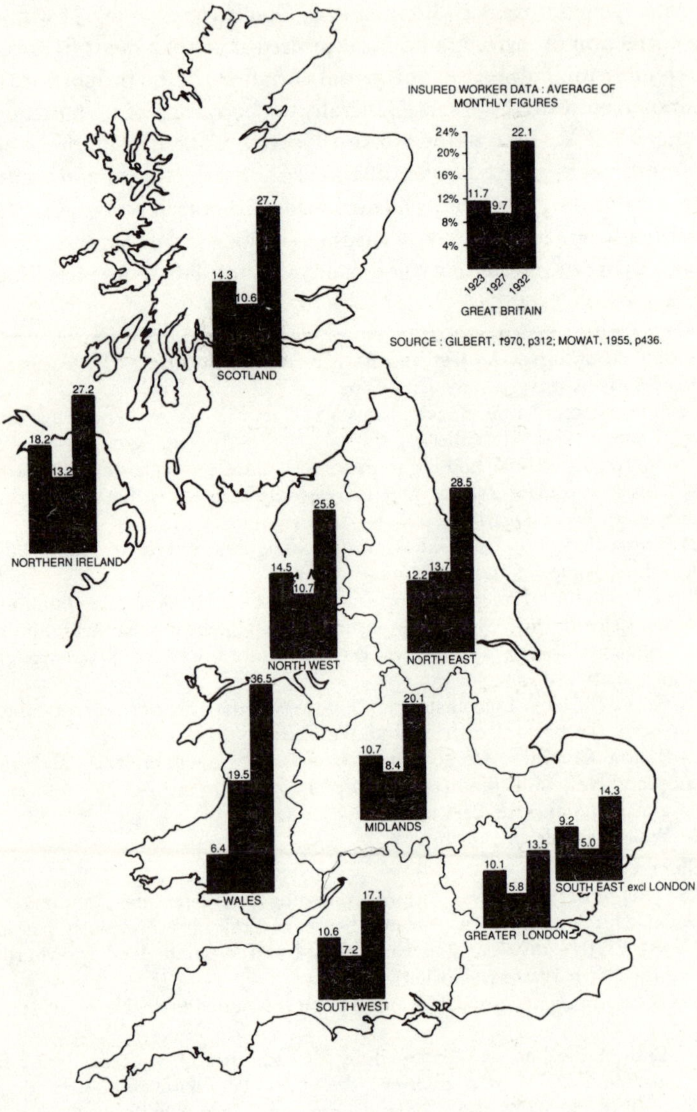

MAP 1.2

UNEMPLOYMENT 1932 : BY COUNTIES

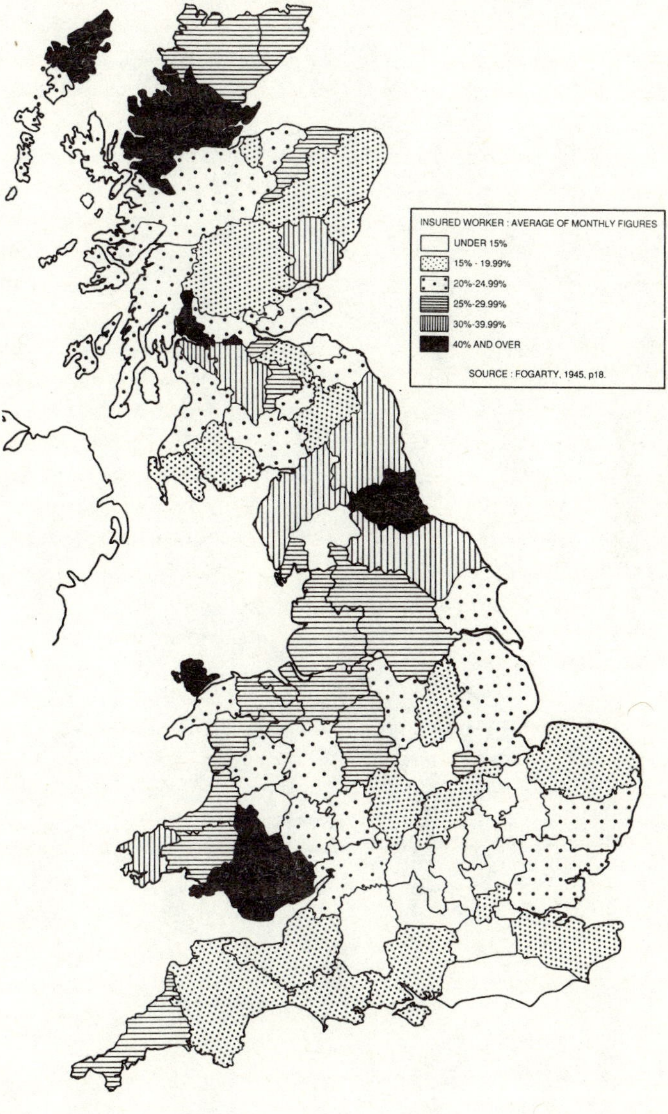

MAP 1.3

UNEMPLOYMENT 1937 : BY ADMINISTRATIVE DIVISION

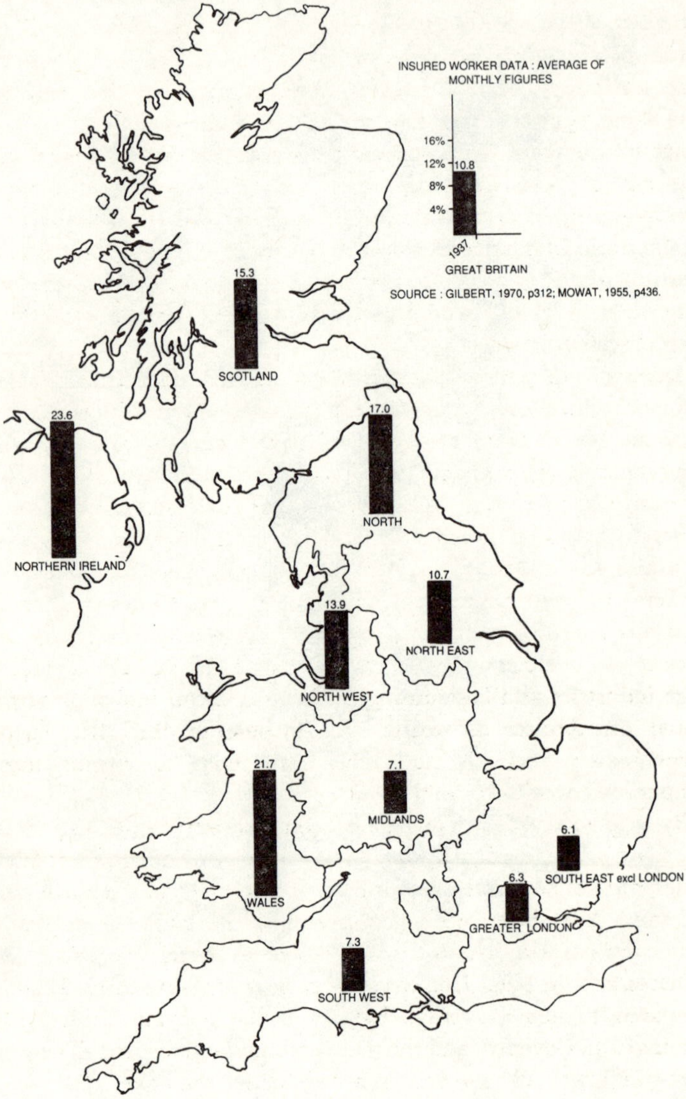

The maps show a pattern that has been remarkably consistent over much of the twentieth century, certainly since the mid-1920s, and perhaps earlier (H. Southall 1986). Thus by 1925, when the south Wales coal economy collapsed, a simple regional pattern between an outer Britain with above average unemployment and an inner Britain with below average unemployment had become apparent. These spatial distinctions remained throughout the rest of the period. As Map 1.2 shows there was more overlap in experience than regional data alone suggests. Thus the east and west Ridings of Yorkshire had more in common with peripheral inner Britain counties like Staffordshire and Cornwall than with the acute and chronic unemployment of south Wales, the north east coast, the worst areas of Scotland and Cumberland. Generally though the regions, especially as constituted in 1937, when the rather misleading north eastern division was redefined, give a good impression of the subregional realities of unemployment.

In essence they show that depression affected outer Britain earlier and more severely, and that recovery came later than in inner Britain. If it is meaningful to refer to 'key facts' of interwar geography then this observation is one of them. It was also an important source of other dimensions of unevenness. Map 1.4 shows the geography of purchasing power in 1936 as published in a marketing survey of the following year (C. Chisholm [ed] 1937, pp47-9). Calculated on the basis of insured workers employed, estimates of family income over £5 per week, more especially over £10 per week, together with numbers of motor car licences and telephone subscribers, with some adjustments for higher wage industries and commuting, it forms a useful indicator of the spatial distribution of wealth and income in the later 1930s. Unfortunately there is no earlier equivalent to permit trend comparisons over the period.

By 1936 however the interregional contrasts were reasonably clear. The south as a whole displayed above average purchasing power while Wales, most of Scotland, the north east coast, much of the north west and south Yorkshire were below average. The midlands displayed some contrasts with average to below average indices typical in the Potteries, and the Black Country, and parts of the north east midlands, compared to above average indices in the buoyant centres like Birmingham, Coventry and the main east midlands centres. The west Yorkshire towns also showed up a little better than average.

More widely the local basis of the data also highlights some significant geographical contrasts. Thus it is notable that many

MAP 1.4

PURCHASING POWER INDEX 1936

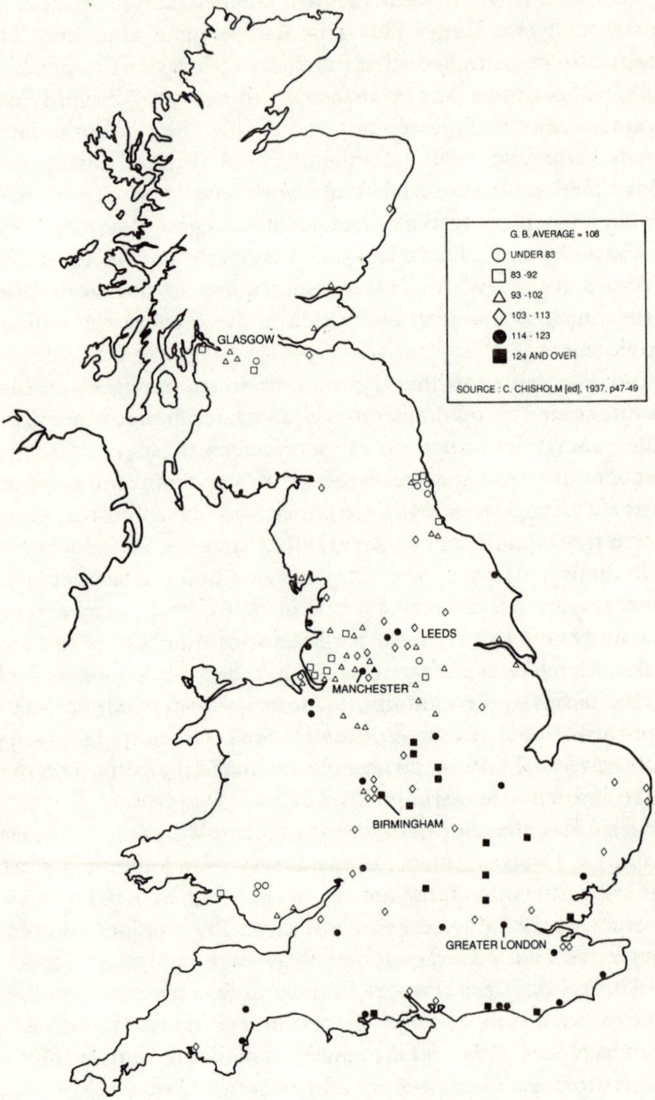

regional centres had higher purchasing power indices than the nearby smaller towns. Manchester for example with an index of 120 compared favourably with Bolton (101), Salford (98), Oldham (95) and Blackburn (89). Similarly Newcastle with 100 can be compared with Tynemouth (83), Sunderland and South Shields (both 79) and Gateshead (77). There were some exceptions to this, most notably Liverpool (with neighbouring Bootle on 90) compared to Birkenhead (95) and Southport (123) in the north. However this pattern was more typical of the larger centres of the south. Thus Southampton and Bristol (both 109) were only average and Greater London, though above average, had a surprisingly low index, below Bradford and Manchester, for example.

These observations hint at some of the varied sources of this pattern of disposable income. In many respects it was a mirror image of the geography of poverty, so that it reflects the higher unemployment of towns in outer Britain, especially in mining and heavy industrial areas. It also reflects the earnings of those in work, some impression of which may be gained from sectoral data. Thus in October 1938 average adult male weekly earnings in motor vehicles, cycles and aircraft manufacture, covering important growth industries concentrated in inner Britain were £4.16, compared to £2.54 for cotton textiles (Fogarty, p11). Average earnings for adult female textile workers, who were very important in the industry, were about a third lower again (Department of Employment and Productivity 1971, p96). Thus the low indices of the Lancashire cotton towns reflected low earnings as well as unemployment. There were also other sources of family poverty related to family size, old age, sickness, absence of a wage earner or dependence on casual employment (B.S. Rowntree 1941). These latter problems were particularly pronounced in the big ports as highlighted in the important social surveys of London, Liverpool, Southampton and Bristol in the late 1920s and 1930s (e.g. H. Tout 1938, especially pp37-46). This was clearly an important element underpinning the regional patterns noted above.

Another key dimension of uneveness was population change. Overall data has been shown in many ways (e.g. Barlow Report, p22; M. Abrams 1945, p22; Law, p58) but it always tends to show the same basic spatial features. In the most comprehensive spatial demarcation, based on Law, who uses regional definitions that readily allow comparisons with later periods and shown in Table 1.4, we see very marked growth in the midlands and south east. By contrast the more rural inner Britain regions, east Anglia and the south west, rather

TABLE 1.4: REGIONAL POPULATION AND MIGRATIONAL CHANGE 1921-39

	% Population Change 1921-39	Total Migrational Change (000s) 1921-31	1931-9
INNER BRITAIN:			
South East	+18.6	+615	+748
West Midlands	+13.8	- 76	+100
East Midlands	+13.1	- 20	+ 32
South West	+ 5.7	+ 27	+ 47
East Anglia	+ 3.1	- 21	+ 9
OUTER BRITAIN:			
Yorkshire E and W	+ 6.2	- 58	- 41
North West	+ 3.6	-154	- 59
Scotland	+ 2.7	-392	- 32
Northern	- 0.1	-231	-149
Wales	- 0.7	-259	-182
(N. Ireland)	+ 2.9	- 62	- 41

Source: Law, p58, p60

lower, below average, growth is apparent. This overlapped with the experience of parts of outer Britain, especially the east and west Ridings of Yorkshire and, to a more limited extent, the north west. However the most peripheral parts of outer Britain, Scotland, the northern region and Wales, performed worst and the last two experienced real declines.

The most active element of interwar spatial population change was migration, also shown on Table 1.4. The interwar period marks a turning point in the history of British migrational patterns. Thus the outward flow to the Empire had dried up by the 1930s and was replaced by an inward flow of returned emigrants, immigrants from Ireland and refugees from eastern Europe (J. Stevenson 1977, pp28-9). Internally the dominant rural-urban flow of the nineteenth century was being overlain by a dominant flow from relatively declining to relatively expanding regions. By the 1930s therefore the inner-outer Britain divide was clearly apparent in migrational patterns. At the subregional level migrational patterns were more complex and the aggregate outward flow of population from all the major urban areas into suburban areas was invariably the most readily apparent trend especially, but not exclusively, in the buoyant regions (Barlow Report, pp160-4; Bournville Village Trust 1941, pp41-50). Rarely however did these spill over regional boundaries so that they are not apparent in regional migrational flows.

Fertility was less obviously related to spatial economic change than migration and has attracted less academic interest until recently. Generally the interwar period saw a continuation of the long term trend of birth rate decline. Thus the average number of children born to parents married in the 1860s was 6.16. By 1900-9 the number had fallen to 3.30, by 1925-9 to 2.11 and by 1930-4 to 2.07 (D. Gittins 1982, p210). However there were marked spatial variations in the extent of this decline. Table 1.5 shows the ten 'key' areas used by Gittins.

TABLE 1.5: MARITAL FERTILITY RATES FOR TEN 'KEY' AREAS 1911 AND 1931

	1911 (%)	1931 (%)	Decrease (%)
Hampstead	117	76	35.0
Burnley	151	80	46.0
Middlesex	157	96	38.9
Montgomeryshire	175	131	27.7
Lincolnshire	187	121	35.0
Edmonton	193	111	45.0
Stoke on Trent	203	119	43.0
Gateshead	204	135	33.5
Bethnal Green	221	120	45.7
Rhondda	235	109	53.7
England and Wales	167	103	

Source: Gittins, p64

Taken in conjunction with the rest of her work it shows that traditional differentials in fertility between working and middle class areas generally narrowed but to a widely varying extent. Thus in textile, especially cotton, districts working class fertility fell to almost middle class levels. There were large falls in coalfield areas, especially in south Wales, though these shifts occurred less rapidly in Durham, Yorkshire and Scotland where fertility remained much higher (pp 109-16). The smallest declines occurred in the heavy industrial areas associated with shipbuilding and related industries, especially on the north east coast and in Scotland, paralleling coalfield developments in such areas (pp121-3). Fertility in some port areas, especially Merseyside, remained high.

The relationships between fertility changes and uneven economic development are not straightforward. Gittins attributes some importance to high (male) unemployment in areas like south Wales, but attaches greater significance to the changing roles of women within society. Thus the important place of women in the labour force in textile districts is contrasted with their relative unimportance in heavy industrial areas. However she gives little attention to religious factors, which were clearly important in maintaining high fertility in areas with large Catholic populations such as Merseyside, parts of Scotland and the north east coast. Whatever the exact sources of this continuing high fertility though, it remained a feature of much of outer Britain, except the textile areas, and, to a lesser extent, south Wales.

Mortality rates were also higher in these same areas, though we must say at once that the generally high birth rates of many declining towns in outer Britain were cancelled out to produce a falling population by migration rather than high death rates. Only in a few areas, mainly in the Lancashire textile districts, where low birth rates were reproducing a progressively ageing population structure, was any natural decrease experienced, and then only in the late 1930s. Having said this it must be stressed that the general issue of mortality and health and their relationship to the pattern of economic change were the subject of many studies (reviewed in Stevenson, pp123-72).

TABLE 1.6: INFANT MORTALITY AND UNEMPLOYMENT 1931

	Deaths Under 1 Year per 1000 Live Births	% Unemployment 1931 Census
Wigan	103	18.9
Liverpool	94	19.6
St Helens	88	16.1
England and Wales Average	62	11.5
Brighton	54	8.1
Oxford	44	4.7
Bath	39	8.1

Sources: J. McNally cited from Stevenson, p143
1931 Census, Occupations, 1934, Table 16

An important debate developed amongst medical officers and social commentators about how far unemployment produced higher mortality (e.g. G.C.M. M'Gonigle and J. Kirby 1936). On specific indicators, such as infant mortality, areas of high unemployment consistently did worse than other areas, particularly areas of low unemployment, as Table 1.6, adapted from McNally's 1935 study, Public Ill-Health, suggests.

Temporal evidence indicated associated variation, especially for neo-natal mortality (M. Mitchell 1985, pp108-12). Standardised death rates also showed the same trends and high and prolonged unemployment was associated with mortality rates some 25-50% above average by the late 1930s (Glynn and Oxborrow, p201). Broadly average rates were experienced in the more heavily urbanised areas with below average unemployment (e.g. London and Birmingham), while the lowest mortality was found in the suburban smaller towns and less remote rural areas with low unemployment (e.g. the outer south east). However many aspects of these distinctions predated the interwar period and have persisted subsequently (e.g. C.A. Moser and W. Scott 1961, pp36-8). The precise role of unemployment as an influence on mortality remains very difficult to establish, and historians have continued the contemporary debate of the 1930s. However it is fair to say that unemployment was one of several sources of economic disadvantage that delayed improvements in mortality in areas that were badly affected (C. Webster 1982; Mitchell).

The last dimension of unevenness we consider here is housing. Map 1.5 shows something of interwar housing conditions, showing a marked regional concentration of overcrowding in the northern part of Britain, especially Scotland and the north east coast. Only London and Plymouth in the south recorded anything like northern overcrowding levels. The remainder of the south and the east midlands had low overcrowding. However this was not a simple inner-outer Britain divide. Thus south Wales was more like southern than northern England or Scotland. Lancashire's cotton districts were again exceptional. The west midlands were an intermediate zone with towns like Stoke, West Bromwich and Dudley more 'northern' and Coventry more 'southern'.

The sources of such differences were complex. Essentially they reflected an interaction of traditional regional and local patterns of housing provision and consumption with unevenly declining fertility and the changing interwar space economy (M. Daunton 1983, pp38-9;

MAP 1.5

OVERCROWDING 1931

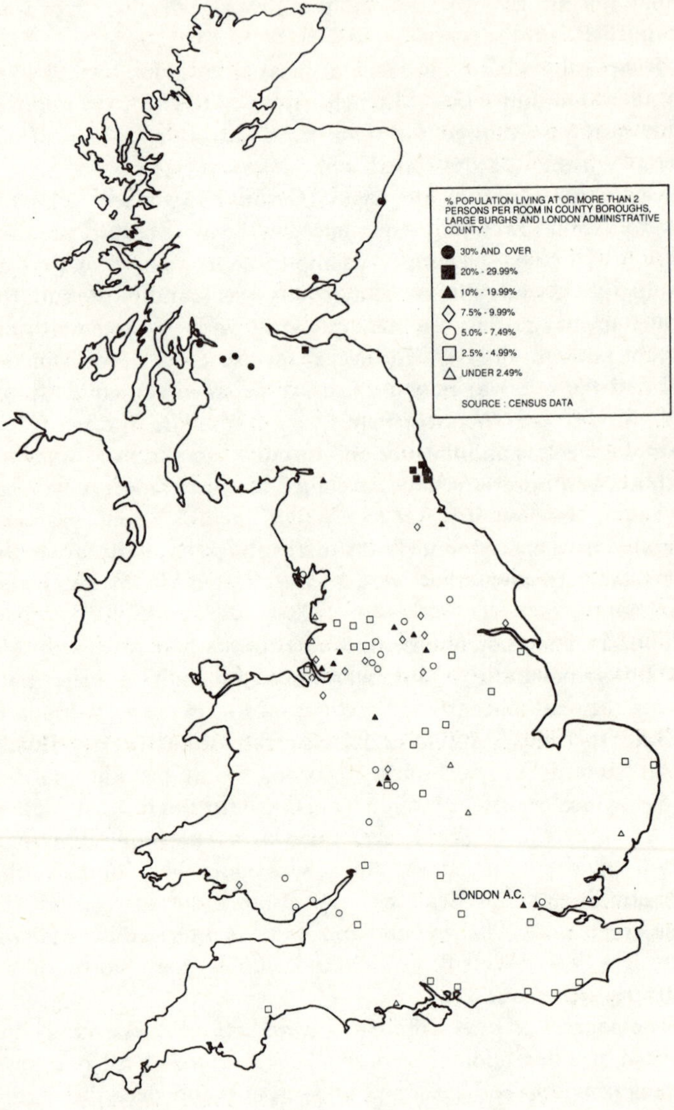

and Chapter 8). Overall the interwar period saw an unprecedented spatial convergence of housing standards under the influence of the new mass media, central state policy reinforced by subsidy provision, and the increasingly national organisation of the housebuilding industry (e.g. A.A. Jackson 1973; CDP 1978, pp46-63). In some areas, particularly in Scotland, traditional housing expectations were incorporated into the new standards (R. Smith 1974, pp217-23). More importantly though the effect of uneven economic development was to limit the extent to which traditionally disadvantaged areas were able to move towards the new higher standards (Ministry of Health Overcrowding Survey 1936; see also Chapters 7-8).

Generally the interwar period was characterised by what historically was a very high rate of housebuilding. Thus the percentage addition to the housing stock in 1921-31 was 17.8% and in 1931-9 it was 25.0%, both above anything previously recorded (Glynn and Oxborrow, p227). In all 4,309,425 dwellings were built in Britain between January 1919 and April 1939 of which 30.8% were built by local authorities, 11% by private enterprise with state subsidies and 58.3% by private enterprise alone (Barlow Report, p67).

Spatially though the absolute and relative importance of the different categories varied. In Chapters 7-8 we will show how and why municipal housebuilding varied. Private housebuilding, especially unsubsidised varied even more dramatically, particularly in the first three quarters of the period, as is suggested in Table 1.7. By the late 1930s there were marked accelerations of unsubsidised private building in outer Britain and the midlands that reduced these differentials (Richardson and Aldcroft, p236).

TABLE 1.7: HOUSES BUILT PER 1000 OF 1931 POPULATION 1919-1936

	South	Midlands	North and Wales	Scotland
Unsubsidised	21	10	8	4
Subsidised	20	32	25	24
All Houses	41	42	33	28

Source: M. Bowley, cited from Richardson and Aldcroft, p177

At the local level the pattern was very much more complex, but variations were clearly huge. Thus in Croydon CB the ratio of all private dwellings completed to 1939 population was 1:10.8; for Merthyr Tydfil CB it was 1:2194 (Croydon CB 1951, p5; M. Swenarton and S. Taylor 1985, p390). Such a variation between an affluent suburban boom town and a depressed area is unsurprising, but within this range less straightforward variations were apparent. Thus Newcastle (1:17.7) and Tynemouth (1:15.8) on the depressed north east coast did rather better than Bristol (1:19.1), Wolverhampton (1:22.6) and Norwich (1:37.7) (S. Ward 1983, p83).

Overall therefore the broad regional pattern between inner and outer Britain was modified by a great deal of local diversity. We could go much further in considering this, as for all the other dimensions of unevenness. However we have probably said sufficient to show how uneven development between the wars interacted with pre-existing geographical patterns to reproduce unevenness across a wide spread of social and economic indicators. We must now draw together the main arguments of this chapter.

Conclusions

In a classic 1933 description, which would bear extension to the whole of Britain, J.B. Priestley identified four different Englands, each representing different phases in the economic, social, political and cultural development of the country. Wisely, he did not seek to portray any clearcut divisions as between north or south, still less between inner and outer Britain, but saw clearly that the pattern was more varied than a simple regional divide. As he commented, the different Englands were 'variously and most fascinatingly mingled, in every part of the country I visited. It would be possible, though not easy, to make a coloured map of them. There was one already in my mind, bewilderingly coloured and crowded with living people. It made me feel dizzy.' (1934, p406).

In this chapter we have suggested that dizziness may be avoided by portraying the uneven development of interwar Britain as two dualities, between export and non-export dependent sectors and between a core and a periphery in an organisational power model. This is of course a gross simplification and, even in our brief examination of detailed indications of unevenness, we have identified a real diversity far greater than the notion of two dualities would imply. Our simple models steady the senses but they should not blind us to the underlying complexities of spatial pattern produced by the interaction of traditional and interwar experience. It is this sense of the need for both generalisation and awareness of real complexity that we carry forward into the remainder of this book. In the next chapter we examine the second of its major themes, state intervention.

2

State Intervention

Introduction

State intervention is an umbrella term embracing all aspects of governmental activity, including local government, public corporations and central government. As we will see in the next chapter a considerable amount of recent theorisation has added a conceptual level to discussion of state intervention, but the focus of the present chapter is more empirical. It gives an overview of state activity within Britain between the wars. Thus we examine the dimensions, functional categories and financial characteristics of state expenditures over time. In more detail we then consider the political and administrative frameworks within which the state existed. Finally we examine the major orthodoxies animating central policy in relation to state intervention and expenditure and briefly consider some of their broader spatial impacts.

Dimensions of state intervention

Table 2.1 shows that state expenditure accounted for roughly a quarter of Gross National Product (GNP) during the interwar period. This contrasted with 10-15% in the 1900-1914 period, a much higher proportion during world war I, peaking at a little over half the GNP in 1918, and an even higher level in world war II. Something of the build-up to this was already apparent by 1938, but the state spending peak in 1943 was very much higher, accounting for very nearly three-quarters of GNP. Thereafter it fell back, more slowly than after world war I, stabilising at a somewhat higher level than between the wars. The interwar years appear therefore as a period of transition in peacetime state expenditure between relatively low spending pre-1914 and rather higher post-1945 spending. Ostensibly wartime conditions would seem to have been important in shifting state expenditure to successively higher planes which then survived, albeit in a rather diminished form, into the following period of peace. Thus world war I appears as a decisive breakpoint in state expenditure patterns, while over the interwar period total spending as a percentage of GNP remained

TABLE 2.1: TOTAL GOVERNMENT EXPENDITURE AS PROPORTION OF GROSS NATIONAL PRODUCT

Year	%	Year	%
1890	8.8	1930	26.2
1900	14.4	1935	24.4
1910	12.8	1938	30.1
1915	35.0	1945	65.8
1920	26.1	1950	39.5
1925	24.2	1955	37.3

Source: Peacock and Wiseman, p166

FIGURE 2.1 : TOTAL GOVERNMENT EXPENDITURE 1920–1938
(at Constant 1900 Prices)
Source : Peacock and Wiseman, 1967, pp 164–5

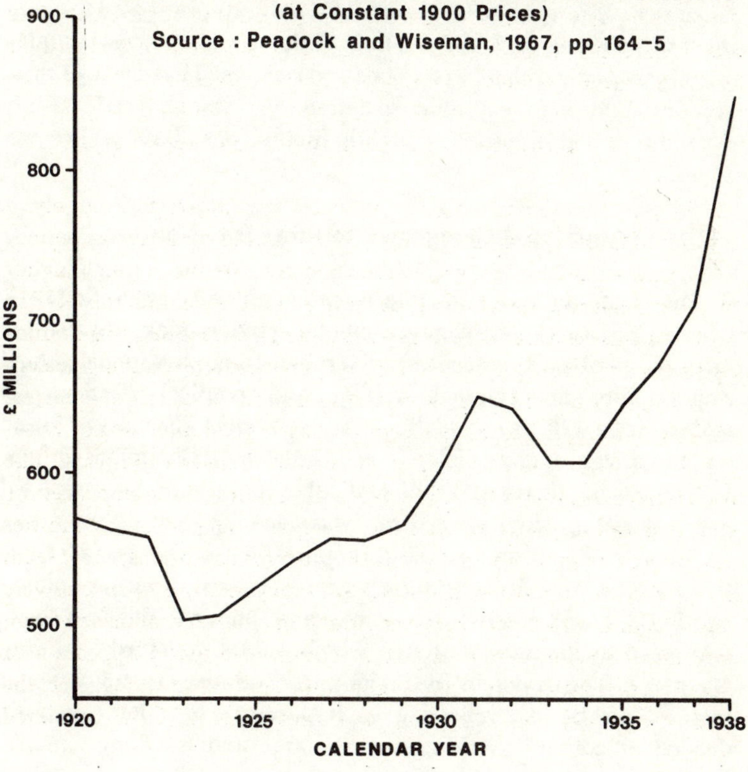

relatively stable. This is generally confirmed by Figure 2.1 which shows the absolute level of state spending at constant prices.

As can be seen there were peaks in the early 1920s, early and late 1930s with intervening, though not very pronounced, troughs. The overall trend is modestly upwards, with the state sector comprising a fairly stable proportion of a growing economy. This absolute growth in spending was heavily concentrated in the current account which made up about 90% of the interwar total, a little higher than prewar. Capital spending also grew, but more slowly.

Another associated and important trend in state expenditure was its changing financial characteristics. Already before 1914 a clear trend towards more state spending in transfer payments and subsidies was apparent. These were 33% higher in 1910 than 1900. By 1920 they were a massive 5.62 times the 1900 level (at constant 1900 prices) and by 1930 7.37 times greater (Peacock and Wiseman, pp174-5). Commensurate with this was the reduced proportion of state spending on goods and services. This formed 87% of spending in 1900, but had fallen to 62% in 1920 and accounted for only 50% in 1930. However, there was a swing back and the bulk of the spending increases in the later 1930s were evidently on goods and services. Thus by 1938 these accounted for 65% of total spending, yet transfer and subsidy expenditure had slipped only slightly from its peak level in the early 1930s.

Functional Categories of State Intervention

By the 1930s the range of state intervention was very wide (D.N. Chester (ed) 1957). Many governmental activities long predated the interwar period. Thus central government had traditionally held responsibility for external trading and political relations. It maintained a well developed diplomatic and imperial network centred on the Foreign, Indian, Colonial and, from 1925, Dominions Offices. It also, via the Board of Trade and subordinate agencies, regulated external trading activity, a task that was assuming greater prominence with the erosion, from 1915, and the final ending, in 1931-2, of free trade and the gradual shifts towards managed external trading relations. These external economic and political relations were reinforced by the armed services, which will be examined further in Chapter 4. The navy took the major part of defence expenditure over most of the period, reflecting its importance to a heavily trade dependent country presiding over a large and far flung Empire.

However the newest service, the Royal Air Force, created only in 1918, had become the main spender by the end of the period (R. Higham 1962, pp326-7).

Another key area in which the state was traditionally closely involved, but in which its exact functions were ambiguous, was in the maintenance of a stable currency. The direct responsibility for monetary management rested in various places over the interwar period, not all within the state sector. Thus the return to the gold standard in 1925 in effect transferred responsibility to a private body managed by a self-appointed group of bankers, namely the Bank of England (P. Williamson 1984). Though the decisions to return to gold, and go off it again in 1931, were made by governments, and Bank of England policies throughout closely reflected those of the Treasury, the 1925-31 period was essentially one of privatised money management. However, the state, via the Treasury, was directly involved in currency management before 1925 and after 1931. The Bank itself was not finally brought into the state sector in the formal sense until 1946.

Internal security and the maintenance of law and order were also well developed traditional state functions. Occasionally these might still be fulfilled, in extremis, by the armed forces, as in the most serious industrial disputes of the 1919-1926 period, to be considered further in Chapter 6, and in Ireland. However in Britain at least a civil law, police and penal service was well established. While aspects of the system were heavily centralised, there was no national police force, though the Metropolitan Police, uniquely under direct central control, did have some quasi-national functions. Its Special Branch was the nearest thing Britain possessed to the state secret police forces found in several European countries in the 1930s. However it fell well short of being a Gestapo. The localisation of policing outside London had some perceptible effects, notably on the management of national protests like the hunger marches, where the desire for local order seems frequently to have outweighed central desires for containment (P. Kingsford 1982, especially p109). However this should not be exaggerated; local variations in law enforcement generally were slight and central powers, greatly strengthened after world war I, were sufficient to ensure a large measure of uniformity (G.M. Harris 1939, pp226-9).

During the nineteenth century there had been a gradual intensification of state intervention in business activity. Thus factories, mines, railways, shipping etc. were subjected to increasingly careful inspection and regulation, largely on safety grounds. As well as this regulatory tradition, the state, largely at the local level, had by 1900 become increasingly involved in the monopoly provision of public utilities, notably tramways, gas and electricity. As we will see in Chapters 7-8, municipal trading was never uniform over the whole country. It was more urban than rural. With the important exception of the north east coast, it was more northern than southern. It was less common for gas than for electricity or trams. The main features of this persisted in the interwar period with some elements of the pattern for municipal tramways reproducing themselves in a new one for motor and trolley buses (H. Finer 1941, pp278-88).

Increasingly though the initiative in such matters shifted away from the local state. Signs of this were already apparent before 1914 with the creation of the Port of London Authority in 1908 and the effective nationalisation of telephones by the Post Office, itself a unique example of central government trading activity, in 1912. Only Hull included telephones in its municipal trading portfolio. During the interwar period however the Central Electricity Board and the British Broadcasting Corporation (both created in 1926) and the London Passenger Transport Board (1933) were important examples of a new state organisational form, the quasi-autonomous public corporation.

However, even by 1939 there was no widespread political tolerance of overt nationalisation on this model for most business activity in which government became involved. With a few exceptions intervention was generally tentative and reluctant, as we will see in Chapter 5. Where possible surrogate or arms length intervention, using the Bank of England or other intermediaries, was preferred. Very rarely was the framework of private ownership and control openly replaced. The actual reasons for such interventions were varied. Strategic and imperial considerations were often present and had featured in all the main initiatives before world war I, including the government formation of the Pacific Cable Board in 1901 and the acquisition of a majority state shareholding in the Anglo-Persian Oil Company in 1914 (G. Jones 1984, pp152-3). Such concerns were also paramount in the formation of Cable and Wireless Ltd. under the Imperial Telegraphs Act of 1929 (S. Pollard 1962, pp158-9). They were also present in the securing of long term British timber supplies by means of the Forestry Commission, established in 1919, and in the increasing involvement of government in civil aviation, culminating in the formation of British Overseas Airways in 1939 (H.J. Dyos and D.H. Aldcroft 1974, pp 400-17). They were detectable too in the government assistance to the Cunard Company in the building of its two giant liners Queen Mary and Queen Elizabeth (Mowat, p446).

As we will see in Chapter 5, much state concern focussed on the problems of the older industries. In general government assisted rationalisation with various levels of subsidies or occasionally by other means. Railways (1921), coal (1930), iron and steel (1932), tramp shipping (1935), cotton (1936) and agriculture (throughout the period, but especially from 1931) all experienced some degree of direct state intervention (Checkland 1983, pp312-30). Less specific measures like the Trade Facilities Acts in the 1920s and 75% industrial derating (1929) were also of some assistance to older industries (U.K. Hicks 1970, pp71-4; D. Mair 1986). The Bank of England was also active in several fields, particularly in non-naval shipbuilding which government 'scrap and build' assistance to shipowners only aided indirectly.

In general there was less intervention in the growth sectors, but several important industries (most notably motor cars) developed behind protective tariffs imposed either during world war I or in the Safeguarding legislation of 1921 and 1925 (Pollard 1962, pp193-4). Some growth areas like chemicals, rayon and aircraft manufacture had been directly stimulated by government during world war I, but these bonds were soon loosened after 1919, in common with those for most other industries. Although the public services were themselves an important area of growth, state ownership in other growth sectors like electricity, oil, telecommunications and broadcasting did not set a general example. And, as we will see in Chapter 9, the emergent idea of the late 1930s that the state should assist the development of new industries in the depressed areas was still viewed as very unorthodox by conventional opinion.

One of the most dramatic and visible areas of large scale state intervention in the interwar period was in the social services (B.B. Gilbert 1970). These had been a growing facet of state activity before 1914. Thus in addition to the historic local responsibilities for poor relief, the state had latterly become heavily involved in primary and secondary education, and was developing significant but still limited initiatives in housing, unemployment and health insurance. Some of these areas of intervention were wider than their explicit focus so that education and poor relief contained the seeds of a system of health care and hospital provision. The social service state of the interwar period extended much wider, particularly in the immediate aftermath of war. For the first time the central state intervened decisively to subsidise the provision of houses on a very large scale by local authorities. Unemployment insurance was extended to cover the majority of the workforce and an unforeseen consequence of high unemployment was that the sound insurance basis of the scheme was lost. There were also significant, if less dramatic developments in health and education provision over the period as a whole. Both however were areas where voluntary effort remained very important, and a comprehensive state welfare system did not appear until after 1939. Overall though the interwar period saw a clear shift away from the contributory principles that had dominated the pre-1914 welfare system. As we will see, particularly in Chapter 6, this move away from contributory or insurance principles was far from complete by the 1930s and was accompanied by rigorous means testing procedures that were widely disliked.

The last broad category of state intervention was in what might be labelled the environmental services, associated with the creation and maintenance of a physical infrastructure including roads, water, sewerage, parks, public cleansing, lighting etc. There was little in this that was new during the interwar period, as we will see in Chapters 7-8. However many of the major municipal innovations and investments in water and sewerage, for example, had already taken place. Thus most urban areas were serviced, at least to a substantial extent, by waterborne sewage systems in 1919. Tyneside (where water was largely supplied by private companies) was the major exception amongst the larger urban areas and some smaller towns, such as Warrington, were also backward in this respect (H.A. Mess 1928, p95). However, interwar conversion schemes in such residual areas were not sufficient to produce dramatic changes in the overall scale of intervention in the environmental services.

Overall therefore state intervention spanned a very wide range of functions. There were only a few fields in which this intervention was entirely new, most of them in the economic sphere. However on some items, particularly some of the social services, state intervention went qualitatively further than it had done before 1914. Moreover in virtually all areas the state sector was quantitatively larger than it had been pre-1914. Table 2.2 shows something of the relative weighting of government spending by functional category.

Most apparent in the longer term is the fluctuation in military and defence expenditure reflecting wartime conditions and the build up to and run down from them. It is particularly noticeable how other expenditure was relatively 'squeezed' by war considerations. Aside

TABLE 2.2: OBJECTS OF GOVERNMENT SPENDING AS % OF TOTAL

	National Debt	Military & Defence	Social Services	Economic Services	Environmental Services	Other*
1910	7.4	27.3	32.8	13.9	5.3	13.2
1915	6.0	74.8	9.7	3.7	1.3	4.4
1920	20.4	32.6	25.9	12.8	1.6	6.8
1925	28.4	12.5	36.3	12.3	3.0	7.5
1930	25.4	10.4	42.3	11.6	3.3	7.0
1935	18.5	12.6	46.5	11.2	3.7	7.4
1938	13.4	29.8	37.6	9.5	3.2	6.4
1950	11.2	18.5	46.1	12.6	2.1	9.5

*Administrative, Law and Order and Overseas Services

Source: Peacock and Wiseman, pp186-7

from this the only other categories to show large scale percentage fluctuations over time were the expenditure servicing the national debt and social services. The former was linked primarily to the impact of wartime borrowing at high interest rates, followed by loan conversion to take advantage of lower interest rates in the 1930s. The trend in social services partly reflects the impact of the shifts in social policy noted briefly above, combined with the peak in unemployment in the early 1930s and consequent expenditure on maintenance payments. It is noticeable how all other categories exhibited a stability tending to slight decline as a percentage of total spending. In most cases this reflects the continuance of already established patterns of intervention. In the only category where this is not the case, 'economic services', it illustrates the tentative nature of government intervention into private industry during the period, manifest in ad hoc expenditures and the absence of any clear spending programmes comparable to those for the social services. The failure of these initiatives to encourage private capitalist restructuring brought more decisive and far-reaching intervention after 1939 when it was acknowledged that rationalisation of most problem industries could only be achieved by greater state intervention including public ownership. One of the key features of the British state in the interwar period was a reluctance to embrace such policy options. The reasons for this were deep-rooted. We can only begin to comprehend them by understanding the political and philosophical context of the interwar British state.

Changing access to state power?

During the interwar period the political framework of mass democracy was erected around the British state. It was not yet complete even by 1939 and relics of former practices remained in the form of business and university dual voting (D. Butler 1963, pp7-13). However the formal significance of these was greatly diluted by the granting of universal suffrage. All men over 21 received the right to vote in parliamentary elections in 1918. Women over 30 received the right to vote at the same time; in 1928 they received equal voting rights to men. This was in sharp contrast to the prewar position. In 1911 only 59% of males over 21 and no women had voting rights in parliamentary elections, though the local government franchise was wider, permitting some women to vote and (after 1907) be elected. However, it was not until the last full decade of the interwar period that parliaments elected on universal suffrage (if not one person, one vote) deliberated on affairs of state. This wider franchise dramatically increased the electorate. In 1918 some 21.4 million were entitled to vote compared to 7.7 million at the previous election in 1910. And despite the loss of Irish votes after partition this had risen to 28.9 million by 1929. This extension of electoral democracy was closely associated with (and indeed part of) the changing political agenda of state action noted above.

But we should not overestimate its influence at least in this period. The power of property and business continued to have potent and ultimately more powerful means of expressing itself within parliament and the state. In many ways the very close interaction of capital and the state that occurred during world war I served to reinforce prewar patterns and was sustained into the peace. One of the principal vehicles of this was the Conservative party which, with the demise of Liberalism in the 1920s, increasingly became the party of business. In the first election conducted on the much wider franchise in 1918 the 383 Conservatives returned included 85 industrialists and 71 representatives of commerce and finance (J. Turner 1984a, p15). Businessmen therefore outnumbered Labour by more than two to one. Over most of the interwar period businessmen made up about 35% of the Conservative MPs who, except in 1929-31, were always the largest single party in parliament. However Haxey, (1939, pp32-9) apparently including Conservative supporters such as the National Liberals, found evidence that 44% were company directors in 1938. He also makes the point that the requirement that Ministers resign any directorships of publicly quoted companies during their term of office did not imply any significant divorce of business and the state given the speed with which they resumed them and usually acquired more because of their ministerial experience.

It is though misleading to look solely to the House of Commons for the direct influence of business. As Turner points out there were strong pressures arising from the increasingly professional nature of politics under mass democracy and the complex nature of business that militated against the big businessman being active in parliament (1984a, pp17-18). However the increasing concentration of the headquarters of large firms in London noted in the previous chapter was partly indicative of a different kind of linkage. This was reinforced particularly by the elevation of many big businessmen to the peerage. Thus the National Government in the 1930s ennobled the chairmen of the Ford Motor Company (Lord Perry), of Imperial Chemical Industries (Lord McGowan), of the London Midland Scottish Railway (Lord Stamp) and of the Ocean Coal Company (Lord Davies) amongst many others (Haxey, p42). Although formally the House of Lords was much less significant than before the 1911 Parliament Act, it still provided businessmen with a voice near the centres of power in Westminster and Whitehall. As well as being available for regular consultation these businessmen peers could be recruited into the process of government without the need for any electoral test. Sometimes this was done covertly or semi-covertly as in Lord Weir's role in industrial planning for rearmament (see Chapter 4). In other cases business peers, or at least those from major business families like Lord Londonderry, were able to directly participate as ministers.

In a slightly different way the Bank of England with its peculiar position both within and yet also outside the state also acted as a direct linkage between business, mainly banking, and the state via the Treasury. More formally business organisations such as the Federation of British Industries, established in 1916, and the National Confederation of Employers' Organisations (1919) provided a means of advancing industrialists' interests within the arena of the state. However, these had not yet become one of the more effective channels of business influence on the state (J. Turner 1984b, pp33-49). Least specific, but perhaps most important, were the social, cultural and personal networks linking business, especially London-based big business, banking and commerce, with senior politicians and higher civil servants. In a real sense there was an identifiable ruling class that survived remarkably well and was in several important respects strengthened during the period between the wars.

Potentially however mass democracy was directly antagonistic to the perpetuation of such a ruling class, or as Aneurin Bevan put it (1952, p5), 'a sword pointed at the heart of property-power'. In some respects this weapon was used in the interwar period, so that the Labour party replaced the Liberals as the main opposition party in 1922 and achieved sufficient strength, though lacking an overall majority, to form two governments, in 1923-4 and 1929-31 (M. Pugh 1982, pp251-63). Geographically Labour was strongest in the industrial north, Wales and Scotland, and weakest in the south; the long-term spatial pattern of British elections was already established by 1929 (G.D.H. Cole 1948, pp217-23). The achievements of Labour in government were profoundly disappointing to many of its supporters. Labour's gradualism and commitment to constitutional methods brought a few major social reforms, of which the most outstanding was probably the 1924 Housing Act. But interwar Labour governments never challenged the capitalist system in any comprehensive way. There were no socialist answers to the central problem of unemployment and the second Labour government in effect had no alternative to the conventional capitalist definition, analysis and solution for the financial and economic crisis of 1931 (R. Skidelsky 1967).

Many on the left despaired of Labour in the 1930s. They argued that its constitutionalism and commitment to gradual reform of capitalism brought an inevitable incorporation and emasculation within the parliamentary apparatus of a capitalist state (e.g. J. Strachey 1934). The dramatic defection of the Labour Prime Minister, Ramsay MacDonald, in 1931 into a National Government rather supported the notion that the authentic voice of the working class would thus be incorporated. The increasing presence during the 1920s of middle and upper class refugees from the other parties, especially the Liberals, was also held to be a further handicap to Labour in mounting any real class challenge to the capitalist system.

However it seems very doubtful if the Labour party's failure to establish a position of real and continuing strength within the state between the wars is explicable solely or even mainly in terms of its own weaknesses as a socialist party. The more extreme left wing made little headway in parliamentary elections. At workplace level revolutionary syndicalist and communist thinking made some advances in the early postwar period, as we will see in Chapter 6, and certainly contributed considerably to the climate of radical reform in 1918-20. But mass unemployment severely weakened the possibilities of such offensive trades union action. Between the ending of the postwar boom in 1920-1 and the late 1930s boom most union activity was defensive action to protect earlier gains, not without some success in most industries.

In many ways we need to explain not why the parties of the left failed but why the Conservatives succeeded so completely as a party of business and property in an era of mass democracy (see generally Pugh, pp223-97 for a recent overview of interwar politics). The answer is partly a straightforward one that the single member constituencies introduced in 1918 usually amplified more modest Conservative majorities in the popular vote. However these basic majorities were still there at every interwar election, including 1929, when the electoral system for once worked in Labour's favour.

Much Conservative policy as implemented reflected the interests of the powerful if not entirely unified business grouping within the party. However the success of Conservative leaders in persuading the electorate that such business oriented policies were in the national interest rather than merely serving sectional advantage was very important. The use of Coalition and National ostensibly non-party labels in 1919-22 and after 1931 also helped reinforce the sense of national rather than sectional interest. The principal Conservative leader of the period, Stanley Baldwin, was trusted by large sections of the British public in a way that Labour leaders or Lloyd George were not. Alone among senior British politicians between the wars, he made very effective use of radio and especially newsreel film in conveying a political message (J.A. Ramsden 1982). That message was generally simple and was as much as personal projection of reassuring calm, confidence and trust as of Conservative policies. But it was undoubtedly important in the maintenance of Conservative political hegemony in a period of great economic difficulty and international uncertainty.

The pragmatism of the Conservatives was also important, manifest most obviously in the willingness to participate, invariably as major partners, in non-party governments. However, the willingness to make gestures towards public opinion was also significant. This could take the form of introducing measures that were popularly desired but in which party leaders had little real faith (such as the Special Areas programme considered in Chapter 9), or by continuing useful measures introduced by Labour, particularly in the housing field, or by withdrawing obviously unpopular proposals such as the proposed reductions in unemployment assistance in 1935. Such pragmatism seemed to reinforce the sense of a reasonable, common-sense approach to government, even though the central thrust of Conservative policies frequently ran directly counter to many of these political gestures. Paradoxically, however, it did mean that some of the most significant interwar initiatives in state intervention were the immediate product of a pragmatic but reluctant Conservatism.

Behind the formal party political scene there were permanent civil servants. Their role in the power structure is very difficult to elucidate or define with any precision, but must have been considerable (M. Beloff 1975; G.C. Peden 1983). Thus there was only one Permanent Secretary of the Treasury during the whole interwar period (Warren Fisher) compared to seven Chancellors. There was considerable policy continuity in the Treasury, and indeed in more junior ministries like Health (e.g. S.V. Ward 1986) that seems to have been primarily sustained by the Permanent Secretary and other senior civil servants. Such tendencies to continuity associated with a disinclination to attempt any radical policy appraisals, at least under normal peacetime circumstances, made higher civil servants the natural allies of the Conservatives. One does not have to subscribe to a 'capitalist conspiracy' view of the state to accept this. Thus Beloff, the Conservative political historian, observes that:

> 'It was not altogether unreasonable ... to argue that while civil servants might impartially advise and execute the wishes of successive ministers of different parties but all basically dedicated to the status quo, they could not be expected to feel the same about newcomers whose class origin and general outlook would also be unfamiliar.' (pp213-4)

He also suggests what Labour politicians have frequently stated more firmly, that civil servants may have acted 'rather to put a brake on collectivism than to accelerate its progress'.

In a wider sense too the Conservatives were the major beneficiaries of the dominant ideology and cultural climate of the interwar period. The new, or relatively new, mass media - national mass circulation newspapers, radio and cinema - were potent means of reinforcing certain sets of values and discouraging others. Thus virtually all newspapers, although less formally linked to political parties than in previous periods, purveyed social and cultural messages that were strongly supportive of the status quo, private property and business, and antipathetic to socialist and collectivist sentiments (C. Seymour-Ure 1975). Even the *Daily Herald*, editorially controlled by the Labour Party (though under business ownership) adopted a very moderate, quite traditional, approach on most issues. The Communist *Daily Worker* which appeared in 1930 was an attempt to provide a real left-wing alternative, but it never achieved mass circulation to rival the other nationals. In the new field of radio, the BBC, from 1926 a state-owned broadcasting service, had a technical independence of government on programme content, though it was obliged to carry government statements. In practice it did not test this independence and invariably followed a line that governments did not disapprove of especially in relation to the General Strike and other major manifestations of civil unrest (A. Briggs 1985, pp96-106). Under the puritanical leadership of Sir John Reith, the moral and cultural values it purveyed were traditional rather than radical.

Finally there was the cinema, which about 40% of the population attended at least once a week during the 1930s (J. Richards 1984, pp11-33). Proportions of cinemagoers were rather higher amongst the young and the working classes, groups generally less accessible to other media. What could be shown in general release was very strictly governed by a system of censorship, technically exercised voluntarily by the film industry, but in effect reflecting state policy (N. Pronay 1982, pp112-22). By 1930 there were 98 separate rules on the censor's list of forbidden subjects. As well as moral concerns, many of the rules related to political questions (pp98-110). Thus it was explicitly forbidden to portray 'relations of capital and labour', 'controversial politics', 'industrial unrest or violence' and 'conflicts between the armed forces of the state and the populace', even though all these issues had featured prominently on the British domestic scene during the previous decade. Royalty (especially the Prince of Wales), the armed forces and the Empire were assiduously protected from potentially critical cinematic portrayal. Again it could hardly be claimed that any of these institutions possessed a real life purity so complete as to warrant this treatment.

Although an alternative cinema developed, its products were denied general release. The results of all this were a mass release output of extraordinary social and political blandness. As the President of the British Board of Film Censors remarked in 1937: 'We may take pride in observing that there is not a single film showing in London today that deals with any of the burning questions of the day' (Pronay, p122). Consensus, capitalism and an uncritical acceptance of the relative positions of ruler and ruled were the dominant values transmitted to mass cinema audiences. Not surprisingly Richards (p323) concludes his penetrating survey of 1930s cinema saying that it 'played an important part in the maintenance of the hegemony of the ruling class'. Given these dominant characteristics, Baldwin's mastery of the new media was no surprise.

Overall therefore the changes in the access to state power produced by mass suffrage were more apparent than real. The ideological climate, the conservatism of state administrators and the political astuteness of the Conservative party combined to reinforce the already deeply entrenched position of capitalism within British society. The possibilities of radical change in how state power was exercised in relation to private capital were accordingly constrained. Far from being Bevan's sword pointed at the heart of property power, the mass democratic state of the interwar period usually looked more like a sword that defended property power, or at least major sections of it. However, this is not to say that the exercise of state power was simply a direct manipulation of government by owners of capital. At the heart of state policies were a series of administrative orthodoxies which, though deriving from the wider interests of British capitalism, acquired a semi-independent existence in the hands of state policy makers and provided a legitimacy and form of rationality for state actions.

Orthodoxies of state policy 1918-1931

Pre-1914 economic policy (as defined principally by Gladstone) rested on three interrelated orthodoxies or sets of assumptions about the proper role of government (Checkland, p184). Consistent with the dominant philosophy of laissez-faire, they were all about what the state should not do. The orthodoxy of the gold standard was about governments not interfering in currency exchange rates. Free trade was about them not imposing barriers to international trade. Public finance orthodoxy was about the state doing as little as possible and not borrowing to do it, unless the resultant debt would be self-liquidating. Although the last years before 1914 had seen some implicit challenges to these orthodoxies, principally in the field of social reform, most areas of state policy after 1918 still bore the impress of all three. In a wider sense they tied the internal economy of Britain on to the back of its external economy in a way that provided no cushion or means of escape. That it worked so well was because Britain's economy was strong internationally and the City of London dominated world financial activity.

With hindsight we can see quite clearly that the First World War shattered the preconditions of these orthodoxies, but this truth did not reveal itself to those who controlled state policy until rather later (Checkland, pp282-302). The war disrupted the whole free trade world system. It also brought rapid domestic inflation which dramatically altered the international exchange value of sterling. Linked with this, its prosecution demanded an end to the minimalist state and was paid for with huge borrowing in a depreciating currency at high rates of interest. Orthodox thinking had always conceded that borrowing would be necessary during wars, but world war I was of an entirely different order to nineteenth century wars and demanded a scale of borrowing that would have horrified Gladstone. As war ended, state policy makers, supported by large sections of business, particularly banking, opinion saw their prime task to restore the pre-war position, implying harsh deflationary measures. However in the immediate post-war period there were strong and at that time irresistible pressures for social reform. As we will see in Chapter 6, the labour movement as a whole was in a stronger position than ever before and was using its strength to secure concessions from both employers and the state (K. Burgess 1980, pp176-90). There were even fears of revolutionary unrest in the wake of the Russian Revolution of 1917.

In such circumstances retrenchment was out of the question. By 1920 however economic and political circumstances were changing, severely weakening the pressures for social reform and an expansive state, and the strategy to restore the pre-war structure began. Under the guidance of the Geddes Committee severe cuts in state spending with balanced budgets and high interest rates were imposed to dampen inflationary pressures (Mowat, pp129-32). A qualified version of free trade was re-established (despite Conservative advocacy of protectionist policies) in a pattern of world trade transformed by war. In 1925 the Conservatives restored the gold standard at the pre-war parity of 4.86 dollars to the £ (D.E. Moggridge 1969; S. Pollard (ed) 1970). The policy was regarded as mistaken at the time by both sides of manufacturing industry, (though in varying degrees) by the economist J.M. Keynes and by virtually everybody since. Its main proponents were concentrated in the City of London, the Bank of England and the Treasury (Williamson, pp106-8). The more perceptive of the bankers, such as McKenna of the Midland (himself a former Chancellor) recognised that the short term implications were continued deflation, downward pressure on wages and unemployment in export industries which would experience the full costs of an overvalued pound (L.J. Hume 1970). But so deeply rooted were the traditional orthodoxies that these adjustment problems could be rationalised merely as a purging of bad habits, an essential precondition for a return to free market purity and true competitiveness that sooner or later had to be faced.

In addition to purely economic considerations, the whole issue became bound up with questions of international prestige and confidence. Even McKenna, debating the issue privately with the Chancellor, Treasury advocates of gold and Keynes in 1925 concluded: 'There is no escape; you have got to go back. But it will be hell' (cited from Mowat, p200). Most of its firmest advocates, particularly Montagu Norman, the Governor of the Bank of England, were less worried about these problems compared to the envisaged benefits for the continued health, prosperity and prestige of British capitalism, which they saw as synonymous with the financial markets of the City of London. In so far as they thought about it at all they saw the pressures on industries to reduce costs by lower wage settlements, higher productivity, labour 'shakeouts' and rationalisation as an act of purification, lancing the poisons introduced by wartime collectivism. In that sense it was quite literally an act of class warfare and played a fairly direct role in precipitating the General Strike in 1926, which we will examine in Chapter 6.

Much has been written about the impact of the gold standard decision, focussing principally on its macro-economic effects. However an interesting study by Jones (1985) has attempted to define some of its spatial effects at a subnational level. Concentrating primarily on south Wales, the north east coast and west central Scotland, the most severely depressed areas of outer Britain, he concludes that the 1925 decision significantly damaged their export performance and thus worsened (but did not create) their economic problems. He finds no evidence to suggest that the domestic consumption industries were significantly affected by cheaper imports leading to substitution for British products. (A range of key items produced by newer industries were of course already subject to a degree of tariff protection by this time which must have discouraged import penetration.) Consequently he finds a clear spatial effect arising from the monetary policies pursued in the 1920s, reinforcing the contrast between inner prosperous and outer depressed Britain.

This spatial impact, generated by one of the most important state policies in the first part of the interwar period, was reproduced in many other aspects of state policy. As we will show in later chapters, state spending under orthodox finance did little to assist and much to hinder the ailing regions. Although pressures for expansive public works policies funded by borrowing mounted during the later 1920s, the 'Treasury view' prevailed. Quite simply this held that:

> '... very little additional and no permanent employment can in fact and as a general rule be created by State borrowing and State expenditure.' (W.S. Churchill, Chancellor, April 1929, cited from R. Middleton 1983, p351)

The theoretical justification for this, in so far as it existed, rested on the Gladstonian view that increased state sector borrowing would 'crowd out' private investment. However, by the later 1920s it is debatable whether Treasury officials actually believed this or simply found it a convenient argument for political reasons to fend off spending pressures that otherwise would be difficult to resist (R. Middleton 1985, pp87-9; G.C. Peden 1984a). As translated spatially though the 'Treasury view' meant that state spending was discouraged most completely in the depressed areas. The financial logic for this was an adaptation of the orthodox principle of self-liquidating debt: If state loan-based spending was creating capital assets, these should be concentrated in areas where growth would ensure an income to redeem the debt. For local authorities who might be expected to implement a large part of such a public works programme (and pay for a significant part of it), that income might accrue as direct payments for services, or as general local taxation. The latter of course ran counter to a strict reading of financial orthodoxy, though was a well established practice by the start of the period. It was still viewed with suspicion, but regarded as unavoidable given the collective nature of much of what was provided. In effect the self-liquidating principle was reworked to give local rateable income something, but not quite all, of the status of direct user payments (S.V. Ward 1984b, 1986).

Thus loan based spending in declining areas, especially where the major object was simply the relief of unemployment, might easily breach this principle and was thus to be discouraged. More practically such thinking was reinforced by the fear that such spending would in any case create assets in the wrong places, or inhibit the free working of the labour market by discouraging migration from areas which private capital was abandoning. The detailed spatial operation of this is discussed more fully in Chapters 6-8, but for the present we can note how the macro Treasury view had a geographical dimension that broadly reinforced the dominant interwar pattern of spatial unevenness. This 'spatial orthodoxy' was never as clearly articulated as the major orthodoxy from which it derived, but it is perhaps significant that it was pursued most explicitly during the period 1925-30 when the attempt to restore the laissez-faire economic policy was being pursued with greatest conviction.

Orthodoxies of state policy 1931-1939

The restored system never worked as intended. The City of London was no longer the single world financial centre able to react to and influence the international economy. The emergence of New York and several smaller financial centres meant that London's actions alone were insufficient to keep the system working smoothly and predictably. Additionally the undervaluation of several important currencies in Europe and Japan and the persistent weakness of British export performance weakened London's position. Overseas investors bought sterling not to buy British products but because British interest rates were high, which made London particularly vulnerable to a crisis of confidence. As Britain's trade position worsened after 1929 and the second Labour government struggled unsuccessfully to manage the consequences of a deepening recession within an orthodox financial straitjacket the danger of such a crisis increased (Williamson, pp117-29). It finally came in 1931, and there was a rapid withdrawal of funds from London, precipitating the fall of the Labour government in August. Despite this a naval mutiny finally destroyed international confidence and Britain went off gold in September 1931.

The pound was allowed to float and depreciated against the dollar. There were no immediate repercussions. Confidence was restored in part by a hefty bout of deflation and expenditure cuts to accompany the devaluation. However, this was simply a cloak of orthodox respectability for a highly unorthodox act. The fact that it was undertaken by a government espousing orthodoxy made it more acceptable (Mowat, p404). Labour would not have had such an easy ride; indeed the former Labour Minister, Sidney Webb's reported comment on hearing of the decision to go off gold: 'They never told us we could do that', speaks volumes of the nature of orthodoxy and access to state power between the wars (A.J.P. Taylor 1965, p297).

Effectively a new orthodoxy of state economic policy was formulated in 1931-2. The Exchange Equalisation Account created in 1932 was a mechanism for the Bank of England, in consultation with the Treasury to buy and sell sterling in order to stabilise its international value, or, in effect, to consciously manage it. Free trade was comprehensively ended in November 1931 emergency legislation, and made permanent the following year (Mowat pp415-9; Pollard 1962, pp190-6). Thereafter about three quarters of imports were subject to import duties. The protective tariffs provided a bargaining mechanism for negotiating selective trading agreements. The first intention was imperial preference, though the 1932 Ottawa Conference intended to implement this did not produce anything like Empire free trade, since the colonies and dominions were anxious not to damage their infant industries by allowing free access for British manufactured goods. However the proportion of British trade with the Empire did increase, accounting for 37.9% of UK imports and 45.6% of exports in 1938 compared to 25.7% and 39.6% in 1929 (Mowat, p437). A string of trading agreements were also concluded in the early 1930s. Argentina, Sweden, Denmark, Norway, Germany and Russia in particular secured quotas for their exports of food and natural products to Britain while offering concessions for UK imports (F.C. Benham 1941, pp129-35). Overall therefore the effect of currency and trade management was to provide a cushion between the internal economy and external events that had not formerly existed.

In effect two of the essential foundations of a state managed economy had been laid, though in fact very little else was built on these foundations before 1939. There were some, not very successful, moves, particularly in the iron and steel industry, to use the granting of tariff protection as a lever to force rationalisation and modernisation, which we will examine further in Chapter 5. But apart from these rather limited initiatives, the only major gesture was the introduction of a cheap money policy so that the bank rate was stabilised at 2% from 1932 until the outbreak of war. Characteristically though this was done for orthodox reasons to discourage the inflow of short term 'hot' money, and to make it easier to balance the budget by reducing debt charges (E. Nevin 1970). Thus lower interest rates enabled the conversion of war loans and had the dramatic effect on spending on the national debt noted above. However, though it certainly was not conceived as such, cheap money was also a reflationary economic policy and from about 1935 Ministers began to consciously regard it in that light.

Its credibility as such was rather undermined by the generally deflationary tone of budgets throughout much of the decade, especially before 1935 (Middleton 1985, pp96-121). This was despite the greater freedom that lower national debt charges gave the Chancellor. After 1934 though the leeway began to be utilised to directly generate more activity in the economy by state spending, particularly in the slum clearance programme, and from 1936 in rearmament. This was done within a continued formal attachment to the principle of orthodox budgeting, even though the practice was somewhat different and large scale borrowing for rearmament was sanctioned in 1937. This amounted to the introduction of unorthodox deficit budgets, even though complete abandonment of orthodoxy did not come until the following decade.

Overall therefore the abandonment of two of the traditional orthodoxies in currency and trade was effectively concealed by the maintenance of public finance orthodoxy. In consequence the state did little, at least until the end of the decade, to counter spatial unevenness by direct expenditure. It is significant that 1937 also appears as a turning point in the state's policies towards spatial development, as we will see particularly in Chapter 9. However, given the earlier shifts in the other orthodoxies, some spatial impacts of these new strategies might have been expected to have occurred earlier. It is difficult though to give any comprehensive analysis of this in the absence of detailed studies of the spatial impact of cheap money and protection. Our observations on this must therefore be tentative.

Nevertheless, virtually all the signs suggest that, with only a few qualifications, outer Britain did rather worse than inner Britain from these new orthodoxies. As a general point we noted in Chapter 1 that economic recovery proceeded more slowly in outer than in inner Britain, suggesting that no dramatic advantages accrued from new currency and trade policies. Given the damaging effect of the gold standard on exporting regions, its abandonment might be thought to have been most beneficial for these areas. However, as Jones (1985) points out, Britain went off gold in a much less favourable climate for world trade than it went on. International trade was very depressed which was hardly conducive to an export surge from areas where productive capacity had been severely weakened by a decade of recession. Moreover the adoption of protection by Britain, a major world trading nation, undoubtedly further encouraged other countries in their own moves towards protection and economic nationalism.

This would obviously damage those regions most dependent on exports.

The trend towards trading agreements with the Empire and elsewhere seems to have had some impacts on the fortunes of particular regions. However these were not always in outer Britain. Thus the limited imperial preference policies were of particular benefit to exports of motor vehicles, which had enjoyed a protected home market since 1915 (Benham, p105). The string of trading agreements with the Baltic countries benefited coal exports, but because French, Belgian and Italian markets were being lost, the latter particularly after economic sanctions were imposed after Mussolini's invasion of Abyssinia, the impact on different coalfields varied. Generally the western export fields, especially south Wales, lost, while the eastern fields and ports gained (Benham, pp147-8; Fogarty 1945, p182). Troubled industries like iron and steel, where import penetration had been a problem, clearly derived some immediate benefits from protection, but these were also spatially skewed towards the new centres of the east midlands, at least initially, as we will see in Chapter 5.

Finally cheaper money, by easing the credit position for industrial investments, might be claimed to have assisted the older industrial areas. Against this though are the doubts of most historians about the extent to which high interest rates alone had deterred investment (Glynn and Oxborrow, p134). Moreover the fact that later in the 1930s special finance organisations had to be established for the most depressed areas strongly suggests that lower interest rates alone were not sufficient (C. Heim 1984; see also Chapter 9). And of course the most obvious manifestation of the impact of cheap credit in further fuelling already buoyant domestic consumption, especially the private housing boom, was heavily skewed towards inner Britain as we saw in Chapter 1. It had though begun to affect some of the larger centres and less depressed areas of outer Britain by the later 1930s. The development of easier hire purchase also largely benefited the new consumer industries of the south and midlands. But insofar as lower interest rates played a part in encouraging government to commence slum clearance, some benefits accrued to outer Britain where there was relatively more obsolescent housing (Richardson and Aldcroft 1967, pp180-5).

Overall therefore, despite some significant shifts in the central assumptions of state intervention from 1931, there appears to have been little fundamental change in the spatial distribution of advantage/disadvantage arising from these policies compared to earlier. The 'Treasury view' on state spending and its spatial derivative was the last orthodoxy to crumble in 1937-9 and it seems significant that it was only at that time that state policies and actions which materially reduced the relative material disadvantage of outer Britain began to appear. Ultimately it was only a shift to an expansive state that offered any mechanism for reincorporating outer Britain, particularly its most depressed areas, into the productive mainstream.

Conclusions

This chapter has outlined the basic dimensions and functions of the British state between the wars and examined the political framework and the central policy rationales that guided its operations. As in the first chapter the main impression is one of incomplete transition. Labourism succeeded Liberalism but could not effectively challenge the political dominance of Conservatism. The orthodoxies of state policy were also still in a phase of transition by 1939. The old orthodoxies of laissez faire had been abandoned in the 1930s but the new ones of a managed economy were not yet in place. While the main purpose of this chapter has not been to examine the spatial dimension, we have noted that in general the more depressed areas of outer Britain tended to be those that derived least benefit from state intervention. This is the theme that will dominate subsequent chapters. In the next chapter we locate our exploration of the relationship between the state and uneven development in a context of some major theoretical questions.

3

Some Theoretical Questions

Introduction

We have already indicated that one of the central arguments of this book is that state intervention reinforced the process of uneven development over most of the interwar period. Later chapters will elaborate this argument in considerable empirical detail, but will also attempt to understand why the state acted this way, and why it began to change in the later 1930s. At one level this understanding can be sought empirically, within the demonstrable attitudes of particular ministries and the performance of particular ministers arguing their case within cabinet. We do not ignore the importance of such factors, but find them unsatisfactory as a complete explanation, because the state was not a closed system operating without inputs from or outputs to the capitalist economy and civil society.

Accordingly we turn, selectively, to recent theorisation about the state and its relationship to the capitalist development process to provide useful insights for our specific concerns here and to link our largely empirical concern with a particular conjuncture of time and space to a wider debate. Implicit in this is the assumption that there is nothing fundamentally unique about the state as an influence on spatial development as opposed to development identified or conceptualised in other ways. In other words the geographer must search for explanation within the same sorts of processes and forces as would a historian, an economist, a political scientist or a sociologist. The geographer will be more interested in geographical space, but cannot presume that the state's actions in space are caused by any unique set of spatial processes. Accepting this we set out some of the main alternative explanatory pathways generated by recent theoretical debates on the state and apply them to the interwar period.

The ideological landscape of most theorisation is what has been termed 'radical political economy'. Though sometimes described as a single paradigm, it is really several distinct approaches, resting on the rather different foundations of Marxist, Weberian and Durkheimian analysis, which have had a marked effect on all the social sciences in recent years. The common label of radical is justified in that they all reject a view of human affairs as being shaped by a series of self adjusting mechanisms such as are presumed by classical economics, pluralist political theory or, in a geographical context, spatial analysis and conventional location theory. Instead they assume that tension or conflict is very widespread or endemic in human affairs and that powerful vested or class interests will act to serve their own purposes to the detriment of other weaker groups. Most of these approaches have been developed since the 1960s, albeit on foundations that were laid much earlier, and clearly reflect a search for understanding of the mounting social and economic problems of western capitalist countries during the 1970s and 1980s. This association with capitalist crisis immediately suggests their relevance to the interwar period.

Three major questions of relevance have emerged from these theoretical debates, each generating other important subquestions, and suggesting three alternative kinds of explanation of state activity in relation to capitalist development. We sketch them here in a simplified form so that their meaning is accessible to the reader, something which cannot always be said for the originals. (The purist will have to forgive a certain crudeness.) Put very simply the three alternative explanations are:

1. The state under capitalism exists to serve and advance the interests of capital.
2. The state under capitalism reflects and embodies the class tensions of capitalist society.
3. The state under capitalism is an autonomous agency in capitalist society.

The implications of these alternatives for interpreting and explaining state actions are very different. (1) implies that everything the state does is explicable in terms of its value to capital. (2) on the other hand implies that some aspects of state activity can be explained as victories for working class action and not simply in terms of their functionality for capital. (3) implies that the state may be influenced by a wide range of external influences but that those performing key state management functions have a degree of independence sufficient to enable them to choose one of several courses of action on criteria which embody internal state priorities as well as external influences. In practice it would be difficult to identify one theorist who would subscribe entirely to one of these alternatives but all lean more towards one than the others. However, in a book like this which is primarily concerned with using theory to illuminate a specific episode of state intervention in relation to capitalist development, it is useful to distil out the main theoretical questions with an exaggerated clarity and hence a high degree of simplification. We are more concerned here with the questions generated and the explanatory frameworks suggested by theories than with reciting them chapter and verse.

The state and the interests of capital: a theoretical sketch

In the 1848 Communist Manifesto, Marx and Engels referred to the state under capitalism as 'but a committee for managing the common affairs of the whole bourgeoisie' (K. Marx and F. Engels 1967, p82). Much recent communist theory of the state under capitalism (B. Jessop 1982, pp32-77), together with more widely influential theorists like O'Connor (1973) and Castells (1977) have rather reinforced this sort of interpretation. However such a perspective is not without its problems and three immediate and important questions arise:

(1) How does the state serve the interests of capital?
(2) What exactly are the interests of capital?
(3) How does capital ensure that the state acts in its interests?

Addressing the first of these questions, theorists working on these lines have argued that the state has two principal functions, **legitimisation** and **accumulation.** The former involves the promotion and maintenance of the conditions necessary for social stability and harmony, the latter the promotion and maintenance of the conditions necessary for successful capital accumulation. Legitimisation is not directly productive for capital but works in its general interests since stability is a necessary precondition of successful capital accumulation. The state's accumulation functions are more obviously related to the interests of capital. However these must immediately be subdivided into activities which directly enhance capitalist production and those which enhance the reproduction of labour (i.e. ensure the continuing availability of a suitable workforce), where capital benefits less directly. Implicit in such a typology of state actions is the view that while all state action might be in the interests of capital, there are other beneficiaries and not all areas of state activity are equally in the interests of capital.

The last point acquires even greater complexity when the second question is considered and it is acknowledged that the interests of capital are not a single definable entity. Classical Marxism recognised the existence of different **fractions of capital** distinguished by their ownership of different means of production, principally land, factories and machinery and money. The 'hostile brothers' represented in these different capitals had common interest in the maintenance of capitalism but beyond that their interests would be quite different. Thus the priorities of landed capital would require high rents which would increase costs to industrial capital. Banking capital might desire high interest rates and overseas financial dealings to the detriment of domestically based industrial and landed capital.

Later theorists predicted that this fragmentation of capital would gradually diminish. In particular land would lose its distinctiveness and finance and industry would be integrated into a new dominant and monopolistic finance capital, which would increase in size and merge ever more closely with the state (Jessop, pp32-77). Ultimately therefore a greater unification of the interests of capital might be anticipated under advanced or late capitalism with big business essentially shaping state policies against the residual smaller non-monopoly capitals and the working class. As Jessop notes (especially pp67-8) such an interpretation is not beyond criticism, though we should also recognise the transitional and incompletely advanced nature of interwar British capitalism, which necessitates caution in the complete application of these later conceptualisations.

The third major question, about how capital ensures the state acts in its interests is in many ways the most crucial question. In the previous chapter we have already outlined some of the empirical groundwork for this question by considering the access to state power. The major question is of course how the notion of a state that basically exists to serve the interests of capital can be squared with mass democracy. Part of the answer advanced is that the introduction of mass democracy served a legitimising function, contributing to social stability and acting as a smokescreen for the major focus on servicing the accumulation concerns of capital. Several important concepts have been advanced to illuminate the main methods by which capital shapes state action, of which the most crucial are **instrumentalism, structuralism** and **hegemony.**

Instrumentalism asserts that it is the presence of a ruling class of capitalists or those committed to capitalism within the state that ensures that business interests are served by the state, so that it becomes a direct instrument of capital. Structuralism places more emphasis on the determination of the political by the economic sphere so that regardless of the composition of the state elite, the institutional and organisational form of the state will be predisposed to work in the interests of capital. Hegemony is rather less deterministic than either of these, asserting that the dominance of capital's interest within state action is in large measure produced by its ideological domination of the general climate of thought and values. Committed capital-logic theorists of the state tend to argue that this will be determined by the economic base and so will tend to play down the independent role of ideological hegemony. However many Marxists, following Gramsci, would now see this as a powerful element in understanding the nature of state power. This however has led many of them away from the simple notion of a capital-determined state and brought them into a more general discourse about the complex nature of the state.

The state and class conflict: a theoretical sketch

Though it is not always possible to make clear distinctions, many Marxist theories have emphasised a view of the state as **relatively autonomous** of capital. This is a key concept which has been widely adopted despite or perhaps because of its vague meaning. In practice it refers to a partial neutrality of the state so that it can serve interests other than those of capital. Class theories of the state have been advanced by Miliband (1969), and Poulantzas (see Jessop, pp153-91), and are important in the context of a study like this which is rooted in particular real experiences because much similar work such as that by Gough (1979) and Melling (1980) has been attracted to such perspectives. In essence the approach concedes that the state under capitalism has a strong predisposition to work in the interests of capital, but argues that state actions can only be understood in terms of class conflict, something which is of course central to Marxist thought. Such an approach is able to make use of much of the conceptual language outlined earlier.

Thus class conflict outside the state, probably in conjunction with capitalist crisis, is held to create instability within society that necessitates the bourgeois capitalist state to defuse this by extending its legitimisation functions. While there are several alternate ways of doing this, ultimately it is likely to involve formal incorporation of working class and other non-capitalist interests into the representational framework of the state. However this incorporation within the state, though it may partially resolve the state's crisis of legitimacy, places the working class in a better position to influence the state's accumulation functions. This is especially so in the field of labour reproductive activities which, although indirectly of benefit to capital, actually has a much more direct bearing on the working classes themselves. This class conflict begins to occur within the state with working class pressures to extend the scope and quality of these reproductive functions of the state beyond the basic level necessary or desired by capital.

However, given capital's tendency to favour state action that directly enhances its own production activities, sooner or later this tension will express itself more widely across the whole range of state activities. This is particularly likely to happen if the scale of expenditures in other fields is such as to damage the private processes of accumulation. Unless capital is able to redress the balance by cutting or shifting the focus of state expenditures then some crisis of capitalism is likely to appear. However it is successful in redressing the balance this may trigger off a wave of class conflict outside the state as the working class attempt to regain losses in the state's 'social wage' within the sphere of private production. This in turn is likely to provoke a new crisis of legitimacy.

It is possible to further elaborate the dynamics of this, but sufficient has probably been said to show that it is less reductionist and, though deterministic, less so than capital-logic theories of the state. It is also profoundly more dynamic since it allows the idea of two sets of antagonistic forces directly shaping state actions. By contrast capital theories depend on changes in capital to explain shifts in state actions. Other influences are only indirectly apparent through the filter of capital. But despite these differences which are important at the level of concrete reality, there is still a considerable amount of conceptual unity at the more abstract level. Many of the same or very similar concepts used in capital theories are employed by class theories, though with some differences in how they are linked and animated. This means that in class theories hegemony assumes a greater importance since there is not the same reductionist assumption that the ideological climate is directly derivable from the dominant structures of the economic base as appears in capital theories. In more sophisticated versions, hegemony involves not simply the domination of a political, intellectual and moral climate of capitalism, but one that incorporates and thereby attempts to emasculate elements of alternative projects. However as we noted for capital theories, such increased emphasis on the climate of thought and the consequent diminution of emphasis on things that relate directly to economic relations, lead into an area where determinacy in the accepted sense is abandoned and where the autonomy of the state itself may play an increasingly important role.

The state as an autonomous agency: a less theoretical sketch

One weakness of the other two groups of theories is the tendency to ignore the state itself. Implicit in the concept of relative autonomy is the notion that the state is capable of acting with a degree of independence of external influences, but this is not something which has been particularly developed in class theories. The tendency has been to assume that the autonomous is less than the determinate part of state action or to argue that state autonomy represents a convenient way of obscuring the true capital-serving nature of the state. However moving further away from the mainstream of Marxist thinking, there is a greater willingness to concede the notion of greater autonomy within the state. Autonomy does not mean that the state is immune to external influences, merely that these do not determine state policies. Expressed thus of course makes this seem very close to a conventional view of the state, and in some respects it is. However Weberian theory in particular has emphasised the key role of state managers (i.e. the bureaucracy and senior state employees), and the kind of institutional and official ideologies which they develop (e.g. E.C. Page 1985). This has led to the development of a managerialist approach to understanding state actions, though it has never been theorised in any complete way that embraces a proper theory of institutions. Neither has the Marxist influenced pioneering work of Burnham (1941) on managerialism been developed, despite occasional more recent examples such as Block (1980). It is not our purpose here to rectify this, but we need to consider some of the main issues raised by this kind of approach. The more important can be summarised as:

(1) The nature of managerial influence on state actions.
(2) The extent and location of such influence.
(3) The circumstances most favourable to managerial domination.

Generally the influence of managers seems to arise from their mastery of the detailed operations of the state and their capacity to act as a cohesive group within the state or at least particular parts of it. Such a cohesive group is characterised by subscription to common sets of values and assumptions to create an **internal bloc** within the state, with its own ideologies and views about the proper course of state action. The most effective exercise of managerial domination over state action in a democratic society depends on it being done covertly while outwardly sticking to the conventional divide between an accountable executive determining policy and state administrators merely implementing. However the absence of any clearcut division between the two means that state managers may exert considerable power at the level of implementation. The translation of broad policy into spatial terms is potentially one such area where state managers may be a key element.

All this implies that it is very difficult indeed to assess the extent and nature of managerial influence or power in relation to other influences. It may only become clear at particular conjunctures when conflicts arise within the state. However an important aspect is the political relation of state bureaucracies, and the extent to which state managers establish a **wider legitimacy** independent of this relationship with politics. This is not equal across all areas of state policy. Long established sections of the state bureaucracy, particularly those antedating democratic politics might be argued to possess such a wider legitimacy, or at least have incorporated such a view into their own ideologies. The armed forces particularly would normally possess such a role, as well as having the unique means of forcibly establishing their own legitimacy by seizing control of the state. Accordingly we could expect a high degree of independence and autonomous influence on state actions within the armed forces. However, other sections of the state might also be able to establish this wider legitimacy through direct dealings with civil society.

Finally we can note that different sets of historical circumstances may favour greater managerial influence or domination of state. Routinisation of established policy areas under stable conditions can normally be expected to be associated with a high degree of managerial influence and control over state action. Conversely though managerial dominance over state action is also enhanced during emergency circumstances, such as war, when normal mechanisms of political accountability are less effective and the imperatives of action predominate (Block, especially p232). Again this relates most obviously to the armed forces, but can be applied across the whole field of the state bureaucracy. Between these two extremes it is possible to argue that the conscious conceding of greater managerial autonomy, in the circumstances of a mass democratic society, may form a conscious defence mechanism of established political interests in an attempt to insulate particular areas of state policy from competing political groups. Thus widely varying circumstances might be expected to accelerate the role of managers in shaping state policies, in ways that were not always reversible. Overall therefore managerialism as an approach has a considerable relevance but its imperfect theorisation and more practical doubts about its ability to comprehend the major dynamics of state policy suggest that it is likely to be a subordinate rather than a central explanation.

We have now briefly sketched out some of the main questions and explanatory pathways that have been produced by recent studies of state intervention and action. It is not the intention in this book to test them in any formal sense. Most in fact are not really testable in the terms of conventional scientific method. Their purpose is rather to act as a series of pertinent questions to ask and conceptual tools to help illuminate the nature of the relationship between the British state and spatial developments in the 1919-1939 period. We must now begin to breathe some life into the concepts we have outlined to emphasise their relevance to the interwar years, so that we can link the theoretical with the larger empirical section of this book. Accordingly we here highlight some of the important linkages that we will be explored further in later chapters.

Concepts and realities in interwar Britain: capital theories

There is no direct equivalence between the conceptual typology of state functions in terms of capitalist interests and the realities of actual state activities. Legitimisation and the dual concerns of accumulation with capitalist production and labour reproduction were omnipresent in real state policies.

State subsidised housing for example was of most obvious importance in ensuring the availability of suitable workforces in the places where they were required (labour reproduction). However such schemes also contributed directly to capitalist production for those sections of business directly involved in the building process and could also be of wider significance in creating a more efficient urban structure, as was often the case with central slum clearance schemes. Finally state housing was also a powerful force in the promotion of social stability and harmony, as the most tangible symbol of the 'land fit for heroes to live in' during the 1918-21 period of great social unrest, and later in the 'great crusade' of slum clearance during the 1930s. The relative importance of each of these elements would vary according to the nature of the policies adopted. We cannot infer it simply from the fact or even the quantity of state expenditure on housing. The focus of housing policy, the detail of allocation and management, the varying reliance on subsidised municipal rather than subsidised private provision were all important variables that would shift the relationship of reality to the main conceptual categories.

We can make a similar point about state intervention in electricity supply. Its most powerful interwar impact was probably on business activity. However the increasing pursuit of the household market by the electricity industry during the 1930s suggests that, insofar as this was reducing energy costs in the home, it was also contributing to the reproduction of labour. Finally the importance of the National Grid as a symbol of progress in an era of depression conferred a legitimisation function, defusing sources of disenchantment with the existing system. As with housing the detail of pricing and marketing was crucial in determining the nature of the state's actions.

Finally we can note that military and defence activity, although primarily concerned with the maintenance of internal and external stability (i.e. legitimisation) was also an extremely important direct contributor to capitalist production amongst the defence contractors and less directly across a much wider section of manufacturing industry. As we will see in the next chapter it also played an important role in reintegrating the formerly unemployed workforces of the depressed areas into productive employment, so that there was also an important reproductive function.

We could easily multiply these examples, but sufficient has probably been said to show that all state activities were multidimensional in their functions for capital. The relative importance of each function would vary according to what exactly was done and how it was done. However it would also tend to vary according to which fractions of capital were involved. The transitional nature of the interwar economy was such that despite some elements of integration British capitalism retained a very fragmented structure. Drawing on our initial survey in Chapter 1 together with the work contained in Elbaum and Lazonick (1986) and Longstreth (1979) we can characterise interwar British capitalism as having three main elements:

1. Banking Capital: Highly concentrated organisationally and spatially. Potentially therefore a very effective instrument for achieving domestic economic restructuring, but committed to an international banking role and generally slow to form long term

links with industrial capital. Very powerful force, especially in the depression years.

2. Industrial Capital: Collectively powerful, but much weakened during the depression years by its rather fragmented organisational structure and overcommitment to declining sectors. Unable to diversify rapidly because of constraints imposed by generally small-medium size of most firms and absence of sympathetic financial structure. Divisions of interest clearly apparent between declining and growing industries.

3. Finance Capital: Emerging big business apparent in the new large firms. Very highly concentrated organisationally and therefore powerful despite its relatively slow emergence. Able to withstand depression comparatively successfully because of large size of firms which permitted easy diversification and conferred increased power in dealings with other economic groupings and the state.

In addition there were relics of a distinct landed capital, though its larger elements were merging into banking capital while smaller landed capitals were being weakened in both town and country.

The requirements from state policies of these different fractions of capital varied very greatly. We have already seen some evidence of this in the previous chapter in relation to the major orthodoxies of interwar state policy. Thus the return to gold was widely interpreted as a victory of banking over industry. Free trade was more complex but again it was favoured by banking together with export-oriented or import-dependent industry; opposition came from import-vulnerable industries. Orthodox spending policies were also of rather more value to the City than to other fractions of capital.

The shifts in macro-policy in the 1930s are more difficult to interpret. Clearly going off gold and the ending of free trade were reversals for banking capital, but as Longstreth (pp172-3) points out, the changes of the period soon laid the basis for a new wave of highly profitable banking and financial activity in the Empire sterling area. However this was not immediately apparent in 1931-2 and the most obvious beneficiaries were some elements of industrial capital and finance capital. The latter was in a particularly strong position to benefit from the more controlled trading climate associated with imperial preference and managed trade relations, and use them to develop monopolistic trading positions.

Integrating this kind of macro-perspective on fragmented capitals with the functions of more specific fields of state activity outlined above produces some interesting connections. While these can be more fully explored in later chapters, it is useful to briefly rehearse some of the main issues here. On state housing activity, banking capital would be more concerned with the legitimisation function, in contrast to the more specific concerns of sections of industrial and finance capital for labour reproduction and in some cases production enhancement. High housing spending that might well be functional for industrial capital and finance capital could be expected to be potentially dysfunctional for banking capital and the residual smaller urban landed capitals. Much of course would depend on how the interests of the different capitals were reconciled both in the detailed operations of policy and more generally.

There was comparable and in some ways greater ambivalence in electricity supply where capital interests were very fragmented on account of the private power companies which were attractive to banking capital, in one or two cases producing finance capital style grouping, and the industrial consumers of electricity. These wanted a cheap and efficient system that required a heavy measure of state intervention if not necessarily ownership. Finally armed forces expenditures would be regarded differently by banking capital which valued the overseas stability conferred by an international naval and military network, but resented high spending to pay for it and those sections of industrial and finance capital that were major defence contractors. As with electricity the issue was confused further by the presence of considerable state manufacturing capacity paralleling the private capitalist sector.

Overall therefore the animation of apparently simple concepts and their application to a real situation soon acquires great complexity. The problem of how these various capitalist interests were expressed in shaping state policies adds to this. In the previous chapters we sketched out some of the empirical side of this question, showing how business, especially finance capital, was strongly represented near the centres of state power, hinting at an instrumentalist perspective. However, we also identified more structural and hegemonic forces were also operating, increasingly shaping state actions in a less visible way. In many ways this apparent inconsistency might be understood in terms of the transitional nature of the interwar state. Thus it was shifting from a non-democratic bourgeois form in which the state was more literally an instrument of capital, to one where mass democracy could potentially undermine the advancement of capitalist interests insofar as they depended on their personal representation within the state. Although, as we have noted, mass democracy did not actually produce a majority Labour government until 1945, the threat was clear. In such circumstances a short term strengthening of instrumentalist tendencies and a longer term shift towards greater structural and hegemonic advancement of capitalist interest might logically be expected. This interpretation would be broadly consistent with the observed position though requires rather more investigation to be firmly established. More work on the lines of that contained in M. Langan and B. Schwarz (1985) would be valuable. However as we noted earlier, the implicitly less deterministic reliance on hegemonic influence shaping state actions leads us beyond the functional rigidities of capital theories.

Concepts and realities: class conflict and managerialist theories

If class conflict themes of the state have any validity then we should expect to see it demonstrated in the interwar period. The 1919-26 period saw the most serious and sustained industrial unrest ever experienced in Britain, greatly intensifying the trend to major strike action already apparent pre-1914. The 1920s also saw the emergence of the largely working class Labour Party as a major political force which showed its potential via mass democracy to capture the heights of central state power, even if it did not actually realise this potential. More widely, working class consciousness, that is a sense of collective class identity based on the workplace polarisation between the worker and the owners, was arguably higher than ever before or since. The experience of war had greatly accelerated the growth of collective workplace activity and had markedly eroded the rather unquestioning working class acceptance of a ruling class with a legitimate right to rule. The 1917 Russian Revolution had also highlighted the fragility of the established order. Conversely class identity in the Marxist sense had not yet been weakened by mass consumerism.

Thus it is entirely possible to see the early post-1918 years as constituting a major crisis of legitimacy for the state, generating greater intervention by the state aimed at restoring stability using both the tactics of coercion (e.g. the Emergency Powers Act) and concession (e.g. welfare legislation). In the longer term the key elements of the strategy of concession might be represented as mass democracy which permitted the emergence of a reformist and constitutionalist Labourism as a mass political force. In effect this converted the instabilities of mass class conflict in the workplace into the more manageable and tractable class tensions within the framework of the state. Mass unemployment also intensified the extent to which the working class sought to express its class identity at the political rather than the economic level, since it shifted the terms of workplace class conflict on to ground that was far less favourable to organised labour. As we saw in the previous chapter, the great bulk of the working class movement, despite the palpable weaknesses of the two interwar Labour governments, largely abandoned extra-state action in favour of class advancement via the ballot box after the early 1920s.

If we accept this kind of class based analysis, then we can indeed claim some aspects of state policy not simply as functional for capital, but as victories won by class struggle both outside and within the state. Referring back to the specific examples considered above, it becomes possible to add another dimension to comprehending how these aspects of state policy and action were shaped. Thus we can highlight the importance of conscious working class action in more consciously creating the crisis of legitimacy that was certainly part of the explanation of the instigation of a mass state housing programme after 1918. The industrial and rent strikes of wartime Britain, especially Clydeside, have become critical episodes in this kind of explanation. Similarly the role of Labour action at local and central level has also been portrayed as critical in shaping the exact character and nature of housing provision. Labour's 1924 Housing Act in particular stands out as one such example of a major working class input into housing policy. The actions of Labour councils or even Labour Housing Committee chairmen in many towns and cities is also seen as an important mechanism of working class action influencing and shaping the character of actual housing policies beyond what was simply functional for capital (see Melling 1980, generally and Chapter 8). The likelihood of different configurations of class interests existing at local and central level also enables us to see class conflict manifest in central:local state relations.

It is more difficult to claim quite such an important role for working class action and class conflict either within or outside the state for electricity supply. However some Labour politicians were eager to promote the idea of electricity as a symbol of socialist progress. The first Labour government also forced the pace of change on this question and thus played a role in the appearance of the National Grid scheme in 1926 (see Chapter 5). Locally many Labour councillors actively used their control of tariffs and marketing strategies to promote cheap electricity supply in working class areas, especially in conjunction with slum clearance schemes (L. Hannah 1979, pp206-7). The growing importance of electricity to the general functioning of the whole economy also gave it a particular importance in the General Strike, and illustrated that a class dimension was present in some sections of the industry, supported in some cases by sympathetic Labour councils (p272).

The class dimension in defence was altogether more confused, as we will see in the next chapter. Thus the working class, in common with other sections of British society, had strong anti-war sentiments, reinforced in some cases by vaguer notions of international worker solidarity and direct experience of the internal strikebreaking role of the armed forces in the early 1920s (see Chapter 6). However the employment claims of workers in defence related industries, especially shipbuilding, were also important and often seemingly took precedence when Labour was in power. Thus Conservative governments pursuing orthodoxy were usually worse enemies of defence spending than Labour governments. The most serious incident of quasi-class conflict directly involving the armed forces, the 1931 Invergordon naval mutiny was the direct result of orthodox finance.

Overall therefore it is readily possible to detect class dimensions within state policies beyond a simple functionality of state policies for capital. The implication however is that if the state was not simple a means of advancing the interests of capital, but was sufficiently neutral of capital to permit other class interests to be advanced, it may also have possessed a greater independence of either side of the class divide. Thus managerial tendencies were strongly evident in the interwar period and have been identified by most commentators on the period (e.g. Checkland, pp282-339). Major state bureaucracies were being created to service the newly expanded state activities in fields like housing and electricity; they already existed for each of the main armed services. Such groups were united in varying degrees by common commitments and ideologies. Their detailed knowledge and expertise within an increasingly complex state institutional framework often made them powerful vested interests in the shaping of state policy and action. Within the electricity supply industry for example there was a pervasive technical ideology concerned with advancing the system rather than consciously serving any set of particular political interests (see Chapter 5). And as we will see in Chapters 7-8, local government officials, acting in conjunction with central bureaucracies could also play important roles in containing local political ambitions, especially those of Labour. In defence, the perpetuation of separate ministries for each of the armed forces created a managerial framework for defence expenditure that itself had important impacts and tended to heighten the power of the armed forces themselves. The navy, which came out of world war I relatively higher in public opinion, was in a particularly strong bargaining position.

The strength of managerialist sentiment within the interwar period is also important. As Marwick and other commentators have noted, there was a widespread anticipation amongst many in progressive circles that the role of experts and professional managers rather than politicians or actual owners of capital would become increasingly important (A. Marwick 1964). New and important pressure groups like Political and Economic Planning were imbued with this kind of progressive managerial ethos (J. Pinder [ed] 1981). It was implicit also in the strategies proposed by J.M. Keynes and the Fabian socialists which were to be important elements of state orthodoxy after 1939.

Something of this ethos was also apparent in the actions of the state, particularly the tendency to create semi-autonomous state agencies to take certain areas of state policy out of the political arena. We noted several examples of this in Chapter 2, and undoubtedly the appearance of bodies such as the Central Electricity Board in 1927 contributed to the strengthening of the technical-managerial style noted above. Even such areas as housing were not immune from this and by 1935 proposals to take it out of the local political arena were actively under consideration. In the event they appeared only in a residual form for the depressed areas of the north east coast and Scotland, where local financial difficulties and horrendous housing conditions had set an unequal task for the local authorities (see Chapters 7-9).

However we should not necessarily accept such quasi-autonomous agencies at face value. The experience of the Unemployment Assistance Board (see Chapter 6) and the North Eastern Housing Association (Chapter 8) is illustrative that managerialism was not apolitical at least so far as the labour movement was concerned. At the very least it makes us question more deeply what such managerialist tendencies actually represented, in particular whether they were simply another more subtle mechanism for advancing the interests of capital by less instrumentalist means. We cannot of course attempt to answer this question at this stage, without more detailed examination of how it operated in practice. However the potency of the managerial idea in the interwar period cannot be denied. It was no accident that James Burnham's 1941 identification of a managerial revolution was a product of this period.

Conclusions

We have therefore set out something of where we propose to look for explanations in this book. It should be clear that each of the major frameworks we have outlined is not without considerable relevance to the period. Each raises important questions that will help guide and direct our thinking in sifting through the Parliamentary Papers, Public Record Office files, local council minutes and all the other primary and secondary sources that are used in subsequent chapters. However, it is as well to re-emphasise that theory is not our primary concern. We do not seek to distil any eternal verities of state action. The concern is with understanding the British state in the interwar period and theory is one subordinate part of the means to that end, not the end itself. Thus equipped with the empirical background of earlier chapters and the theoretical frameworks of this we can move on to examine the relationship between particular aspects of state action and uneven development.

4
Defence Expenditure

Introduction: the position in 1919

Britain in 1919 was a major world power, reflecting the strategic role it had developed to service and enhance the economic supremacy of British capitalism in the late nineteenth century. This involved a heavy reliance on world trade and was associated with the acquisition of a widespread and extensive empire. Traditionally therefore its navy had played the dominant role in securing its major trade routes, maintaining the international stability consistent with a high volume of seaborne trade and holding the empire together. The army was normally less important, usually performing a colonial or occasionally a European role. From Britain's point of view the Great War (world war I) had been an acute manifestation of the mounting economic and strategic rivalry with Germany that had been apparent for some years previously. It had provided the opportunity to secure important economic interests and trading routes out of the unstable Austro-Hungarian and Ottoman empires, particularly the latter. It also appeared to confirm British naval supremacy.

Britain in 1919 therefore presided over an enlarged empire, having secured important German and Turkish possessions outside Europe, but soon found that the relative decline in its world economic position had not been stopped by the defeat of Germany. Thus Britain had an enlarged area to defend but lacked a commensurately stronger economic base to sustain that defensive role. Other spending pressures, combined with financial orthodoxy and a genuine and widespread revulsion against the horrors of the Great War were to have important implications for defence spending. Increasingly, therefore, Britain lacked a strategic capacity consistent with its world power pretensions.

1919–39: an overview

Figure 4.1 shows the course of interwar spending on the armed

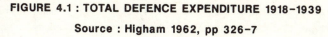

FIGURE 4.1 : TOTAL DEFENCE EXPENDITURE 1918–1939
Source : Higham 1962, pp 326–7

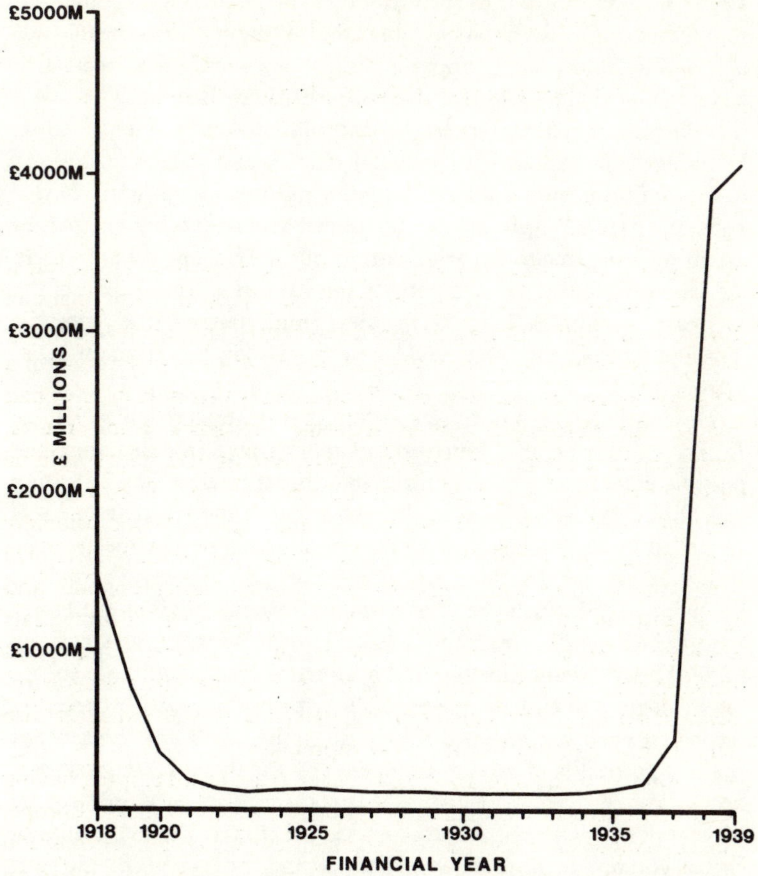

services. There was a period of 'demobilisational insecurity' after war ended, associated with a sharp fall in spending. This gave way to a fairly stable 'peacetime equilibrium' of low spending from the mid-1920s until the mid-1930s. Thereafter the 'mobilisational change' of rearmament brought rapid rises in spending (R. Higham 1965, pp330-3).

The immediate reason for demobilisation in 1919 was the formulation of the so-called 'ten year rule', which said that no major war was expected for that period. Originally enunciated by Lloyd George in 1919, it was formally stated as government policy in March

1922 and consistently endorsed until 1932 by the Committee of Imperial Defence (CID), the major originator of strategic policy advice for the state and the armed forces (B. Collier 1957, pp6-7). Its source was simply the absence of any credible enemy. Thus the decisive defeat of Germany and its apparent eclipse as a world power seemed to have removed the only real domestic threat to Britain. The 1920s therefore were characterised by international agreements, as at Washington in 1922 to secure naval limitation and at Locarno in 1925 to secure European stability (S. Roskill 1968, pp300-55; A.J.P. Taylor 1965, pp221-2). Within the much reduced armaments budget greater attention was given to imperial matters outside Europe. There was an increased recognition of the potential naval threat from Japan in the far east, and this long term view underpinned the sporadic development of Singapore naval base from 1923 (R. Higham 1962, pp108, 127-8).

However it was not until 1931-2 that these fears were realised in the Japanese invasion of Manchuria (Collier, p24). By this time the possible emergence of a new European threat in Germany and Italy was also recognised. It was in this context that the ten year rule was cancelled in March 1932. However continued hopes for the recently convened Geneva disarmament conference and the general climate of financial restraint delayed any action on this cancellation until after 1934, when the disarmament talks collapsed. By this time Germany under Hitler's chancellorship had been named as the ultimate enemy for strategic planning purposes (Collier, pp24-6). Japan became the secondary enemy, active within an eastern theatre of war. This meant that the possibility of two simultaneous and widely separated wars was now acknowledged as realistic. Matters were worsened in 1935 by Mussolini's invasion of Abyssinia which menaced the main lines of British communications between Europe and the far east. By the later 1930s the increasingly open territorial ambitions of Italy and especially Germany in Spain and central Europe reinforced British moves towards progressively higher armaments spending.

However this account, based on spending trends and strategic policy advice, lends a clarity and purpose to government policy that was not actually there. At the same time as rearmament was progressing, political and diplomatic means of avoiding war were being pursued in the form of appeasement, which meant acquiescing in the realisation of the territorial ambitions of potential enemy states (Taylor, pp389-438). The value of appeasement has been much disputed, but some commentators have justified it as buying time for adequate rearmament. Certainly the later acceleration of war production brought many important technological developments in weapons systems. This was particularly true for aircraft, which by the 1930s had become the critical element in strategic thinking.

The growth of the air menace 1919-39

The interwar period was a transitional period between the traditional British reliance on seapower to sustain its economic and strategic world role and the emergence of the aircraft as the dominant delivery vehicle for modern weapons systems and the ultimate determinant of victory or defeat. The potential threat of air power had been recognised in 1912 when the first anti-aircraft guns were installed in Britain (Collier, p9). The Great War had expanded the imaginations of politicians and strategic planners about the potential of aircraft, particularly the high speed bomber armed with high explosive bombs. Gradually the concept of the strategic bombing offensive crystallised, whereby industrial production would be disrupted and civilian populations demoralised by sustained bombing. This offensive weapon then became a defensive strategy on the principle of deterrence.

During the interwar years the bomber came to be seen as a master weapon by both public and strategists, particularly as aircraft speeds increased (U. Bialer 1975). Fighter interception and ground defences seemed to offer no effective answer. All the experience of the period, in US trials against battleships, in RAF colonial experience, in Spain and Abyssinia, seemed to reinforce this (Taylor, pp390,437-8). No one seriously questioned Baldwin's 1932 pronouncement that 'the bomber will always get through' (Higham 1962, p158). In the events of the 1940s though such views were not justified. There were important improvements in air defences with the introduction of greatly improved interceptor fighters and the development of radar (Collier, pp35-46). Neither was strategic bombing as effective in undermining civilian morale and disrupting war production as was assumed. However, this was only apparent with hindsight. It did not influence interwar strategic thinking, which was dominated by the bomber menace. This had many consequences, the most serious of which was an underproduction of fighters, though a more specifically spatial effect came in November 1934, on the eve of rearmament. Recognising that some parts of the country were more vulnerable than others to bombing, the Air Council produced an air safety zonal classification of Britain into safe, unsafe and dangerous (PRO AIR9/67). The

MAP 4.1

AIR VULNERABILITY AND STRATEGIC MANUFACTURING CAPACITY 1935

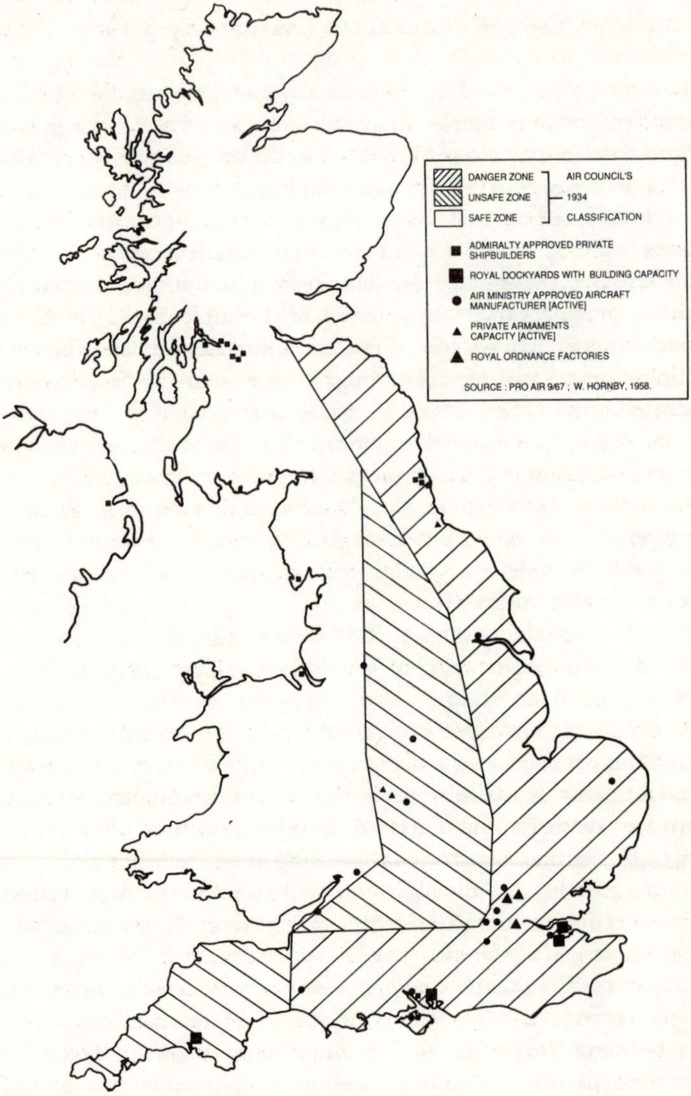

classification, shown in Map 4.1, remained operative until 1940 when assumptions about bomber take off points decisively changed.

The specific purpose of the zoning had been to encourage the relocation of aircraft firms from the dangerous zone, though it influenced thinking about locations of all strategic production in the rearmament period. As can be seen, relatively little strategic production, especially of the new priority of aircraft, was then in safe locations. Thus only 25% of the total employment of Air Ministry approved airframe and aero engine contractors was in the safe zone in April 1935 (derived from W.J. Reader 1968, p210 and P. Fearon 1979, p224). Those that were (Bristol, Gloster and Avro) were only just over the line. By contrast, 55% was in the dangerous zone. In addition the three existing Royal Ordnance Factories (ROFs) at Woolwich, Enfield and Waltham Abbey, the only major centre of ammonium nitrate production for explosives at ICI Billingham, the Royal Naval Dockyards at Portsmouth, Chatham and Sheerness and the private shipbuilding yards of the north east coast and the Solent were all dangerously located.

As will be shown later this classification did much to produce shifts in the geography of defence production during rearmament. However, to understand the significance of these shifts, it is necessary to examine the preceding spatial pattern of defence spending in more detail. We examine first the main armed service spender for all but the last two years of peace, the navy.

The geography of naval expenditure in 1919

Warship building and repairing capacity in 1919 was characterised by the parallel existence of a state sector in the six home Royal Dockyards and a private capitalist sector in the form of the Admiralty approved private yards, of whom 16 were actively building warships for the navy in 1919. Historically the Royal Dockyards had fulfilled all the navy's building and repairing requirements (W. Hornby 1958, pp64- 5). However during the nineteenth and early twentieth centuries this role had altered with the ever growing requirement for larger and more sophisticated warships, and the emergence of a large scale private capitalist shipbuilding industry. The navy had secured an increasing proportion of its vessels from approved private yards, whose emergence was actively encouraged by the Admiralty. The Dockyards, though retaining a significant building capacity, concentrated increasingly from 1905 on repair and refit work, over which they retained a near monopoly. Thus the newest Dockyard at Rosyth, which only became operative during the war, had no building capacity. Pembroke and Sheerness were suitable only for small vessels, and such building as went on was concentrated in the south at Portsmouth, Devonport and Chatham. However in 1919 the naval tonnage building in private yards was more than ten times that building in the Dockyards (Navy Estimates, 1919-20).

The spatial impact of this is clear as can be seen in Map 4.2. Before spending was cut from wartime levels, the bulk of naval spending was concentrated in northern England and Scotland where most of the approved private yards were located. This did not mean that all the impacts of that spending accrued to the main contractor. Somewhat later (in 1934) it was revealed that a £2.5 million cruiser contract created orders for hundreds of firms in 81 towns (L. Jones 1957, p111). Unfortunately the Navy Estimates specify only the contractors for the hull and the machinery. Nearly always the machinery was supplied locally, in many cases by the same firm (the exceptions were usually the Royal Dockyards). More generally the high degree of regional economic specialisation apparent in the shipbuilding areas suggests that most component materials for a warship would be supplied from nearby, or from other warship building centres or from other northern heavy industrial centres, particularly the armourers' centre of Sheffield.

Thus the three most highly specialised armaments firms existing in 1919, Vickers, Armstrong-Whitworth and Beardmore had the capacity to build, engine, arm and armour plate their warships within their own organisations, which usually meant from capacity close to the slipway. At Beardmore's, operations were heavily concentrated at Dalmuir, with strong backward linkages to the Glasgow region (J.R. Hume and M.S. Moss 1979). Armstrong-Whitworth vessels launched at Walker-on-Tyne might be engined there or by the nearby firms of Parsons or Hawthorn-Leslie, and would be armed upstream at the Elswick or Scotswood ordnance works, perhaps with some links to the old Whitworth works at Openshaw, Manchester (J.D. Scott 1962). Vickers' warship operations were highly concentrated at Barrow, which also undertook much subcontracting work for heavy gun mountings though there were strong company linkages to Sheffield. While high value equipment like range finders and radios were usually produced elsewhere, these were, as yet, a relatively small part of total contract value. Overall therefore we can be reasonably confident that the bulk of naval spending on building in 1919 provided profits for firms and employment for workers in the north and Scotland. A rather lower volume of building expenditure, but large amounts of repair and refit work sustained large workforces at the southern Dockyards and rather fewer elsewhere.

The Changing Geography of Naval Spending 1919-39

Map 4.2 also gives an outline of change. In 1922 the Washington naval treaty brought cancellations of submarine contracts and a drastic curtailment of proposals for new construction, particularly of battleships and battlecruisers, which only private yards had the capacity to build. Only two such 'treaty' battleships were completed during the interwar period. The general pattern though was of a sharp decline in the amount of new building, and within that a relative and absolute shift to construction in the Royal Dockyards. Thus the building profiles of the Dockyards show a peak in the middle of the period with low points at the beginning and end, in sharp contrast to the experience of the private yards. This had a very marked spatial effect with the south faring much better than the north and Scotland on account of this abnormal concentration of work in the Dockyards. The spatial effect was compounded because refit work became even more heavily concentrated in the Dockyards (Higham 1962, p194), and because the only two non-southern Dockyards, at Pembroke and Rosyth, bore the brunt of state sector cuts and were closed.

The fact that the two private warship builders on the Solent (Thornycroft and J.S. White) were as badly affected, relatively speaking, as northern and Scottish yards only partly modified the spatial impact. Similarly a slightly higher than average tendency for Dockyard subcontracting to the private firms in 1932 had a marginal impact. But the main conclusion remains that within a general climate of naval expenditure cuts, the south was relatively protected and in several respects did better than at peak national periods of building. Thus as building accelerated with rearmament, the private yards once more secured large contracts, notably for five new King George V class battleships laid down in 1937, two each on the Clyde and Tyne and one at Cammell Laird, Birkenhead. By 1939 a pattern closer to that of 1919 than 1932 was evident.

We have already considered the reasons for the temporal fluctuations in building activity. The reasons for spatial fluctuations are less immediately apparent. The principles by which work was allocated between different yards and areas was the subject of great

MAP 4.2

ROYAL NAVAL VESSELS BUILDING 1919, 1926,1932 AND 1939

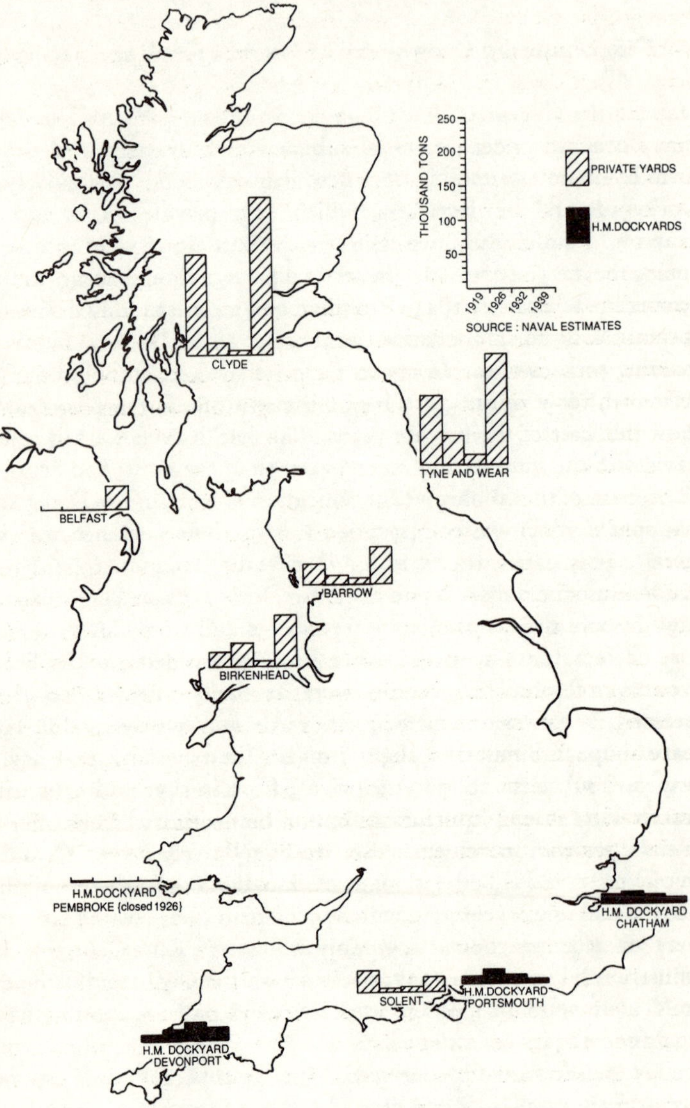

political interest amongst MPs with warship building constituencies. Many parliamentary questions were asked, though failed to produce any complete delineation of how exactly the process took place. However within the general context of cuts the Admiralty seem, quite consciously, to have given preference to the Dockyards, allocating work to them without any necessity to tender competitively against private yards and in many cases evidently without any tender at all (e.g. Hansard, 249 HC Deb 5s, c1274). The Admiralty firmly believed that Dockyard prices were a reliable yardstick against which private firms could be assessed. Yet private firms were often well aware that Dockyard costs were consistently higher than their own. Vickers, for example, privately estimated Dockyard prices 1925-34 at £220 per ton compared to £201 in the private yards (£210 excluding the two battleships) (Scott, p184). Rearmament increased this differential spectacularly, but the Admiralty continued to use Dockyard costs as a marker, with predictable results for private contractors' profits (W. Ashworth 1953, pp108-13). Overall though sufficient has been said to show that cost criteria do not explain the spatial shifts in allocation of naval work.

A more credible argument is that the Royal Dockyards were favoured to maintain strategically important production in specialist naval yards. This was virtually admitted in the parliamentary discussion of the 1928 Navy Estimates (214 HC Deb 5s, c2139-40, 2190). Such a view essentially regarded the southern Dockyards as core capacity with specialist, skilled workforces to be kept working even under low spending conditions so that capacity and skills could be retained. By contrast the private yards were seen as more peripheral, a spare and rather elastic capacity. In Admiralty thinking, they needed only a few orders to prevent wholesale deterioration and allow reactivation should future mobilisation be necessary. Thus after the initial postwar rundown, the decline in southern Dockyard employment was less severe than in other shipbuilding centres and a fairly stable employment of 30,000 (+/-2500) was maintained from 1927-36, at a time when unemployment in the private shipbuilding industry was very severe (Navy Estimates). In this context the trend to build more warship tonnage in the Dockyards from the mid-1920s would seem to reflect an insufficiency of repair and refit work to fully occupy the slimmed down core workforce in the southern Dockyards. Accordingly extra building work was allocated to meet this shortfall. And even when lulls in work occurred temporary layoffs were uncommon (May Report 1931, p81).

Only occasionally were such principles apparent in the allocation of work to private yards, usually at times of political sensitivity to unemployment or the priorities of rearmament or both. Thus in 1924 the first Labour government deliberately placed orders for material and stores with contractors in 'blackspot' unemployment areas (Statement of 1st Lord on 1924-5 estimates, p7). Vickers at Barrow benefited particularly, receiving a large order for the reconditioning of gun mountings. By late 1934 the coincidence of abandonment of the ten year rule and heightened political concern about unemployment brought a greater than usual willingness to tinker with usual contracting practice on employment grounds. Thus Vickers-Armstrong (by now merged) were persuaded by government to direct work on a cruiser contract to their yard on Tyneside, where shipbuilding unemployment was 70.4% rather than concentrating it solely at Barrow, where it was a comparatively modest 22.4% (PRO CAB24(251)CP253(34)). This was very much a turning point. Earlier the same year the Admiralty had fiercely resisted pleas for preferential treatment from Clydeside and in 1933 the Cabinet had steadfastly refused to give Palmers of Jarrow an order to protect it from closure (R.H. Campbell 1979, pp170-1; F.M. Miller 1976, p464).

As rearmament got into full swing though, the strategic necessity to secure capacity meant that 'uneconomic' orders were given in early 1939 to several smaller yards that otherwise might have been closed (Hornby, p40). However by that time severe damage had already occurred, especially to labour skills, technical development and new investment. To understand this we must examine intra-industry changes in more detail. We begin with the state sector.

Rationalisation and the royal dockyards

In 1925 it was announced that the two non-southern Dockyards, Rosyth and Pembroke, were to be placed on a care and maintenance basis (Pembroke and Rosyth Dockyards, 1925). This followed a period of intense in-fighting between the Admiralty and the Treasury. The latter (under Winston Churchill), pursuing orthodox financial policies, had been pressing for cuts while the Admiralty had been pushing an ambitious cruiser building programme (Roskill 1968, pp445-55; Higham 1962, pp127-8). The Admiralty fought very effectively and, after nearly thirty cabinet meetings on the issue, the Treasury capitulated, insisting though that cuts be made elsewhere. Rosyth and Pembroke were the price of that victory. Shortly afterwards Pembroke Dockyard was completely closed, though Rosyth eventually reopened in 1938.

The decision to close these two in particular was a complex one. It was justified principally on grounds of size, flexibility and naval strategy, though such arguments were hardly conclusive. Certainly Rosyth with 6687 employees in April 1918 and Pembroke with 3479 were much smaller than Chatham (11,494), Devonport (15,837) and Portsmouth (16,576) (170 HC Deb 5s c1421-2). However the very small yard of Sheerness was retained. On flexibility and naval strategy Rosyth was rejected because it was a 'capital ship' Dockyard, designed specifically to meet the requirements of a North Sea anti-German battleship based strategy. Clearly in the 1920s this no longer seemed relevant, though it left a physical legacy of ships that needed servicing. Thus Rosyth was the only Dockyard where the Navy's largest ship, HMS Hood, could actually dock. There were also some important arguments against closure of these two: Both were likely to be safer from an aerial bombing point of view than the remaining southern yards. This point was made in the parliamentary debate on the issue in 1925 (189 HC Deb 5s c854-932). Air defence schemes drawn up in 1923-5 had placed the southern Dockyard towns in or near a front line air fighting zone (Collier, pp15-20). Moreover the eventual reopening of Rosyth partly reflected increased fears about southern vulnerability. Even Pembroke was again pressed into service using floating docks during world war II because of the risks of using the southern Dockyards (Hornby, p296). Finally, we can note that Rosyth was actually the most modern yard, completed only in 1916.

There was also another, less obvious, set of reasons for their closure that relate more to the cultural priorities of naval rather than commercial management practices. The Admiralty successfully resisted several attempts during the 1920s to introduce commercial and civilian management and the Dockyards remained firmly under naval control (Hornby, pp73-5; Roskill 1968, pp455-6). In this context local traditions and cultural attitudes to the navy were very important. Portsmouth, Chatham and Sheerness Dockyards all dated from Tudor times; Devonport from the seventeenth century. All were 'naval towns', important recruiting centres where local populations were sympathetic to naval concerns, motivated by a strong sense of loyalty to the navy. Although trades unionism was typical in all Dockyards, the southern towns did not have the rather more polarised class structures associated with capitalist labour relations (e.g. M. Waters 1984). There were different demarcations of labour skills in the

Dockyards as compared to the private industry (Balfour Report IV 1928, p394). On these kind of criteria Pembroke and especially Rosyth were unusual. Neither possessed the traditions and cultural orientation towards the navy of the others. And unlike any other Dockyard, Rosyth had experienced quite serious labour problems during world war I (Industrial Unrest Commission 1917, pp4, 11-2). It was also regarded as poor recruiting territory.

Such cultural reasons were reinforced by more straightforward spatial factors. Thus the peacetime climate of expenditure restraint tended to prioritise locations near to the centres of power. In contrast to the advantages of dispersal during war conditions, it was more useful in peacetime to have close access to the Admiralty. This was paralleled by the increasingly southern concentration of Admiralty research stations. Thus in 1920 the Admiralty Engineering Laboratory was founded at West Drayton, Middlesex. The following year the Admiralty Research Laboratory shifted to nearby Teddington, having originated in wartime in a remote Scottish location. Other establishments dealing with weapons and communications research were located near Portsmouth while establishments shared with the other services also tended to be near London. In such a context the southern Dockyards, especially Portsmouth and Chatham, were better placed to assist with prototype development than those elsewhere. Overall therefore a complete explanation of Dockyard rationalisation would emphasise naval tradition, local culture and the wider management structure of the navy, all of which prioritised the southern Dockyards. The changes in the capitalist warship building industry were based more on the rationale of profit, but this did not prevent the restructuring process being complex.

The impact on the capitalist sector

By 1939 two of the 16 yards active in 1919, Beardmore and Palmer's of Jarrow, had ceased to exist. The fixed capacity of the warship industry declined by about a fifth between 1930 and 1939 (Hornby, p40). There had been a major merger of Vickers and Armstrong Whitworth, and several ownership changes (J.R. Parkinson 1960, pp29- 30; Scott, pp164-6). But considering the extent to which demand was depressed, there was remarkably little quantitative change in the fixed capacity of the private warship building industry. Instead private builders responded by allowing capacity to deteriorate, by not investing, by colluding with other builders and, to a lesser extent, with the Admiralty and, most important of all, by shedding labour.

Of course the warship industry was not really distinct from the merchant shipbuilding industry, nor was private warship building solely for the Royal Navy. Accordingly it is difficult to specify the impact of naval expenditure alone. Several writers though have emphasised the small effect of naval cuts on levels of shipbuilding unemployment (e.g. R.F. Bretherton et al 1941, p71). However this does not mean that naval spending was unimportant for profits. Slaven's study of the mixed yard of John Brown of Clydebank 1919-38 shows that naval contracts (with an average on-cost profit of 9.3%) were over three times as profitable as merchant work and brought over 47% of total profits while accounting for under 23% of total costs (A. Slaven 1977, pp202, 207). A conflicting interpretation about pre-rearmament profit levels is given by Ashworth though it is less well supported by evidence than Slaven's study (Ashworth, p106). Generally the evidence of other business histories support Slaven. Thus Vickers at Barrow remained open largely on the strength of Admiralty contracts (Scott, p184). And the two yards that were closed survived as long as they did because occasional naval orders had helped offset severe losses in other fields (Hume and Moss, pp182, 216; E. Wilkinson 1939, pp141, 157- 8).

The relatively high profits gained even on occasional naval contracts were then important in avoiding the need for large scale restructuring. Another factor was the widespread collusion over contracting between shipbuilders. Opinion differs as to when this began, but it seems likely that it was occurring covertly from about 1925 (Scott, p184; Slaven, pp199-200). By the rearmament period the Admiralty was sufficiently convinced that competitive tendering had been a facade for several years to abandon it in many cases, though Ashworth believes that active collusion had not actually begun until about 1935 (pp106-7). Much, of course, depends on what this collusion really involved, but even in the 1920s remarkably close prices were being tendered by different yards, suggesting that some measure of price fixing was already present. Several accounts suggest that the Admiralty was also drawn into some parts of this process, with contract rotas being referred to in 1926 (e.g. Slaven, p200). The 1934 US Nye Committee on the Munitions Industries also released correspondence from Vickers that indicated remarkably close contacts with the Admiralty contracts department and suggested that contract fixing on the basis of personal friendships occurred (Scott, pp242-3). Strictly speaking there was no explicit evidence of corruption, but certainly a rather cosy relationship did exist between the private builders and the Admiralty that many, particularly on the left, found very unsettling. Private yards often consciously recruited managers with Admiralty connections; politicians with ministerial potential or experience were often recruited as directors (Haxey, pp62-3).

Despite such expedients though some rationalisation was unavoidable. The Bank of England, in an act of 'surrogate' state intervention, forced the merger of Armstrong Whitworth and Vickers in 1927, resulting in the temporary closure of the Walker yard (Scott, pp183, 186). In 1930 the industry collectively formed National Shipbuilders Security Ltd (NSS) with Bank of England support (H.M. Hallsworth 1935, pp250-2). It bought and scrapped the capacity of firms in difficulty. Sites were prevented from being used again for shipbuilding by 40-year restrictive convenants. In fact it was mainly used on non-Admiralty approved firms, though Beardmore's Dalmuir yard was closed by this means in 1930 and Palmer's in 1934. NSS also held the Vickers-Armstrong yard at Walker on a temporary care and maintenance basis (L. Jones, pp135-8).

Rearmament brought a halt to this limited restructuring. The Admiralty was concerned rather to involve more firms in contracting. By 1939 Harland and Wolff of Belfast, already on the Admiralty list, were actively building for the navy for the first time in the interwar period. Other smaller Scottish yards were also being used. The increasing use of Belfast though was indicative of how air safety zoning considerations were beginning to have an effect. More generally this played a part in the late 1930s' swing back to private builders and away from the Dockyards. Apart from the Tyne and Solent the private warship builders were well located. It is perhaps significant that the Solent builders recovered less than the other private building areas since they shared the acute vulnerability of the Dockyards. However, a severe problem of the rearmament period was labour shortage. The shipbuilding industry had comprised 269,970 workers in 1923; by 1935 it had fallen to 157,230 (Hallsworth 1935, p256; 1938, p358). Skills that were saleable outside the industry (e.g. electricians) were in particularly short supply. The interwar experience left the industry with low wage rates, serious labour mistrust of management and poor working conditions in open yards (P. Inman 1957, pp34-5, 328-33). None of these eased the labour shortage problem and contributed to a climate of labour unrest by the end of the 1930s. Some areas were able to draw in labour from acutely depressed districts nearby. Thus

Barrow drew in labour from west Cumberland but Tyneside remained a problem, especially after the two battleship contracts were placed (Scott, p224).

Profits meanwhile rose dramatically. Although Excess Profits Tax, introduced in 1939, recouped some of this (G. Peden 1984b pp139-42), the scale of profits was astonishing. It was not until 1941 that the Admiralty realised this. A subsequent analysis of contracts for 32 ships placed 1936-8 showed a median rate of on-cost profit of 28% with three ships showing profits of over 70% (Ashworth, p108). The most expensive contract, a £3.5 millions battleship showed a profit of nearly 42%. Although the shipbuilders contested these figures, their own sample still showed an average profit of 19%. A long term wrangle ensued that is beyond the scope of this work.

Overall therefore the costs of naval cuts were borne largely by the workforces of the private shipbuilding areas. The few naval orders that were allocated for private builders in the depression years were usually sufficient, under conditions of collusion, to give modest profits to the yard owners. However they denied any long term employment stability and greatly reduced the bargaining power of shipyard workforces. They also inhibited any larger scale rationalisation of warship building capacity than actually took place. Rearmament brought demonstrably huge profits to warship building firms though the benefits of these were slow to spread to workforces.

Naval expenditure and uneven development

We have established that naval spending reinforced the spatial impact of the interwar depression. The south was relatively protected; the north and Scotland bore the brunt of cuts. In essence this pattern was shaped by two major sets of forces, at least until rearmament. These were banking capital and the Admiralty itself. Lesser influences were exerted by the warship and armaments builders and the labour movement. The priorities of banking capital involved the maintenance of Britain's position in the world and the security of its overseas investments. Traditionally therefore the navy played an important role in the protection of such investments. However, a more obvious interwar priority was the maintenance of the international stability of sterling which, as incorporated by the Treasury into state policies, led to the climate of spending restraint noted in chapter 2. In a period in which it seemed that stability in Britain's strategic and economic position in the world could be maintained by treaties and agreements, the navy, by far the most expensive service until the late 1930s, became a target for expenditure cuts.

On the other side (usually) was the Admiralty which exhibited a high degree of autonomy in its operations. Thus the major spatial impacts of spending cuts seem to be attributable, almost completely, to Admiralty actions, motivated by managerial decisions on self-defined naval rather than capitalistic criteria of profit or even wider strategic criteria. Obviously the Admiralty's autonomy was not complete, but it was remarkably effective in fighting Treasury pressure for cuts in the 1920s. It provides a clear example of the 'wider legitimacy' discussed in chapter 3, and Beatty, the first Sea Lord and hero of Jutland, used his public popularity to great effect in these battles with the Treasury. (Significantly, when the Treasury did eventually gain the upper hand and forced the Admiralty to accept orthodoxy so that it imposed pay cuts on the navy, the outcome was a pyrrhic victory: The resultant Invergordon mutiny precipitated the abandonment of the gold standard.)

During the pre-rearmament period industrial capital and the labour movement had relatively little impact. We have noted the indications of very cosy relationships between armaments firms and Admiralty procurement sections and the above-average profits of naval work. But this was no instrumentalist manipulation of state defence policy by industrial capital. Had it been so it is inconceivable that the spatial allocation of naval expenditure would not have been different. The reality was that the private industry was on the defensive for most of the interwar period, losing its share of a depressed market to the protected and favoured southern Royal Dockyards. All attempts by the capitalist sector to secure the civilianisation and commercialisation of the Dockyards in the 1920s foundered on the rock of naval resistance.

Labour's impact on defence policy was limited. As a party of peace it disliked armaments spending, but in office it baulked at cuts because of the unemployment implications. (Paradoxically the Admiralty had its worst battles with Conservative Chancellors, even more paradoxically with Churchill.) As a party of peace and socialism, Labour preferred that armaments manufacture should be in state hands. This meant that Labour (with the Liberals) opposed the Rosyth and Pembroke closures, but acquiesced in the increased concentration of work in the southern Dockyard towns. Similarly they were inhibited in calling for more contracts for the private industry in the north and Scotland even though these were their natural centres of support; the southern Dockyard towns fairly consistently returned non-Labour MPs. Overall therefore the influence of the labour movement, such as it was, tended to reinforce the Admiralty line before rearmament. Rearmament had the effect of prioritising production, thus immediately strengthening the position of industrial capital and ultimately that of labour. Conversely the power of banking capital and the Admiralty was weakened. Some, though not all, of these trends were paralleled in the other armed services, which we now examine.

Army and RAF expenditures: before rearmament

Unlike the navy, rearmament in the army and RAF necessitated considerable new investment and creation of entirely new workforces. This had long term implications for the space economy beyond those of the immobile warship industry, where the spatial impacts were largely those of contract allocation and rationalisation decisions. Army and airforce expenditures had similar kinds of effects on the older industries, but less prominently than the navy. However, because of the amount of new productive capacity necessary for rearmament, they also had important long term impacts. At the risk of drawing a false distinction, it is on these that we focus.

Like the navy, industrial production for the army spanned both state and capitalist sectors. Both though were much reduced by 1935 (Hornby, pp77-83). The three state-owned ROFs were mainly research and development rather than mass production sites. ICI's private explosives and ammunition capacity at Billingham, Ardeer and Birmingham was barely used (W.J. Reader 1975, pp253, 263). The story of Birmingham Small Arms and the big gun firms of Vickers-Armstrong and Beardmore was similar. Discreetly though, and in various ways, the state had subsidised such firms to retain some capacity against future strategic requirements (Hornby, p147). The aero industry was entirely in the capitalist sector. The state-owned Royal Aircraft Factory at Farnborough in Hampshire, important in world war I production, was shifted to a solely research function and retitled the Royal Aircraft Establishment (Fearon 1974, p247). Instead the Air Ministry retained a 'ring' of approved contractors (Reader 1968, p210; Fearon 1979, p224; D.E.H. Edgerton 1984). As we saw earlier, they were heavily concentrated in inner Britain, especially as earlier northern manufacturers either left the industry (e.g. English Electric in 1926) or moved southwards (e.g. Armstrong-

Whitworth from Newcastle to Coventry in 1927) (K. Richardson 1975, p56). Despite the defection of English Electric, there were still a rather large number of firms in the 'ring' for the volume of work. They survived in a hand-to-mouth fashion on development contracts, short production runs, elaborate subcontracting schemes, and sometimes bizarre expedients such as making milk churns, growing mushrooms and keeping pigs (Fearon 1979, p229). Unlike the other armaments industries, aircraft production before rearmament was not heavily capitalised. It was still run by enthusiastic designer/pilots and relied on skill and hand labour rather than mass production. The changes in the aircraft industry necessitated in the late 1930s were accordingly dramatic, reflecting the technical changes in aircraft design as well as the quantitative pressures of rearmament.

General features of rearmament production for Army and RAF

British output of military aircraft rose from a yearly average of 612 in 1928-33 to 2827 in 1938 and 7840 in 1939 (Fearon 1979, pp225, 237). The state was heavily involved in this expansion of production, though it did not directly become a producer as it had in world war I. However, over 42% of the new investment in the aircraft industry 1936-9 was state investment in the 'agency' factories owned by the state but operated by private firms (Ashworth, p250). Additionally private investment by 'shadow' firms (not normally aircraft producers) was state guaranteed. Finally, of course, as customer the state's insatiable demand for aircraft allied with improved stage payment procedures (Fearon 1979, p234) was an effective guarantee to other private investment.

Organisationally several important innovations permitted this rapid expansion. The first was the 'shadow' scheme. This had been first suggested in the 1920s, but its adoption in 1936 reflected the recommendations of an advisory group of industrialists led by Lord Weir, a former Air Minister, head of a Glasgow engineering firm, and architect of the national electricity grid (see chapter 5). It involved recruiting firms outside aircraft production to shadow the aircraft firms and offer the possibility of very rapid production build ups if this proved necessary (Reader 1968, pp189ff; Hornby, pp218-22). It was also felt to be a means of introducing mass production methods to the aircraft industry. Thus most of the early firms recruited into the scheme were motor car firms which were felt to have the necessary management skills and experience (Hornby, pp218-9). After 1938 emphasis shifted to expansion in the main aircraft industry and subcontracting. The shift reflected substantial private investment in the aircraft industry, improvements in its management skills (Fearon 1979, p235), a reluctance of some aircraft firms to co-operate with the shadow scheme (I. Lloyd 1978, pp161, 170-85) and difficulties with some proposed shadow firms (P.W.S. Andrews and E. Brunner 1955, pp219-22; Reader 1968, pp255-68). Increasingly therefore agency agreements were used to equip new factories on fully mass production lines, fed by increasing amounts of component subcontracting (Hornby, p196).

Meanwhile dramatic changes were also taking place in army production which carried much of the explosive and shell manufacturing for the other services. More was invested by the War Office 1936-9 than the Air Ministry and the Admiralty combined (Ashworth, pp249-51). Some 70% (£18.9 millions) was directly on state sector factories and 16 new ROFs had been approved by March 1939 with nine already open, employing 32,900 compared to the usual peacetime ROF complement of under 9000 (Hornby, pp83, 91). Most of the private expansion that occurred was also assisted, mainly as state-owned agency factories. Thus in 1937-9 ICI, the most prominent contractor, began 18 new agency factories (Hornby, p149). There were many others from within and outside the traditional armaments industry (e.g. Andrews and Brunner 1955, pp222-5). Overall therefore a large number of new factories were operating or being built by the outbreak of war. Within a relatively short period a substantial reorientation had taken place with far-reaching spatial implications.

The changing geography of Army and RAF production 1935-9

A series of pressures peculiar to the mid/late 1930s were operating on location decisions on the new rearmament factories. One was the air safety classification defined in 1934 and outlined earlier. On this basis the Air Ministry sought the relocation of the most vulnerable aircraft factories (PRO AIR 9/67). The War Office similarly sought the replacement of the three historic ROFs in London and the CID the duplication of ICI's Billingham explosives capacity (Hornby, pp160, 293; Reader 1975, p263). A second pressure was the growing concern about the depressed areas (see chapter 9) with a mounting general pressure from both labour and business and more specific Ministry of Labour pressure on service departments to consider sites in the depressed areas. Finally the aircraft industry was forced to come to terms with the technical changes in aircraft design and the shift to mass production. These required metalworking and engineering labour skills and created labour problems for expanding firms remote from major engineering centres.

The outcome of these varied pressures is shown in Map 4.3. Generally most new armaments capacity was better located from the air safety point of view than the pre-1935 industry. However, many compromises were necessary. Thus the new Birtley, County Durham, ROF in the dangerous zone was developed because its existing buildings meant it could be brought into production quickly (Hornby, pp293-5). Other engineering ROFs like Nottingham were constrained by labour requirements. Most of the rest like Chorley, Bridgend, Glascoed, Pembrey, Bishopton and Irvine had western locations within the safe zone. It was more difficult though to exert equal control over private firms, even when factories were state provided. Thus War Office agency factories were provided for BSA and Nuffield Mechanisation in unsafe Birmingham. But the greatest difficulties were experienced with aircraft firms and their shadows. The Air Ministry's proposed relocation of the dangerously located firms foundered on the opposition of the firms themselves. Many were already moving for other reasons, so that Boulton Paul moved from dangerous Norwich to safe Wolverhampton in 1936, largely to secure sufficient skilled labour (Fearon 1979, p234).

West London based Fairey also acquired a branch factory in Stockport in 1934, on the safe/unsafe boundary, tapping the north western surplus of engineering labour (A.D. George, undated, p11; Inman, pp22-3). Short Brothers of Rochester solved the labour problem in another way by forming a close association with Harland and Wolff shipbuilders in safe Belfast (Fearon 1979, p234). But the Air Ministry was quite unable to get any firms to move solely on vulnerability grounds. Moreover it did not always take its own guidelines seriously, and admitted a new firm, Airspeed, to the 'ring' in 1936, despite its location in dangerous Portsmouth (Fearon 1979, p235).

The shadow scheme offered some means of shifting capacity from the most vulnerable areas. However this was limited by the initial reliance on the motor car industry. Southern firms like Ford were not used because of the acute vulnerability of its Dagenham factory in east London (Hornby, p291). Most early shadow aircraft factories were therefore in Birmingham and Coventry, which were unsafe rather

MAP 4.3

NEW STRATEGIC MANUFACTURING CAPACITY 1935-9

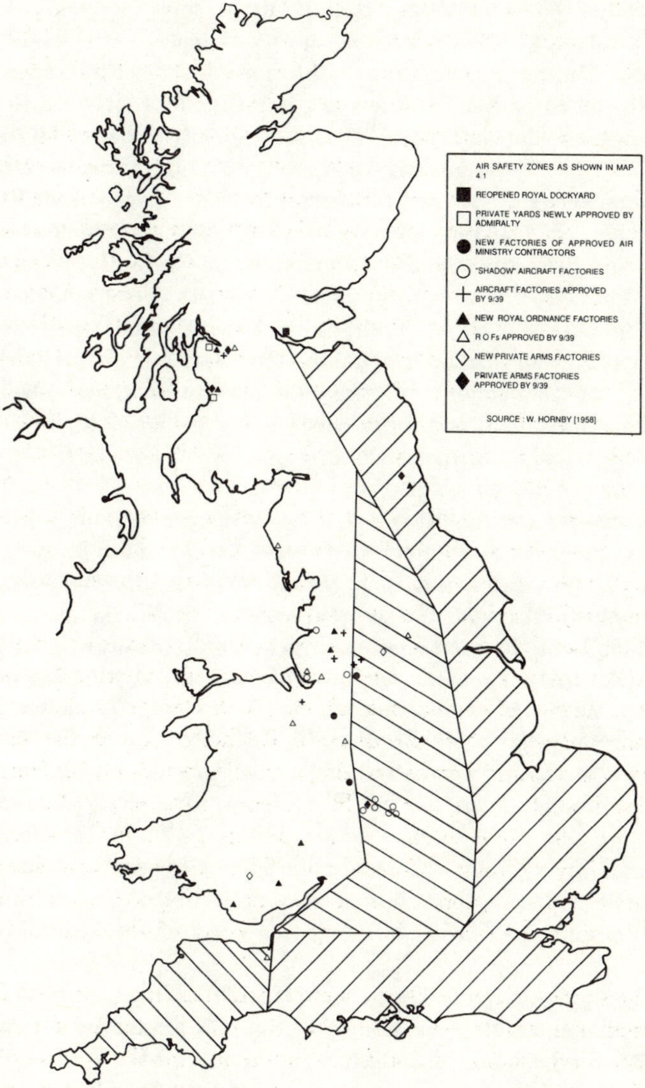

than dangerous. Thus the huge Nuffield shadow Spitfire and Wellington factory at Castle Bromwich, Birmingham, was an improvement on the main Supermarine and Vickers factories at Woolston and Weybridge. However the intensive use of the already prosperous west midlands created labour shortages and as the European situation worsened began to look foolish on vulnerability criteria. During 1937 a shift to the north west became apparent initially when parliament rejected a Berkshire location for a Rootes shadow Blenheim factory and it was subsequently shifted to Liverpool (Hornby, pp289-90; Fogarty 1945, pp237-8). Other smaller shadow factories were soon located in Lancashire, and in 1938 Rolls Royce compromised between the Ministry of Labour's preference for Liverpool and its own for Burton to develop at Crewe (Lloyd, pp177-81). The same year major shadow schemes were agreed with Metropolitan-Vickers at Trafford Park, Manchester and English Electric, Preston (the latter signalling the re-emergence of the firm as an aircraft manufacturer). By 1939 the north west was the favoured location, but already some firms were looking further afield, and it was decided to build a further Rolls Royce agency factory at Hillington, Glasgow (Lloyd, pp190-9).

What then was the net spatial effect of rearmament, in particular the new factories, on the depressed areas? A recent quantitative study based on a social accounting matrix suggests that the pre-war employment effects were most pronounced in traditional trades such as shipbuilding, iron and steel etc. rather than yet in the growth of new industries (M. Thomas 1983). Table 4.1 shows the associated

TABLE 4.1: REGIONAL DISTRIBUTION OF EMPLOYMENT CREATED BY REARMAMENT 1935-8

	(a) % of Employment created by Rearmament	(b) % of Insured Population 7/38	(a)/(b)
London and South East	33.09	35.74	0.93
North and North West	13.14	22.37	0.59
North East	6.55	4.13	1.59
Midlands	21.06	16.41	1.28
East	4.98	3.22	1.55
Wales and South West	11.47	6.80	1.69
Central Scotland	8.26	7.50	1.10
Rest of Scotland and N. Ireland	1.37	3.82	0.36

Source: Estimated by M. Thomas, p569

assessment of the regional pattern of employment benefits to 1938. Though some of the regional aggregates are unhelpful, the regions deriving disproportionate benefit seem to have been Scotland, the north east (i.e. the West and East Ridings with north Lincolnshire), the south west and Wales, and the midlands. These were some of the original aircraft industry locations and the first wave of shadow factories. The later emphasis on the north west presumably only showed up in employment terms after 1938.

However in another long term sense the importance of these new rearmament investments cannot be quantified. Essentially they ushered the large scale multi-plant, multi-locational firm into the British economy on a greater scale than previously, with a production process more spatially divided than had been common even in the large scale firms that already existed. Viewed in this light rearmament was an important catalyst in the evolution of British capitalism. Thus it enabled private firms to develop the complex planning procedures, management strategies and production techniques necessary to make identical products at different locations without very skilled workforces. In particular the important distinction between the main site where decision making and research and development were concentrated and the branch factory where large scale production was concentrated was clearly visible. This separation is not just apparent with hindsight. Clearly the Air Ministry and War Office did not consciously conceive their war production with these long term things in mind. However, these issues were certainly in the plans of some of the firms, most explicitly Rolls Royce (Lloyd, pp189-90). And, of course, there were similar splits already evident in the state sector with research and development in the south and mass production sites increasingly in outer Britain.

Overall therefore we can consider rearmament as an important early stage in the spatial transformation of the British economy. Thus although it brought revival of traditional industries in outer Britain, it also laid the foundations of a shift to branch factory economies providing a reserve of unskilled and semi-skilled labour for manufacturing products which were researched, designed, developed and financed elsewhere, principally at this time in the south. The midlands as in other respects appear as an intermediate zone.

It is important not to claim too much for this; there were a few earlier signs of the process and much did not occur until the 1950s and 1960s. But it remains the case that what the state did and showed industrial capital how to do in the 1930s and 1940s, private capital began to do for itself in the 1950s and 1960s.

Conclusions

Essentially we have argued that the state's defence role in the interwar years was of short and long term importance for the British space economy. The Admiralty's impact was predominantly short term, intensifying depression in the north and Scotland, protecting the south and from 1934, reinforcing regional recovery with new rearmament orders. This strategy undoubtedly contributed to the long term problems of shipbuilding, particularly labour relations and adoption of new technologies. However, it was War Office and Air Ministry policies that laid the basis for a longer term transformation by introducing multi-plant multi-locational production systems on a large scale that transcended traditional regional specialisations.

To explain why such impacts were apparent is less easy. We have already noted the tensions between Admiralty managerial priorities and the orthodox logic of financial capital as decisive elements in determining naval expenditures and policies before rearmament. Industrial capital became stronger as rearmament proceeded. There were clear similarities with War Office activity, except that industrial capital was throughout weaker, and rearmament strengthened state managerial objectives for production. Thus a more 'rational' spatial pattern of War Office production soon appeared in sharp contrast to that in the aircraft industry, where capitalist criteria dominated the early rearmament period. Thus CID's initial decision to expand the aircraft industry and rearmament itself had encouraged substantial stock exchange investment in the industry. Accordingly individual business priorities shaped early locational decisions. The Air Ministry lacked any leverage to influence these until it began directly funding expansion, by which time war threats and labour shortages were also encouraging more 'rational' locations.

The longer term spatial impacts seem to have a more accidental quality. The impetus and encouragement given to the efficient operation and management of a spatially divided production process was an effect rather than a cause or rearmament policies. Some individuals perceived this longer term effect at the time, but most saw it in the 1930s simply as coming to terms with necessity, rather than the articulation of a new spatial model of capitalist production. The state's interwar influence on industrial organisation was not of course wholly or even mainly confined to defence production. In the next chapter we examine the more explicit attempts of government to promote industrial rationalisation.

5

Industry, Rationalisation and the State

Introduction

One of the most profound challenges to the dominant orthodoxies of a laissez faire economic policy was evident in the major industries of Britain. Most of the older staple industries were in trouble, experiencing declining export markets or import penetration. We saw in Chapter 2 that macro-economic policy did little to assist the trading prospects for these industries especially before 1931. However there were also severe structural problems of overcapacity, obsolescent plant, multiplicity of ownership and managerial problems in all of them. In such circumstances the functional requirements of capitalism were for restructuring or rationalisation of ownership and production. At the same time the newer industries were often developing in ways that replicated many of the structural and organisational problems of older industries. Ownership was often fragmented; new large scale production technologies and 'scientific' work practices appeared only slowly. Almost inevitably therefore the state, despite the prevailing ideological commitment to laissez faire, was drawn, usually indirectly, but occasionally directly, into the question of rationalisation. This chapter focusses on this intervention and its spatial impact. We concentrate on the experience of the older industries, though for comparison we briefly consider the development of the newer industry of electricity supply, where state intervention was more overt, decisive and effective in securing 'rational' organisation. First however we examine the more typical pattern of tentative, 'arm's length' intervention in iron and steel.

Iron and steel in 1919

Until the 1870s the British iron and steel industry had been world leader. The half century preceding 1919 was characterised by a loss of this pre-eminence to the United States and Germany, and a rather makeshift adaptation to the new techniques and methods of the industry (D.L. Burn 1961, pp1-392). Organisationally there had been some amalgamations, especially around 1900 and, with state inspiration and encouragement, during world war I (J. Vaizey 1974, pp9-12). By 1919 most firms were part of loose federations of companies concerned not just with iron and steel but also iron ore, coal, shipping, shipbuilding, armaments and heavy engineering. Iron and steel was often not the main focus of these groupings, a characteristic which had advantages in wartime boom conditions. A few firms continued to derive real benefits from these connections in the 'black decade' of the 1920s. Most notable was Colvilles, the leading Scottish firm, which was tied up with Harland and Wolff shipbuilders (P.L. Payne 1979, pp144-5; 187). However many firms found themselves severely affected financially by the problems of related companies, especially in coal, after 1919.

Another important feature of the organisational structure of iron and steel firms was the persistence of the small family firm model of decision making and management (Vaizey, pp22-3). Modern corporate practice and well developed managerial structures were largely absent, in contrast to the US and German industries. Typically firms were run in a fairly dictatorial fashion by a senior family member or by a direct family nominee. Ownership and management remained very closely interlinked. This favoured age, because senior family members tended to have accumulated the largest holdings, so that the captains of the industry were a gerontocracy. This posed several problems. It was not simply that a chairman's ear trumpet could slow the proceedings of company boards, as it did in at least one case, but more that old animosities, rivalries and prejudices persisted and were major obstacles to any effective restructuring and modernisation (S. Tolliday 1986, especially p86). Generally managerial practice remained intuitive rather than scientific. Thus the prominence of a Chicago firm of consultants, C.A. Brassert and Co. in the industry's restructuring efforts from the late 1920s clearly indicates a lack of sufficient homegrown expertise to attempt informed, extended and rational self analysis. Scientifically trained metallurgists were few; middle managers were virtually non-existent; marketing managers were unknown.

Despite, or perhaps because of, this persistence of family structure and absence of scientific management, labour relations were good (J.C. Carr and W. Taplin 1962, pp273-88). This was despite working conditions that were always unpleasant and often extremely dangerous. Also there were often close linkages on the part of both capital and labour between steel and other industries with a history of very poor labour relations, particularly coal. However a critical factor was the relatively high wages paid to iron and steel workers, reflecting the high skill and reliability requirements of the industry (Vaizey, pp26- 7). Additionally the main union essentially adopted the outlook of the senior skilled workers who retained considerable works floor control of the labour process and subordinate workers. Thus the persistence through the interwar period of practices such as 'nattying', involving regular payments from skilled to unskilled workers in their work gangs, perpetuated elements of a traditional subcontracted labour system that was elitist and destructive of any strong sense of class solidarity within the industry (C. Docherty 1983, pp46-7). In a very real sense these 'unscientific' work patterns, survivals from a traditional industry, were direct parallels of the boardroom survival of the family firm.

Whether or not traditional business forms and practices assisted the promotion of good labour relations, they were increasingly inappropriate to the multi-locational character of the firms. Spatially the industry as a whole and the operations of many individual firms were dispersed by 1919, reflecting the several phases in the evolution of the industry and amalgamations. The largest company was the United Steel group, formed during world war I with two Sheffield steel makers as a nucleus. However it also embraced haematite ore fields and acid steel capacity in Workington, Cumberland and had basic capacity and jurassic orefields in north Lincolnshire at Frodingham, Scunthorpe, together with south Yorkshire coal interests (P.W.S. Andrews and E. Brunner 1951, pp102-18). The Guest, Keen and Nettlefold (GKN) group formed in 1902 linked iron and steel making with nut, bolt, screw and other steel manufacturing. The latter were based mainly in the west Midlands, but there had been some shifts to south Wales where iron and steel making was concentrated inland at the Dowlais works in Merthyr Tydfil and at a much newer and more favourably located works at Cardiff (Carr and Taplin, pp267-8). Baldwin's was another migrant to south Wales from the west midlands, showing a similar pattern of a more modern coastal capacity at Port Talbot. However other Welsh steel users were adopting a different strategy in securing controls over supplies by playing a leading role in the opening up of north Lincolnshire. Thus Lysaghts, originally of Bristol, then Wolverhampton, had in 1896 concentrated steel making at Newport, but then integrated back to ore supplies with a major new combined iron and steel works at Normanby Park, Scunthorpe, completed in

1912 (K. Warren 1970, pp109-12). Richard Thomas and Company, a steel and tinplate manufacturer based around Swansea had taken the first stages in such a strategy by the acquisition of iron works at Redbourn Hill, Scunthorpe, in 1907, to which steel making capacity was added during the war.

On the north east coast, there was rarely any great distance between the different plants of the four main groups, Dorman Long, Bolckow Vaughan, South Durham - Cargo Fleet and Consett. The latter, though badly located on an inland hill site without local ore, was a single site operation as was Bolckow Vaughan at Eston on Teesside. However the other two each had several plants reflecting an accumulation of former companies and their imperfect integration into a single operation. Dorman Long was in the worst position with the West Marsh, Acklam and Britannia Works in Middlesbrough and Clarence Works across the Tees, and its wartime built development at Redcar. South Durham's operations were in Hartlepools but with a large scale development owned by an associated company at Cargo Fleet, Middlesbrough, completed only in 1913 (Burn, p229; 360; Carr and Taplin, p358).

Other iron and steel districts exhibited similar tendencies so that overall the industry in 1919 was a jumble of firms that, though quite large, were small by international standards. They retained many traditional small firm organisational characteristics, particularly at individual plant level. Some clear spatial trends were apparent as historic sites gave way either to locations in coastal positions, where imported ore was available, or, increasingly, on the jurassic ore deposits of the east midlands. However there was considerable sluggishness in the industry's responses to process innovation and particularly in the exploitation of the midland ores. With the greater fuel economy of works such as Normanby Park, these non-coalfield centres now offered the prospect of very low cost production, even with their low grade ores. These general questions of the organisation and structure of the industry were to remain key issues during the interwar period.

The pattern of change 1919-39

Figure 5.1 shows the main production trends within the iron and steel industry 1913-39. This shows that despite the characteristic picture of iron and steel as a declining industry, production was substantially higher in 1939 than it had been in the postwar boom 1919-20 and even

FIGURE 5.1 : UK PRODUCTION OF IRON AND STEEL 1913–1939
Source : Carr and Taplin, p 306, 346, 366, 429, 484

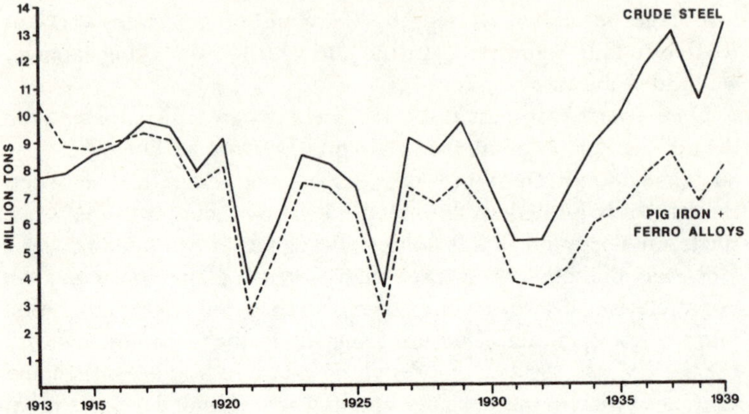

in the peak wartime year, 1917. However for much of the period steel production was running well below this level. Thus the 1920 peak was only topped twice in the rest of the decade, and the 1917 peak was not topped until 1935. Generally the period 1920-32 was one of occasional peaks interspersed with some poor or even catastrophic performances. Only from 1933 and especially from 1935 were real production advances being sustained. Some of these same trends were apparent for pig iron production, but generally iron making did less well, only topping the 1920 peak once (in 1937) and never matching the levels achieved 1913-8. This difference between iron and steel reflected two things. Partly it was a continuation of the long term shift to steel making. It also reflected the mismatch that had developed between UK blast furnace and steel making capacity, which was being filled by scrap and imports of pig iron.

Generally though the growth performance of the whole industry was good by world standards. This was matched by considerable improvements in output per man (Buxton 1979a, p16), associated with major job losses in the industry. These losses were concentrated at the heavy steel end of the industry. Thus the 1924 Census of production recorded just under 185,000 workers in pig iron manufacturing, iron and steel smelting and rolling. By 1935 this had fallen to just over 150,000, a decline of over 18%. The drop was biggest in pig iron manufacture, representing over 40% of the 1924 workforce. Ministry of Labour insured worker data generally confirms this impression, as do the numbers out of work in the iron and steel trades.

Thus over the 1927-32 period, unemployment in the industry was normally about twice the national average; in the worst years more so. In July 1932 for example 46.2% of the insured workers in the industry were unemployed. However there was considerable improvement as the industry subsequently recovered.

The changing geography of iron and steel

Table 5.1 shows the changing geography of production over the period 1913-37. It shows clearly the declining relative importance of the three main older regions on the north east coast, south Wales and Scotland.

TABLE 5.1: REGIONAL DISTRIBUTION OF STEEL MANUFACTURE 1913-37 (EXPRESSED AS % OF TOTAL)

	1913	1929	1937
North East Coast	28	23	22
South Wales	23	24	20
Scotland	19	16	15
Sheffield	11	13	13
Lincolnshire	3	8	10
Lancs, Cheshire, Flint etc.	7	8	8
Black Country	5	6	5
North West Coast	5	2	3
Northants etc.	0	0	3

Source: Burn, p484

This was associated with regional depression (especially in Scotland and on the north east coast), the loss of export markets (especially in the north east), a shortage of modern blast furnace capacity (especially in Scotland and south Wales) and more generally with the obsolescent and high cost nature of much of the plant in these areas (Tolliday 1986, pp85-92). Within these regions however some limited changes were being experienced. Some of the oldest and highest cost plant was closed and new investment occurred at certain favoured locations and was refused at others. Something of this pattern can be identified in Map 5.1. In south Wales the shift to coastal locations continued with major reconstructions at Port Talbot and Cardiff and closures of virtually all the valley works. A singular exception was the new Ebbw Vale works

MAP 5.1

IRON AND STEEL MAKING SITES 1937

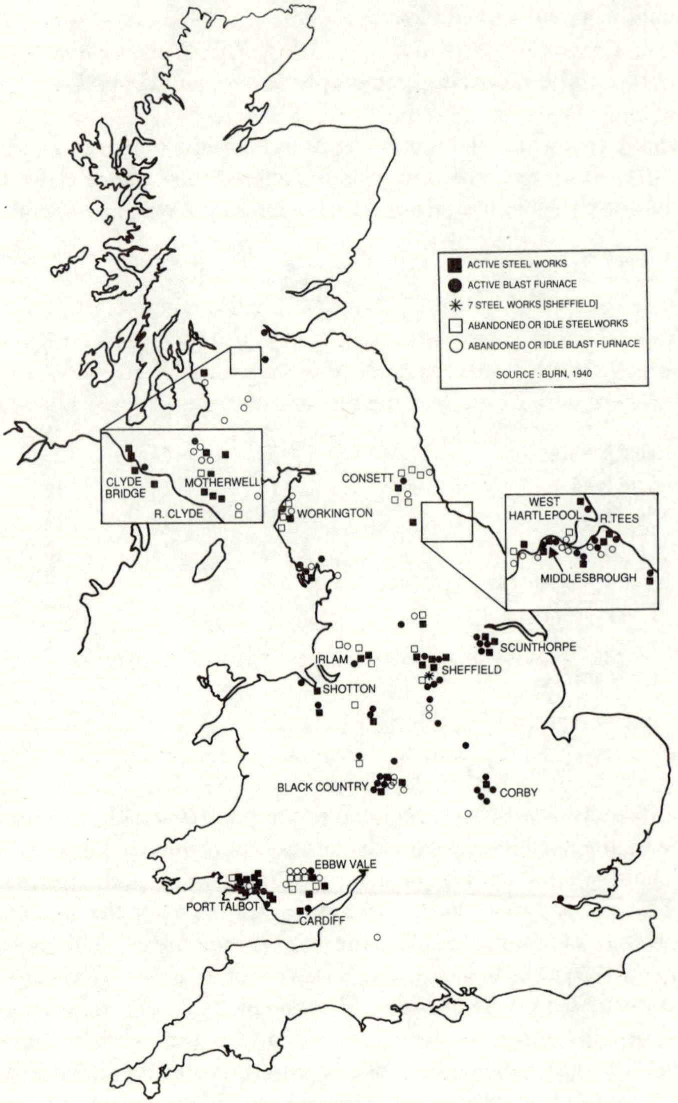

of Richard Thomas developed from 1936 (Warren 1970, p179). Here the developing concerns with depressed area policy were manipulated to great effect by William Firth, of the Richard Thomas company, to push through a controversial strip mill project against steel industry opposition. By locating in Ebbw Vale rather than Redbourn (as originally proposed) Firth gained Stanley Baldwin's personal backing for the project on the eve of the 1935 election at which regional unemployment was a key issue (Pitfield 1974; Tolliday 1986, pp91-2; Warren 1970, pp172-82).

Ebbw Vale though had many unique features. It was more usual for firms to consolidate on the most favourable of their pre-existing sites. This happened in Scotland, where Colvilles created a single integrated plant from two separate works at Clydebridge. Despite this though many relics of the older dispersed production pattern persisted. The proposal for a single integrated Firth of Clyde location came to nothing. In the north east some smaller plants around Teesside and elsewhere were closed, but the regional centre of gravity remained in that district. Despite its unsuitable location, Consett also remained important. Moves to establish a major new integrated works in a port location on Tyneside at Jarrow in 1934-6, on the site of the closed Palmer's shipyard referred to in Chapter 4, came to nothing because of Teesside opposition. This created bitter disappointment in the heavily depressed town and was the immediate provocation of one of the most famous social protests of the interwar period, the Jarrow Crusade (Carr and Taplin, pp534-7; IDAC 1937, pp24-8; Wilkinson, pp172-213).

However the general tendency to reinvest at selected existing locations within the traditional regions rather than shifting wholesale to new locations did not prevent the marked absolute growth in steel production referred to earlier. Only the north west coast was actually producing less in 1937 than 1913; even there improvements were apparent in the 1930s (Burn, p484). Of the remaining areas, there was relative stability in Sheffield and Lancashire, Cheshire and North Wales (primarily Lancashire Steel at Irlam and Warrington and John Summers at Shotton) and in the west midlands. The only areas of significant growth were in the east midlands. Thus at Scunthorpe there were major investments by United Steel at Appleby - Frodingham, while Whitehead's transferred a bar mill from Tredegar in south Wales to Redbourn in 1933 (Warren 1970, p176). Meanwhile earlier Welsh migrants to Lincolnshire, Lysaghts (from 1921 under GKN ownership) at Normanby Park and Richard Thomas at Redbourn

Hill continued to develop, the latter rather less successfully (Vaizey, pp133-6; Warren 1970, pp172-4). Much more spectacular changes occurred in Northamptonshire where the new integrated works at Corby began large scale steel production in the county in 1934-5 (Vaizey, pp72-5). However the east midlands only accounted for just over an eighth of steel production in 1937 though a somewhat larger proportion of pig iron and an immensely larger proportion of ore production (Warren 1979, p122).

Viewed from the perspective of steel production therefore the geography of the interwar industry showed considerable locational stability. Thus many regional features of the existing pattern were retained, with a few important examples of shifts; towards Corby and Scunthorpe, away from Welsh valleys and Cumberland-Furness. However, though the issue of production has dominated most discussion, such a focus tends to understate the spatial uneveness produced by interwar changes. The reason is that the very efficiency improvements that enabled marked production increases at existing centres were associated with large scale labour 'shakeouts'. Although employment was identified by IDAC as a major social factor in the

TABLE 5.2: REGIONAL CHANGE IN EMPLOYMENT IN HEAVY IRON AND STEEL MAKING 1924-35

	% Change	Absolute Change (000s)
West Midlands	-37	- 9
Wales*	-30	-10
Scotland	-29	- 7
North East Coast	-19	- 5
Rest of England	-16	- 3
Yorkshire (excl. Cleveland)	- 2	- 1
Lancashire and Cheshire*	+20	+ 2
Great Britain	-18	-34

*Adjusted data: see text

Sources: Census of Production 1930, II, pp28-9, p34;
1935, II, p17, p28

reorganisation of iron and steel, there was no quantified discussion of it (IDAC, pp67-76). Table 5.2 attempts some rectification of this. However the regional categorisations adopted in the pre-1935 Census of Production are rather unhelpful for our purposes. Thus west Cumberland is included with the east midlands while Shotton 'shifts' from Cheshire to Wales in 1930-5 on account of boundary changes, necessitating some adjustment of the raw data. Nevertheless a pattern of very marked decline is apparent in Wales, Scotland, the north east coast and the west midlands. However, whereas in the last area there was a considerable growth in closely related iron and steel using trades that more than offset the decline in iron and steel making, this was not true of the other regions. All showed a marked decline across all the iron and steel trades (Census of Production 1930, p10; 1935, pp4-5). By contrast Sheffield, the only real centre in the West Riding showed employment stability and the rest of England below average decline, even allowing for the marked decline in west Cumberland (Fogarty 1945, pp194-5). Lancashire and Cheshire (excluding Shotton) displayed a surprisingly high increase, also apparent, if less strongly, across all the iron and steel trades. It is very difficult indeed to disentangle any employment data on growth in the expanding districts of the east midlands, but by 1939 there were nearly 20,000 employed in iron and steel, including ore extraction (K.C. Edwards 1949, pp143-4). Over half these were in the Scunthorpe area and a fifth in the Corby area. In consequence these were amongst the fastest growing areas in the country in the 1930s, the more unique because they were dependent on heavy industry (Fogarty 1945, pp296-8; 314-5).

Overall therefore the industry's changing geography reproduces many features of the inner-outer Britain divide. The major developmental prizes were located in the east midlands, at least until emergent regional policies began to legitimise stabilisation in outer Britain in the later 1930s. We must not though mistake this for the beginning of state intervention (cf. Pitfield 1974). The uneven development of the interwar steel industry was throughout a product of the interaction of three major interests - industrial capital, banking capital and the state. We must now examine this interaction.

Uneven development: steel, banks and the state

During the postwar boom 1919-20 the banks and major financial institutions were tempted into unprecedented short term lending to the steel industry (Carr and Taplin, pp356-60). As boom turned to slump profits collapsed and bankers found themselves as reluctant finance capitalists, nursing frozen loans and constraining the activities of both industrial and banking capital (Tolliday 1986, p94). Simultaneously the combination of a high cost, inefficient industry, foreign tariffs, industrial disputes (mainly in associated industries) and an overvalued pound meant that export markets were lost and foreign steel products flooded into the UK market. This was itself depressed as major consuming industries like shipbuilding experienced serious difficulties. There were fluctuations but the major trend was against British manufacturers (Carr and Taplin, pp366-73; 429-38). The banks saw steel's problems in structural terms - too many firms, too much inefficient capacity, and overmanning - rather than being a product of the general macro-economic climate created by laissez faire economic policies, which they supported. Generally therefore the bankers sought to exert pressure to solve the structural problems. However, the capacity of individual banks dealing with particular firms to force industry-wide restructuring was obviously limited (Vaizey, pp48-9). The 1929 merger of Dorman Long and Bolckow Vaughan, forced by Barclays, who were bankers to both, was unusual (Carr and Taplin, p449). Inevitably therefore the Bank of England was drawn in, particularly since the Governor, Montagu Norman, the Treasury and virtually all interwar governments were anxious to avoid the direct state intervention that otherwise would become necessary (Tolliday 1984, pp60-1). The Bank was an ideal intermediary for 'arm's-length' state intervention, maintaining a facade of apparent non-involvement and thus sustaining the legitimacy of free enterprise capitalism and 'natural' evolution of market forces (B. Schwarz 1985, pp95-100).

In 1928-30 two further intermediaries, Securities Management Trust (SMT) and Bankers Industrial Development Company (BID) were established to handle the Bank of England's industrial reorganisation activities. Brassert's were commissioned to provide rationalisation proposals, and in 1929 produced a regional scheme based on six very large integrated plants, three existing at Middlesbrough (Dorman Long), Cardiff (GKN) and Irlam (Lancashire Steel) and three new on the Firth of Clyde, at Frodingham and Kettering, Northamptonshire (Vaizey, pp51-3). The state generally endorsed this scheme and covertly lent it authority in the nominally secret 1930 Report of the Committee on Civil Research (Vaizey, p66; Burn, pp436-8). Some limited implementation of rationalisation was made in 1928-30. Thus the steel interests of the major armaments manufacturers, Armstrong-Whitworth and Beardmores, whose problems were considered in Chapter 4, were organised into the English and Lancashire Steel Corporations. However these fell well short of Brassert's proposals and perpetuated many traditional problems (Tolliday 1986, pp94-8). The failure of banking capital to achieve large scale restructuring can be attributed partly to the traditional caution of the bankers themselves. Lacking any real feeling for industrial matters they remained too wedded to short term financial considerations to become true finance capitalists on the German or American models. The only financier who did show any real flair in handling steel's problems, Clarence Hatry, was a fraudster (Vaizey, pp55-6; Andrews and Brunner, pp159-61). Undoubtedly though the pressures of banking did accelerate the cost reduction exercises that went on with plant closures and labour shakeouts.

The resistance to large scale restructuring came largely from industrial capital. A few firms (notably Stewarts and Lloyds, Richard Thomas and United Steel) felt they could use restructuring to achieve stronger market positions. But the majority feared the loss of firm identity, and the very messy process of massive writing off of capital and amalgamating with old rivals and enemies (Tolliday 1984, pp67-9; Vaizey, p70). In any case the steel makers doubted whether the industry's problems were really structural. They increasingly blamed laissez faire economic policy, particularly free trade which allowed foreign 'dumping' while overseas tariff walls kept out British exports. The pressure for tariff protection began first amongst the north east coast manufacturers, and occurred last in areas and firms dependent on imports. Thus Colvilles, who needed large scale pig iron imports to meet their shortfall in blast furnace capacity, did not switch to favouring protection until 1930 (Tolliday 1984, pp53-4). By then only the smaller finishing firms continued to favour free trade.

All this was anathema to banking capital with its commitment to the liberal world trading economy, but by 1931-2 the pressure was irresistible. The Conservatives had already fought (and lost) an election on tariff reform in 1923, so that protectionist sentiments were present at the political level. The depression, the Conservative dominated National government and the ending of the gold standard provided the necessary circumstances for tariffs. The introduction of first temporary and then permanent protective duties on most imported iron and steel products under the 1932 Import Duties Act represented a major turning point. It was a shift in favour of industrial capital and against banking capital. It also marked an overt break with the laissez faire tradition of non-intervention. This had already been breached covertly by 'arm's-length' intervention via the Bank of England, but was still theoretically intact. But no sooner had the state stepped in than it abdicated power to the industry itself. The Import Duties Advisory Committee (IDAC) was established to oversee the protected industries, and advise on tariff and reorganisation matters. It was a small specialist group of civil servants headed by Sir George May, a prominent government adviser (Tolliday 1984, pp64-5). But its starting point was that the industry, rather than the state, should make decisions about restructuring, in conjunction with BID, SMT, etc. However since the latter's position was now weaker, it meant that the very industry that had resisted attempts at restructuring was now given most control over the process.

The immediate result was the British Iron and Steel Federation (BISF) created in 1934 (IDAC, pp17-20, 102-16). This was an improvement on previous attempts to overcome the fragmentation of industrial capital in steel, but it amounted to nothing less than a state sponsored cartel. It gave further encouragement to the kinds of technical improvements already under way, with associated job reductions, but its main impact was to stabilise rather than restructure, especially as demand revived in the late 1930s. It allocated quotas to existing firms on a regional basis and in various ways subsidised high cost producers (e.g. Burn, pp473-8, 483-515). The effect therefore was to allow BISF to determine the reorganisation agenda in the later 1930s. BID was still involved, but banking capital no longer had the leverage it had before protection. They hoped that the BISF independent chairman, Sir Andrew Duncan, plucked from the Central Electricity Board, could recreate electricity's rational development in the less conducive climate of steel (Tolliday 1984, p72). But protection had reduced many of the pressures for major restructuring. The industry revived, profits rose, the debts to the banks were unfrozen, and the relieved bankers no longer had to pretend to be finance capitalists. Montagu Norman continued to be interested but the pressures that had drawn him in during the 1920s were now much reduced. This changing balance of power within capital is crucial to understanding why there were so few dramatic shifts on the lines envisaged by Brassert and endorsed by the state in 1929-30. Thus the typical post 1934 restructuring was relatively small reconstruction, often on suboptimal sites. This merged with the mounting state concern about the depressed areas, though it had rather different origins and employment consequences, as the Jarrow Crusade demonstrated. Less jobs were lost than the 1929 Brassert scheme implied, but even the limited rationalisation that occurred continued to bring job losses in the 1930s, if at a slower rate than in the previous decade.

Why the state did not act more decisively and chose only to intervene overtly on regional rather than industrial criteria is problematic. The ideological climate clearly did not encourage overt state intervention in industrial structure (but neither had it encouraged the overt intervention of protection during the 1920s). More remarkable though is the lack of effective pressure for intervention from industrial capital within the steel using industries and the labour movement.

By the later 1930s there was a growing reaction to the BISF cartel, especially from the new steel using industries. Thus Lord Nuffield, the car manufacturer, criticised the high prices of British steel and in 1937 described the Federation as '... an absolute ramp. Big cigars and nothing to do.' (Burn, p495). But such pressure was rather insignificant in the 1920s, partly because major steel users then were often closely implicated in the existing structure and practices of steel making through interlocking ownership and control. In addition steel users valued the heterogeneous range of product grade and quality that the non-rationalised industry produced (IDAC, pp41-50). A wider industrial antipathy to standardisation helped to perpetuate an old fashioned steel industry. The limited impact of labour partly derived from the traditionally elitist employment structure of the industry noted above. However by the 1930s the unions were pressing state ownership as the only effective solution (Vaizey, pp54-6; Ingot 1936).

Such pressures made little headway. Thus the 1929 Labour government had floated the idea of a public utility company for steel, but the Bank of England threatened non-co-operation from the banks, which was sufficient to sink it (Tolliday 1984, p61). In the later 1930s, labour began to have more impact, but mainly on the depressed area question especially at Ebbw Vale (Warren 1970, p176). Overall though the impact of labour on the interwar rationalisation of the steel industry was very slight. They carried many of the consequences but had little influence on the causes. This was particularly evident at Corby, the most dramatic new development in the interwar steel industry, which we now examine in greater detail.

Corby: a case study of uneven development

About the same time as Brassert recommended Kettering as a location for one of the six major integrated plants, Stewarts and Lloyds asked the same firm for advice on their future strategy. The firm was primarily concerned with tube manufacture, a field of growing demand especially in the south and midlands, though production was mainly in west central Scotland in several plants. Company leadership was mainly Scottish, but the firm also had a significant presence in the midlands. It had also shifted its headquarters from Glasgow to London in 1927, indicating a somewhat different frame of reference to most Scottish steel firms (Vaizey, pp37-9). Most important amongst its various holdings were ore fields and blast furnaces in Corby, acquired by takeovers in 1903 and 1920.

In 1930 Brassert recommended Corby's development as a large scale fully integrated iron and steel works using the basic Bessemer process with associated tube works and facilities for making other steel products such as sheet for Midlands markets, this last a new departure for the company (Vaizey, pp73-4; F. Scopes 1968, pp58-63; 67-79). Most of these recommendations made sense to the board because its current operations were not fully integrated. It had iron making capacity at Corby and tube factories mainly in Scotland, but between it had very little steel making capacity. Its works at Bilston and Redbourn were unsuitable for major expansion (Carr and Taplin, pp532-4). In particular its requirement was for basic Bessemer steel that was especially suitable for tube making. However very little of this type of steel was then made in Britain and the firm was forced to rely on imports. Accordingly during 1929-30 Corby was decided on for a major expansion scheme that was endorsed by banks and, in general terms, the state. At this point though the deepening depression began to affect the demand for steel and the project was shelved.

When protection was introduced the Corby project was rapidly reactivated. Tariffs gave a particular advantage to the east midlands because they penalised regions like Wales and Scotland where ore exhaustion and run down of blast furnace capacity generated a dependence on imported pig iron and scrap. BISF action subsequently eroded this advantage (Burn, pp475-8), but a more telling point was that protection mainly excluded the cheap basic steels of the type made in the east midlands. Thus the increased market share available to British producers on account of protection accrued particularly to the east midlands (Burn, pp489-90). This has a double relevance for

Stewarts and Lloyds because of its former reliance on imports (Scopes, p85). Macdiarmid, the company chairman, favoured a rapid resuscitation of the Corby project, and he clearly wanted to go along with Brassert's original proposal to extend the company range beyond tubes (Vaizey, pp72-5). However this was opposed by virtually everyone involved including BID and the rest of the industry, fearing undercutting in markets other than tubes (in which the firm, with Tube Investments, formed a duopoly). In his own words, Macdiarmid 'allowed BID to understand that it was purely a tube scheme and that we had no intention of destroying the Bank's frozen credits' (cited Vaizey, p75). Finance was thus forthcoming and the scheme went ahead. As demand revived though, he was subsequently able to ignore this commitment and the development was scaled up as it proceeded.

In November 1932, while demand for steel was still very depressed, Corby was announced. There were contradictory assurances to shareholders that tube production would be concentrated at this low cost location and to workers that Lanarkshire job losses would be minimised (Pitfield 1974, p167). However although a Scottish presence was retained, mainly to keep the BISF regional quota allocation (Vaizey, pp74-5), the first closures of older plants were announced in February 1933 and more job losses followed. The largest single decline was at Rutherglen where 1200 job losses were announced in February 1936. However this Scottish rundown was not simply a scrapping of obsolete plant; a plate mill was dismantled and transferred to Corby. The issue of labour migration also soon became important as the works came into production in 1934-5. Thus in 1932, 739 men had worked at Stewarts and Lloyds Corby orefields and blast furnaces. By November 1936, 3890 were employed (IDAC, pp72-3). Of the additional workers about a third, mainly those employed in the tube works, came from other, mainly Scottish, works of the company. About half of the remainder were recruited locally and the rest from other districts. Thus nearly 2000 workers migrated to Corby in 1932-6. As we will see in Chapter 6, this labour mobility was encouraged over most of the interwar period and the Ministry of Labour operated an assisted industrial transference scheme to subsidise such moves. Most of the moves of Stewarts and Lloyds workers and families from Lanarkshire to Corby were assisted in this way (IDAC, p73).

This rapid influx created major pressures for growth in what was formerly a village of some 2000 people. The pressures became even more intense as the demand for steel increased very rapidly in the late 1930s and 1940s when Corby was able to press its advantages of very low cost production. Ultimately in 1950 Corby was designated a New Town under the 1946 Act and its development entrusted to a centrally appointed Development Corporation (M.S. Grieco 1985). However even at this early stage there was active assistance from local and central state agencies in the urban development process. Housing was mainly provided by the company partly because the housing finance arrangements then prevailing made it difficult for the local authority to undertake non-slum clearance schemes (see Chapters 7-8). In any case it was difficult for a small rural district council like Kettering to fund such a major housing project. Finally private speculative builders were reluctant to build low rental housing that steel workers could afford. The only such venture, by the First National Housing Trust (on which see also Chapter 8) was a failure (Scopes, pp116-7).

By 1937 some 1300 company houses had been built rising to 2253 by September 1939 (IDAC, pp73-4; Scopes, p118). These had secured 100% mortgage advances, mainly from the Halifax Building Society and Prudential Assurance under the terms of the 1933 Housing Act (O.R. Hobson 1953, p112; Scopes, p117). This involved local and central government guarantees of the 'extra' advance. The local guarantees were provided with some initial reluctance by the county council which was also active in educational provision and in making necessary improvements in water, sewerage and road systems to facilitate Corby's growth (Pitfield 1974, pp171-2; IDAC, pp73-5). The Central Electricity Board and the district council also undertook spending to link Corby to the electricity grid system.

Overall therefore there was considerable local state intervention to facilitate Corby's development. There was a growth in local rate revenues but this did not occur in step with the demands for expenditure and under the derating provisions of the 1929 Local Government Act, the works themselves were only liable for 25% of the rating assessment. In the longer term the continued growth highlighted the need for coherent planning, something which had been very difficult in the circumstances in which Corby was developed (Scopes, p118). Already by 1937 major environmental problems associated with open cast ore stripping around Corby were identified and restoration had become a major issue (IDAC, pp75-6; Fogarty 1945, pp298-9; J. Sheail 1983).

Compared to later events it is tempting to see Corby's pre-1939 development as an example of non-intervention. However we have shown that state actions, not necessarily consciously, did play a significant part in encouraging its development. The general state sponsorship of the rationalisation idea, including a move into Northamptonshire, protection, labour transference and state involvement in the urban development process were all important to Corby's growth. It remained primarily a decision of private capital determined on capitalist criteria, but the state had influenced and reinforced some of the criteria.

The experience of Corby had many unique features. It highlighted the process of uneven development more dramatically than most other interwar changes in the industry. There were no other wholesale interregional shifts of that kind; marginal changes and intraregional shifts were more typical. But they raised many of the same issues, albeit in a more muted fashion. The role of the state was similar: the indirect nature of state influence, the aversion to direct intervention in industrial structure, the use of non-state intermediaries and overt state involvement on non-industrial criteria were all quite typical. It amounted to 'arm's length' or surrogate state industrial intervention. It pointed a contradiction between the functional and the ideological requirements of interwar capitalism. Functionally laissez faire had ended, but ideologically it remained to haunt state policy towards industry. Steel in fact was fairly typical of several older industries. There was rather more overt intervention in coal, a little more in cotton and rather less in shipbuilding (M.W. Kirby 1973; 1974; 1977; 1979J.R. Parkinson 1979). But there were instances of more direct and decisive intervention in industry. Electricity was one such case.

Electricity generation: the making of the grid

Unlike steel, electricity was a new industry. It was based on British consumption and was untroubled by competition in export markets or imports. Its growth record was very impressive and sales of publicly supplied electricity rose from 1 kilowatt hour per capita in 1895 to 77 in 1919 to 486 in 1939 (L. Hannah 1979, pp427-8). It was a new industry in the sense that many of those controlling it in 1919 had links back to the early days of its economic development. Organisationally it was characterised by highly fragmented ownership and control with over 600 supply undertakings serving what were usually rather small areas in the early postwar period. 68% of electricity sales in 1914 had been from municipal authorities, with the remainder by private supply companies (H. Finer 1941, p58). The latter dominated the supply industry in London, the north east coast and the less urbanised areas while municipal supply was normal in most of the major provincial conurbations. In contrast to the trends to larger scale operations that were apparent in the US and German supply industries before world war I, the typical British supply undertaking displayed only slight tendencies to concentration. Before 1914 the Newcastle Electricity Supply Company (NESCO) had created an interconnected regional supply system on the north east coast, and there were a few voluntary interconnection schemes during and immediately after the war (I.C.R Byatt 1979, pp115-22; Hannah 1979, pp57-8; 81-4). But by international standards these were small scale. Thus by the mid-1920s the NESCO system was selling about 800 gigawatt hours of power yearly, and the south Lancashire interconnection scheme about 650, compared to 3000 in the Ruhr scheme and 1500 in the Bavarian power zone (Hannah 1979, p85).

The obstacles to interconnection were partly institutional, with a profound mutual mistrust apparent between private and municipal suppliers and well developed localist sentiments within the municipal sector (e.g. Hannah 1979, pp84-6). However there were also important technical arguments. Thus some experts doubted the economies of scale claimed for large scale operation, predicted frequent breakdowns on large interconnected systems and favoured more localised patterns of development around small power stations. Perhaps most serious of all was the combined institutional/technical problem of frequency variations in generating practice. While 50 Hertz (Hz) was gradually becoming standard, especially in the municipal sector, some 17 different frequencies still existed in 1924 (Hannah 1979, pp88-9). NESCO and parts of south Lancashire used 40Hz. There was some 85Hz and 100Hz in London and on the south coast. 25Hz was very common in the midlands, south Wales and Clydeside. Although frequency changes on interconnected systems were technically possible, cost considerations ruled this out. Therefore large scale interconnection schemes were effectively impossible without standardisation.

Some voluntary efforts towards interconnection, regionalisation and standardisation under the 1919 Electricity Supply Act continued despite the difficulties (Hannah 1979, pp80-5; Finer 1941, pp275-7). A few joint authorities and boards of varying effectiveness were created, but inevitably the lack of standardisation meant that new, non-standard, investments were necessary to meet the expanding demand for power, especially in the west Midlands and on the north east coast. By the mid-1920s there was widespread political and business concern at the absence of any rational pattern of development for electricity supply. The first Labour government promised more action but lacked the majority or the time to achieve anything. The incoming Conservative government under Baldwin, for all its commitment to orthodox policies of non-intervention, was pragmatic, and recognised the need for decisive state intervention in the industry. Thus the President of the Board of Trade remarked to a Cabinet Committee in 1925 that

> 'electricity ... is so inefficient today in this country that it has always been amazing to me that the Labour Government did not attempt to nationalise it' (cited Hannah 1979, p84).

The discussion of which this was part led to the 1926 Electricity (Supply) Act, one of the more important pieces of interwar state intervention and certainly the most decisive act of direct state involvement in industrial rationalisation. Less than eight years later the generating side of the industry had been totally transformed, becoming a model of rational development in industry (PEP 1936). A national 'grid iron' of high voltage cables, mainly carried overhead on pylons covered all Britain except the north of Scotland. The larger and more efficient power stations were utilised to supply most of the power to this grid, as it soon became known. The less efficient stations were either used for peak or standby loading, or closed. The whole system was overseen by a new state body, the Central Electricity Board (CEB). This did not actually replace any existing supply undertaking, but owned the grid transmission system, controlled the operations of those power stations it selected and was closely involved in planning new capacity. Much remained to be done on the distribution side of the industry until after 1939, but the generating side became a symbol of efficient and rational industrial development.

CEB and uneven development

Spatially the grid permitted considerable concentration in electricity generation, from over 500 stations to 144 (PEP 1936, p26). Though CEB selected more stations than it strictly needed in order to secure local co-operation more easily, the result was undoubtedly a less dispersed pattern of generation than would otherwise have occurred. However it is important to recognise that until late 1938, when rearmament created excessive demands in the south, it did not operate as a truly national system, rather as a series of regional grids with interregional emergency tie lines (Hannah 1979, p148). Normal practice was still to move coal from the coalfields by railway or coastal shipping to the load centres where power stations were still located. Such a scheme of organisation, though it produced a more even development of generating capacity, probably worked to the disadvantage of outer Britain since a truly national supply system would have involved a far higher concentration of generating capacity on the coalfields.

The idea of such a concentration was consciously considered by the CEB, particularly building pithead generating capacity in south Wales to meet the demands of south east England as an alternative to the development of new metropolitan power stations like Battersea and Fulham (Hannah 1979, pp138-9). It was rejected because of fears of greater vulnerability to labour unrest when power stations depended on the output of one particular coalfield and, implicitly, because of the existence of a highly developed transport system. Thus the grid lines, although operating at much higher voltages than previous local schemes, were still, at 132 kilovolts, lower than was desirable for efficient long distance transmission without excessive leakage. They were not intended to form a major means of achieving interregional energy flows and did not significantly alter the regional energy economy (Hannah 1979, p211). What this means though is that we cannot attach great direct significance to the grid as an often-implied cause of the gravitation of new 'footloose' industry to off-coalfield inner Britain locations (e.g. Pollard 1962, pp129-30). Indirectly the scale economies associated with enhanced power station efficiency certainly had some impacts in this direction, but industrial power costs still remained higher in the south than elsewhere.

However even discounting these more extreme allegations, the state in the form of the CEB and the grid must be judged as maintaining and reinforcing the prevalent pattern of regional uneveness. This was simply because its policy was, in effect, to accept the existing spatial distribution of demand for power and reproduce this in its investment strategies. It was never intended to be used (as it was in the USSR and elsewhere) as a positive means of shaping or at least modifying patterns and processes of spatial development at a national level. Although some of the justifications of this were technical, it also implies something very important about the relationship of the state to the capitalist development process, even in a field where the state was acting in a very interventionist way. We can understand this more clearly by examining why state intervention was so unusually decisive in electricity supply compared to other industries.

The sources of intervention

Clearly an important factor was the existing high level of state sector ownership represented by municipal trading. Ideologically this was important since interwar governments committed to laissez faire strategies were presented with an already predominantly state owned industry as fact. Much of the moral agonisation that accompanied even quite tentative steps in other industries was simply not necessary for electricity. It was important practically because local authorities were, to borrow a phrase used in a different context, rather more 'plannable instruments' than private companies. Although municipalities possessed considerable autonomy in relation to central government, important legal and financial linkages such as the loan sanction and the district auditor existed that were particularly relevant to enforcing coherent large scale patterning on the industry's development. Although possessing regulatory controls, central government had no comparable leverage to exert on private companies.

In fact some of the private companies, notably those controlled by George Balfour, were very resistant to the objectives of the CEB (Haxey pp73-7). Had the private companies been in a stronger overall position, it is quite likely that they could have frustrated rationalisation at least in the state directed form it actually took. However even this is debatable, because in an industry like electricity supply, the wider interests of capital were in many ways more important than the particular interests of capital within the industry itself. Thus, in contrast to the position in iron and steel where user industries were heavily committed to the non-standardised output of an old fashioned industry, electrical manufacturers and industrial capital generally wanted an efficient and standardised national system (Hannah 1979, pp96-100). Significantly the CEB national grid proposals were drawn up by a committee headed by the major Scottish industrialist, Lord Weir (later involved in the industrial planning for rearmament, as we saw in Chapter 4) (Ministry of Transport 1926). Within the Federation of British Industries (FBI), Weir was able to counter the influence of Balfour and persuade industrialists at large that the CEB offered the best assurance of a cheap and efficient power system. Thus while Balfour had been able to shape FBI policy in its response to the 1919 Act, the palpable failure of the voluntary reorganisation he promised had reduced his credibility by 1926.

Undoubtedly a scheme for full nationalisation would have engendered more opposition, but the 1926 Act did not involve any private companies losing assets. In fact it actually increased the relative contribution of big private power stations to national electricity output and by 1938 the companies accounted for 37% of sales compared to 32% in 1914 (Finer 1941, p58). Moreover in its operating style the CEB had much of the character of a large private corporation rather than a municipal or state body. It was headed by another businessman, Sir Andrew Duncan. Under his lead, CEB developed a large measure of independence of government, raised funds on money markets rather than via government sources, was motivated by profit and cost considerations and generally created a non-governmental ethos for the supply industry that combined business and engineering practice (Hannah 1979, pp100-4).

Socialist principles were little in evidence, despite the outward correspondence of the scheme with the Fabian project of state socialism. However the great popular appeal of the cheaper electricity promised by Weir and its potential for improving working class life, meant that the labour movement generally backed the 1926 Act (Hannah 1979, pp98-9). Politically though most of the benefits accrued to Baldwin who, though splitting his party on the issue, instinctively and pragmatically recognised the value of decisive state intervention to sponsor popular technological advance, thereby appropriating a potent symbol of modernity and progress into a Conservative ideology that was top heavy with traditionalist values. The manifest effectiveness of the CEB and its operations on quasi-capitalist non-state lines counteracted the ideological damage of pressing state action in the face of very vocal if minority capitalist interests.

Conclusions: the state, industrial restructuring and uneven development

For all the important contrasts between steel and electricity, they reveal some basic similarities in that the state's prime concern was to protect and secure the general interests of private capital. In the case of electricity these were best served by overriding the narrow sectional interests of private capital within the supply industry. In the case of steel, which was more typical of the industries that the state became involved in, the problem was that there was no consistent agreement within capital as to the form that restructuring should take. However virtually all sections of capital agreed that they did not want the state playing a positive interventionist role beyond protecting and legitimising their own, often contradictory, interests.

Since interwar governments lacked the political and ideological commitment to act independently of this position they, in effect, accepted it and rarely, if ever, acted against the interests of the currently dominant fraction of capital within the industry. Before protection they backed Montagu Norman's bankers schemes; after they increasingly endorsed industrial capital and the BISF. In both industries the state's actions can only be properly understood in terms of the fragmented logics of capital. At no point was state intervention ever challenging the fundamental legitimacy of the capitalist development process. Its main effects were rather to reinforce and underpin that process as at Corby or in the operations of the national grid. Only by the late 1930s were there any signs of serious attempts to spatially modify the process to accommodate objectives other than those of capitalist interest. Labour was one of these influences but not yet a major one. In the next chapter we consider why the labour movement had such a limited impact on uneven development between the wars.

6

The State and Labour: Strikes and Unemployment

Introduction: the state and labour to 1919

The labour policies of the British state in the interwar period were dominated by two issues: labour unrest and unemployment. The former was particularly a feature of the 1919-1926 period, the latter was endemic from 1920 but especially in the 1930s. It was though their scale rather than the problems themselves that was new. Already before world war I the foundations of state intervention in the labour market were laid, reflecting business interest in reducing the inefficiencies and frictions in the labour market, the growing labour desires for some state protection and promotion of workers' interests and welfare, and the desire of many progressive intellectuals for both.

Thus in 1914 the state was involved in the settling of industrial disputes initiated under the voluntary 1896 Conciliation Act but occurring in a more direct way after 1910 (E. Wigham 1982, pp1-33). It had promoted two ineffective works programmes for the unemployed (1905 and 1909), had introduced voluntary Labour Exchanges (1909), Trade Boards to fix minimum wages of low paid workers in the 'sweated' trades where workers (mainly women) were poorly organised (also 1909), and a compulsory unemployment insurance scheme for six industries subject to cyclical unemployment (1911) (D. Read 1972, pp171-88). The Liberals had also legalised most normal trades union practices and rendered them immune from the 1901 Taff Vale and 1909 Osborne judgements which had threatened the basis of their operations and strength (Read, pp194-207). In general the state tried to appear neutral in labour relations, though the reality of this was increasingly doubted by labour movement leaders, especially during the years of heightened labour unrest 1910-12 when troops and police were widely used to undermine strike action.

The guise of state neutrality became even less credible after 1914 as government involvement in the wartime labour market increased

(Burgess, 1980, pp153-94). Government became a major direct employer as basic industries were brought under state control and new national munitions factories were established. More widely the necessity for efficient war production made labour productivity and strike avoidance into imperatives for state action. Large numbers of businessmen were recruited into government to run this new state directed economy. At the same time ever greater powers were used to direct and control labour. New Ministries of Labour and National Service were established in 1916 and 1917. Official trades unionism was also incorporated into the state war machine and was emasculated to the extent that official strike activity was banned (Wigham, pp34-46). However there was a flourishing of local unofficial activity and much disruption occurred. In response government and capital made important concessions in the form of real wage increases, rent and some price controls, and allowed idealistic visions of a more equitable postwar Britain to develop.

Basically war had greatly heightened the bargaining power of labour. Although there was a continually shifting balance of advantage both between capital and labour and within the labour movement itself, labour as a whole emerged from the war much stronger than it had been before (A. Marwick 1967, pp299-300). Trades union membership stood at nearly 8.1 million in 1919, almost twice the 1913 level, and it was still rising. Working class living standards had never been higher, and it seemed that the promises of permanent change were about to be implemented.

As war ended the moderate element of the labour movement began to gain the upper hand as the reconstructed constitutional Labour Party was relaunched. However this did not mean that the more extremist elements had disappeared. Syndicalist ideas were still widespread. These proposed the use of a general strike as a political weapon to overthrow government or at least to force major policy changes. Though evident before 1914, they had been greatly strengthened as a mobilising philosophy for the mass of workers by the wartime coalescence of capitalism and the state. The state seemed the clear and obvious target of industrial action. Such ideas received some encouragement from the October 1917 revolution in Russia and that country became more directly important by 1919 in providing a focus for calls for political strike action to stop British military intervention.

All this then was part of the position by 1919 that is important to understanding the pattern of interwar labour policy. This chapter examines first the spatial features of labour unrest and the state's response to it, before considering what is usually seen as the key feature of interwar Britain, unemployment and the geography of the state response to it.

The geography of industrial disputes

Figure 6.1 shows working days lost by industrial disputes 1911-40. It illustrates how the high level of disputes in the prewar years were partially contained in world war I before peace brought a wave of disputes on a scale greater than ever before, especially 1919-23. Most disputes were related to wages and conditions, but there was an undercurrent of pressure for political strikes in this period especially about Russia and coal nationalisation (G.A. Phillips 1976, pp8-20). No major strikes rested solely on such political demands, but the strength of syndicalist sentiment and its emphasis on the role of the general strike continued to be important, especially in the perception of government.

These issues soon reached a head in 1921 when there was a major coal dispute which, at the outset, had threatened to become a strike of the 'Triple Alliance' (miners, railwaymen and transport workers). In effect this would have been a general strike capable of bringing national life to a halt. It did not materialise because of the worsening economic situation after the 1919-20 boom, and a weakening of the influences for direct action. However in 1926 there was widespread sympathetic strike action in support of the miners, who were faced with wage cuts following the withdrawal of a government subsidy to the industry. This was in the form of a nine day stoppage, usually known as the General Strike. During this year, which was preceded by a comparative lull in industrial unrest, days lost were at a totally unparalleled level, mainly on account of the prolonged coal dispute, though the General Strike accounted for 15 million days. Thereafter industrial unrest was always at a lower level, especially 1927-8 and after 1933. A series of major disputes in the textile industries, mainly cotton, largely accounted for the low peak in 1929- 32 and a number of smaller disputes in the even lower peak in 1937. But generally the 1930s were a decade of industrial peace and by their end Britain's strike free record was admired by overseas observers, particularly from the United States (Wigham, pp81-2).

There are no clear indicators of the geography of industrial disputes and the only reliable statistics are available on a sectoral basis (B.R. Mitchell and P. Deane 1962, p72; Mitchell and H.G. Jones 1971, p51).

FIGURE 6.1 : INDUSTRIAL DISPUTES IN GREAT BRITAIN : WORKING DAYS LOST 1911–1940

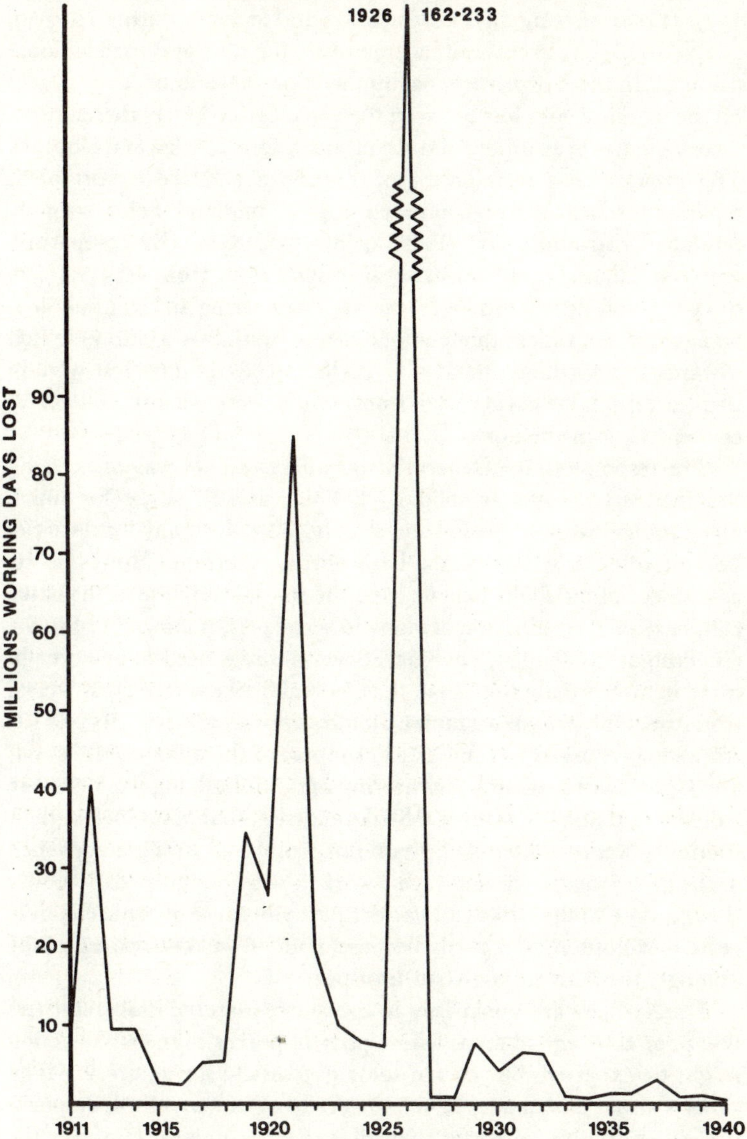

Source : Dept of Employment and Productivity, 1971, p 396

However, given the regional specialisation of the interwar economy, several spatial characteristics are immediately apparent. Thus of 397,177,000 working days lost in strikes and lockouts during 1919-39, 262,740,000 were in coal mining, mainly in the 1921 and 1926 national disputes. In these two years coal mining alone accounted for 55.2% of all the working days lost between the wars. Immediately therefore we have a picture of an outer Britain concentration of strikes and lockouts. The greater labour militancy of Yorkshire and the export fields especially south Wales compared to the midland fields strongly reinforces this impression (R.P. Arnot 1953, p471). By comparison with coal all other industries appear insignificant. However, 12.2% of days lost were accounted for by metals, engineering and shipbuilding, an aggregation which, though not clearcut spatially was still weighted towards the north, Scotland and Wales. 10.7% of days lost were in textiles especially cotton and wool which were almost exclusively concentrated in the north.

The response to the General Strike offers another way of assessing the intensity of labour solidarity. There is still scope for much geographical work to be done on this, because the many local studies do not offer any systematic basis for comparison. However the assessment of the Plebs League as to the spatial response to the strike call, based on a distillation of many local reports, is shown in Map 6.1 (R. Postgate et al 1927, pp28-32). Several things need to be borne in mind in interpreting this. First, the General Strike was not a universal stoppage. Only transport, metal, building, printing, electricity and gas workers were asked to come out in support of the miners (M. Morris 1976, p22). Subsequently engineering and shipbuilding workers were called out, though the General Strike ended at that point, before their solidarity was really tested. Several important and strong unions such as the postal, telephone and textile workers were not utilised. Secondly the response to the strike call varied, partly because of confusion over certain exclusions, and partly because of union weaknesses, especially amongst the seamen and road transport.

Finally there are weaknesses in the source material itself and there was poor coverage in areas where poor responses to the strike action might be expected, but also in some potentially strong areas. Many reports also relate mainly or solely to railway unions, whose response was invariably much better than that of other unions. However the overall assessment seems to be generally consistent with the secret Ministry of Labour reports to government (as opposed to government propaganda) (M. Gilbert 1976, pp161-2; Morris, pp28-30). It remains

MAP 6.1

RESPONSE OF WORKERS CALLED OUT IN GENERAL STRIKE, 1926.

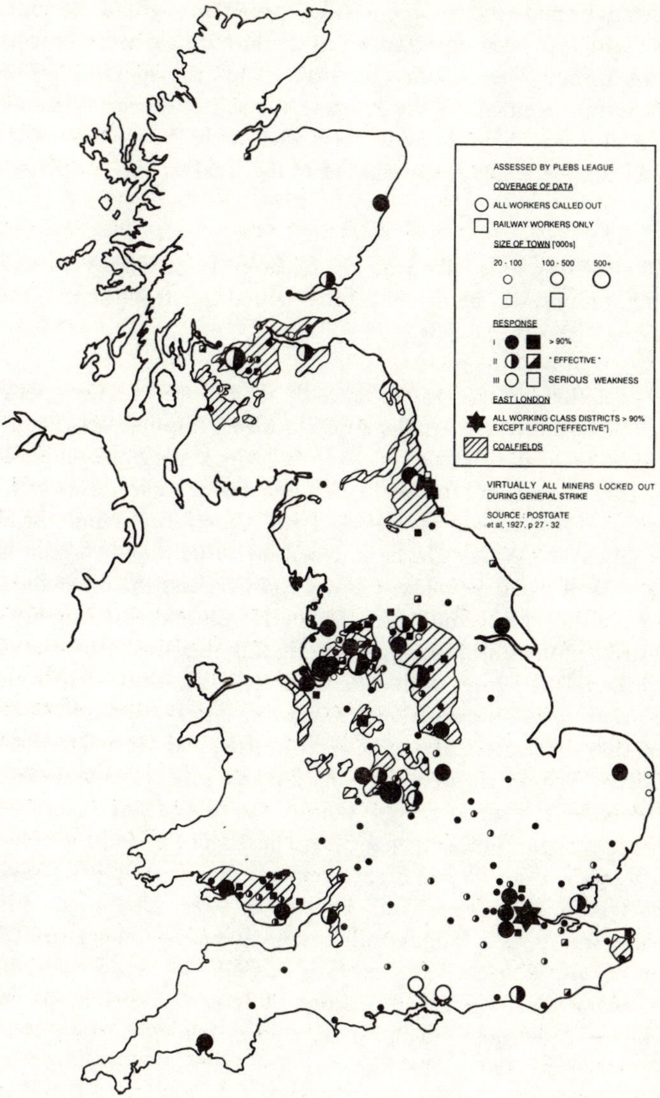

therefore the most widespread and most detailed assessment available. What it showed was the importance of the railway workers who together with the dockers, most public transport workers (and of course the miners) formed the backbone of the strike. Spatially this is important because it produced a wider spread throughout the country than might have been expected. Whereas the coalfield areas, especially in outer Britain, were predictable strongholds, the dockworkers were an important element in the strike in the south, especially London. Above all it was the railway workers who made the strike a national one. As the Plebs League remarked of the weakest region, the south west:

> 'The railway lines, like iron bones, hold the strike together, and other unions, when affected, cluster round the strong centres of the railway branches.' (p65)

After 1926 there were many fewer national disputes and no repetition of the General Strike. Smaller more localised disputes became more common. Daly and Atkinson (1940) undertook a regional analysis of such strikes and came to conclusions not dissimilar to those we have identified for national disputes. They show that outer Britain, especially south Wales, Durham, Northumberland and Cumberland was the most strike prone part of the country, and the inner Britain, especially the 'rural' south (i.e. the south west and east Anglia) was least strike prone. Insofar as they explain this, they link it to differences in industrial structure, with older industries altogether more strike prone than newer industries. However they assert, without apparent proof, that strike proneness in newer industries was also worse in outer than inner Britain. Subsequent work has though cast some doubts on this confident assertion, and pointed to important instances of increasing labour militancy in southern based 'newer' industries by the late 1930s (N. Branson and M. Heinemann 1971, pp104-32). However the full implications of this only became apparent after 1939. During the interwar period labour militancy was heavily concentrated in outer Britain, above all the export coalfields, whose workers, more than any others, carried the brunt of interwar cuts in pay and conditions. How then did the state react to this sectoral and spatial pattern?

The role of the state: general characteristics

We have already noted that revolutionary syndicalism was an element but not a dominating feature of early postwar labour unrest. However many sections of the British state were convinced that sooner or later it would face some revolutionary threat whose imminence would be signalled by major disruptive strike action with political aims (K. Jeffery and P. Hennessey 1983, pp5-9). As well as this immediate political threat there was a closely interrelated economic threat by the unions to the mounting desire of government to disengage itself from the wartime economy and re-establish the preconditions for a return to normal peacetime capitalism (J. Foster 1976). Both involved the state in severely curtailing the industrial power of organised labour. It was also useful for government to link them together in discussion, since the more strikes could be portrayed as constitutional threats to the public interest and the stability of the state, whatever they were in reality, the greater the likelihood that they could be defeated. It became easier to mobilise large sections of public opinion against the strikers and, quite often, frighten the trades union leaders themselves with constitutional enormities (e.g. Bevan, pp20-1). In such circumstances the armed forces could be used and civil liberties curtailed to literally break the strike and 'save' the country while retaining widespread public and even trades union support.

This then was the dominant tone of the state's response to industrial unrest 1919-26, and it was generally successful in containing labour power and permitting the basic preconditions of capitalist accumulation on the pre-1914 model to be re-established. However the ultimate dominance of this state strategy was not always apparent at the time. In the immediate postwar boom a more conciliatory state strategy towards labour was launched at the National Industrial Conference in 1919 (R. Lowe 1978). The left and many less committed academic commentators have dismissed this as a more or less cynical gesture to engage and distract the attention of the labour movement at a potentially revolutionary conjuncture. Certainly state enthusiasm diminished dramatically as boom turned to slump in 1920-1 and the balance of advantage swung in capital's favour. However in a more modest way the conciliatory role of government continued assisting in the settlement of disputes, reinforced by the 1919 Industrial Courts Act. This too declined though from 920 interventions in 1920 (compared to 1607 strikes or lockouts beginning in that year) to 40 interventions in 1935 (compared to 553 disputes) (Labour Report

1925, p10; 1935, p80).

This was a secondary theme; it was in the handling of big strikes that the underlying strategy became more clearly apparent. In 1920 the Emergency Powers Act was passed which enabled the government to declare a state of emergency when actual or likely large scale industrial action interfered or seemed likely to interfere 'with the supply and distribution of food, water, fuel or light, or with the means of locomotion, to deprive the community, or any substantial portion of the community, of the essentials of life' (10 and 11 Geo 5. Ch 55, 1,1). Wide ranging powers to make emergency regulations were conferred by the Act which in some ways continued powers available under wartime Defence of the Realm Acts. Already before the Act was passed though, an Industrial Unrest Committee, a Cabinet Strike Committee and a more enduring Supply and Transport Committee had been formed to handle questions of planning for disputes and organisation during them (R.H. Desmarais 1971).

During 1919, when these committees came into being, the simplest solution was to use the armed forces, not yet run down to peacetime levels. They could be used to keep the peace as happened in Glasgow and Liverpool in January and August 1919 when serious rioting occurred (Higham 1962, pp39-40; Marwick 1965, pp294-6). However service personnel could also be used to replace strikers. Thus in July/August 1919 the pumps of Yorkshire collieries were manned by naval ratings. These industrial and directly strikebreaking roles were rather disliked by the armed forces and in any case became less practical as demobilisation took place (Jeffery and Hennessey, pp49-50). Gradually therefore a more formal emergency organisation was developed, using service personnel but with regional Civil Commissioners and local Volunteer Emergency Committees (Jeffery and Hennessey, especially pp38-41; p73). Volunteer defence forces and mobilisation or armed service reservists were tried in 1921, but fears of thereby arming Communists, Sinn Feiners and strikers meant that this was not subsequently repeated (pp64-5). However the ideological value of allowing an outlet for volunteer activity 'to save the country' was acknowledged, and by the time of the General Strike, this was incorporated either as Special Constables or in unarmed industrial roles.

Two states of emergency were declared prior to the General Strike in 1921 and 1924, the latter by the first Labour government, illustrating how far it had been incorporated into state orthodoxies (Desmarais 1973). In neither case though had it been necessary to put the emergency Supply and Transport Organisation (STO) into action. However it did mean that by 1926 the system was well developed and well organised. Plans and detailed sets of instructions existed to cope with the role of the armed forces, the securing of vital supplies, the mobilisation of volunteer effort etc. Some of the initial crudities were ironed out. Amongst the civil servants who handled them they were known as 'Emergencies Made Easy' or 'Strikes without Tears' (Jeffery and Hennessey, p88). This contrasted very sharply with the almost complete lack of preparation in the Trades Union Congress when the strike was called.

The state and the general strike: spatial features

The full STO was finally mobilised just before the miners lockout began and two days before the General Strike (Jeffery and Hennessey, pp102-23). Troops and warships were moved rapidly to locations where they would have maximum effect. In accordance with plans drawn up since 1920 railways were not used for troop movements, because it was recognised that if they were on strike such movements would be impossible, and if they were not (as was the case over the weekend 1/2 May 1926), troop trains might precipitate action to disrupt their passage into the main industrial areas (p105). Instead movements by road and, in the early stages, by sea from naval bases were favoured. The latter had the particular advantage that they could be conducted in comparative secrecy and with no risk of meeting opposition enroute.

Map 6.2 shows the main features of army and navy dispositions and movements during the general strike emergency. What comes out particularly from this and other evidence is that government effort did not concentrate on the areas where the strike was most solid, but on the major ports and centres of population (Phillips, pp189-217). In the case of Liverpool and Glasgow no doubt this was partly memories of 1919, but similar treatment was now accorded to Hull, the south Wales ports, the Firth of Forth etc. The explanation would seem to be their dual importance in the securing of vital supplies like flour, potatoes and yeast and as 'areas of contention' where there were large numbers of strikers and sympathetic non-strikers but were also likely to be some relatively uncommitted and unsympathetic workers and significant and largely unsympathetic middle class populations. From the state's point of view it was easier to undermine the strike in non- coalfield areas compared to coalfield strongholds with their more

MAP 6.2

REGIONAL MILITARY DISPOSITIONS DURING THE GENERAL STRIKE MAY 1926.

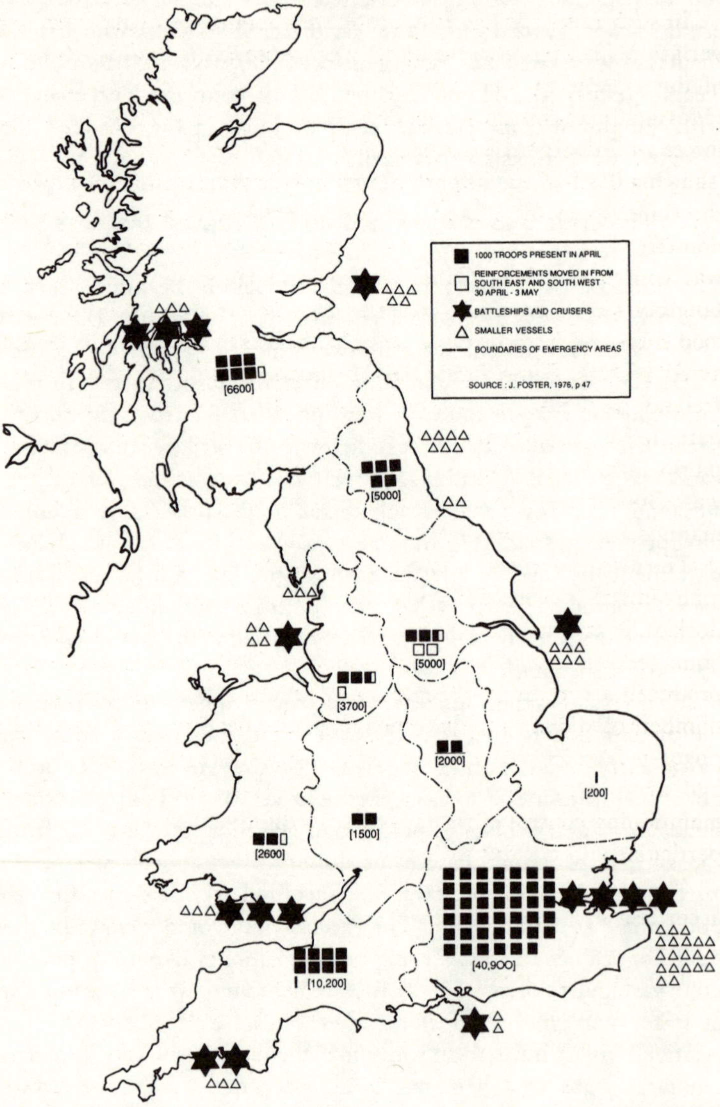

homogeneous class structures. In some such areas (especially in south Wales and parts of Scotland), radical Councils of Action were developed by strikers that represented a near complete transfer of power from the constitutional state to what were effectively local soviets (J. Klugmann 1976, pp85- 94; Postgate et al, pp33-51).

In such areas the agencies of the state tended (though there were variations in different areas) to co-operate especially in the early stages of the emergency and in consequence they were relatively quiet (Mowat, pp315-6). However in the major ports the role of armed forces was much more important. The presence of warships, literally 'showing the flag' was important in simply demonstrating the power of the state. Even the inland port of Manchester did not escape this domestic variety of gunboat diplomacy as the destroyer HMS Wessex was sent up the Ship Canal (Jeffery and Hennessey, p115). More tangibly naval crews also acted as guards for volunteers unloading food ships and in some cases brought them into the docks by boat to avoid pickets. Some items notably yeast, petrol and the mails to Ireland were also moved by warship. In the London docks, the batteries of six submarines were used to provide electric power for pumps, cranes and cold stores when the public supply from West Ham was shut down. More conventionally many power stations were manned by naval ratings.

The army's role was also important in the capital where, although many districts were deeply hostile to the strike, the sheer size of dockland in east and south London represented a large and homogeneous area of very solid support. Initially pickets on the docks produced a very successful blockade, and in a dramatic move large numbers of soldiers were marched in, drums beating (K. Jeffery 1981, pp391-2). Armoured cars were used to escort the first food convoy out, and army experts enthused about the value of such vehicles in maintaining control of the streets, something which was regarded as particularly important in London.

More generally the scale of engagement of the army was such that according to General Officer Commanding London District:

> 'Commanding Officers were unanimous in stating that the General Strike was the best training for war young officers had obtained since the war ... (cited Jeffery, pp392-3).

Essentially the role of the armed forces was the demonstration of overwhelming state power rather than actually using it. Unlike the wave of pre-1914 industrial disputes (and the means test demonstrations in Belfast in 1932) no-one was shot in any disturbances. In fact the strike passed off with comparative calmness, and any anger by strikers was directed mainly against volunteers and, to a lesser extent, the police. Some 3000 arrests were made (Morris, p87), but the overall impression is of the remarkable calmness of the nine days. The fundamental reasons for this are complex and deep seated. However the role of the state would seem to have been a key factor in producing both this atmosphere of calm and, more importantly, a successful outcome for capital. Ideologically it had been able to make the strike into a constitutional issue and thus raised great fears, not least amongst trade union leaders themselves, about the dangers of a trades union victory. It had also demonstrated an overwhelming repressive power without actually using it, and many union leaders feared that prolongation would produce much more violence which could still not produce victory. Accordingly the continuing crisis of legitimisation during the early postwar years was resolved to the advantage of capital and the state.

Organised labour, the state and uneven development

How then does all this relate to the larger themes of this study? In a fundamental sense it is important because the 1919-26 period demonstrated that the state, while not intervening in all disputes between capital and labour, would actively intervene in major disputes to ensure the victory of capital. And, given that the most organised labour was in the north, Wales and Scotland, this victory was not aspatial. However it remains debatable how big the victory of 1926 was. Certainly the Trade Disputes and Trade Union Act of 1927 seemed to be a legislative expression of victory banning general and many sympathy strikes, but it fell well short of earlier bills under contemplation (Phillips, pp274-9). In fact the government had been deeply struck by the collective strength of organised labour revealed by the General Strike. Thus the Ministry of Labour observed that it was 'an extraordinarily impressive demonstration of working class solidarity' (cited from Jeffery and Hennessey, p111). Employers too soon found that they could not be entirely free in using the return to work as a pretext for cuts in pay or conditions or victimisation of union activists. Certainly such things occurred but there was also much bitter resistance and more localised strike action to emphasise the point (Mowat, p327). In the longer term relatively few groups suffered cuts in real wages (H.A. Clegg 1985, pp559-62). There were important exceptions, particularly the miners and, to a lesser extent, the textile workers. More generally workers in the older export oriented industries of outer Britain fell back in wages compared to those in the newer and more sheltered industries (and they also suffered much higher unemployment).

But overall 1926, if it left the balance of advantage with capital, had delivered no decisive knockout to the labour movement within capitalist society. What it did finally squash was the widespread sense within and beyond the labour movement that it had the desire and capacity to radically and permanently transform the process of capitalist development in some direct, large scale way. Instead most wartime collectivism was dismantled. The state sword was forged into a capitalist rather than a socialist ploughshare.

Thus the spatial patterning of the interwar economy was an expression of the processes of capitalist development reinforced by the state and largely uninhibited by any conscious desires or pressures arising directly from the labour movement. It remains highly speculative what would have happened if labour had retained or improved on the strong industrial position it had in 1918-20, but it seems likely that the interwar problems of gross uneveness in development would have been tackled more energetically than they actually were. At the very least state subsidies would have maintained employment in the declining staple industries. In the event though the challenge of labour was contained and its influence limited to marginal amelioration of uneven capitalist development. One of the most acute interwar manifestations of this in relation to labour was in the field of unemployment.

Unemployment and the state: major policy features

The keystone of state policy on unemployment was the making of payments to maintain the unemployed and their dependents. Linked with this central element the Employment Exchanges, as well as being a local agency handling payments to the unemployed, became increasingly important in attempts to match the unemployed with suitable employment. This increasingly drew them into transference (i.e. labour migration) and industrial training schemes. There were also some rather limited public works schemes under the Unemployment Grants Committee (UGC) 1920-32, the Special Areas Commissioners after 1934, and one or two other minor initiatives (to be considered more fully in Chapter 9). All these however paled into insignificance compared to the main policy of maintenance payments. Many contemporary and more recent commentators have tended to describe this as indicative of an absence of policy, but as Miller (1976) has shown this is misleading. Fundamentally the state paid to maintain the unemployed, and encouraged them, not infrequently to the point of coercion, to adopt personal attitudes, develop skills and move to locations that would improve their chances of securing any employment. However it was assumed that the main source of any permanent reduction in unemployment would derive from the normal workings of the economy.

The option of large scale public works on the pattern of the USA, Germany and Sweden was rejected mainly because it was thought too expensive (F.M. Miller 1974, pp166-7). Thus on the 'fair wage' basis utilised by the UGC £1 million of public works expenditure was reckoned to create roughly 4000 man years of employment. At the standard rate of unemployment benefit in 1932 the annual cost of maintaining 4000 unemployed was only £240,000 (Holman Gregory, Final Report 1932, p335). Such pre-Keynesian analysis ignored multiplier effects, but it is important less for its accuracy than for the fact that this was government's yardstick. On the other hand, even at times of greatest stringency it proved politically impossible for governments to significantly reduce the level of unemployment pay for any length of time, still less to ever actually withdraw the commitment. The scheme itself was initiated in 1920-1 partly to defuse what was seen as a potent source of domestic unrest (B.B. Gilbert, pp51-97). Although the threat diminished later in the 1920s, as it did in other fields of labour unrest, the original political perception was evidently justified. Thus the few occasions that long term reductions were attempted (notably 1931-2 and 1935) they were met with quite severe disorder and were probably the most serious threat to the fragile social peace of the 1930s (Miller 1979, p348; W. Hannington 1936, pp230-42; pp298-320). The Communist-led National Unemployed Workers Movement, although it never represented more than a tenth of the unemployed, was an important force and was effective in mobilising opposition to such unpopular policies towards the unemployed (Hannington 1936; P. Kingsford 1982). At these times many employed workers could be recruited in support of the unemployed often either because of their own experiences of unemployment or because means testing of an unemployed member of their household had important implications for them.

More formally the trades unions also consistently opposed any cuts and wanted fairly generous rates of support, in part because they prevented employers taking full advantage of the existence of high unemployment in wage bargaining (S. Glynn and S. Shaw 1981, pp125-6). As the Holman Gregory Royal Commission Report on Unemployment Insurance remarked, a little opaquely, but still unmistakably:

> 'The effect of unemployment relief is indirect. It influences wage rates by disinclining the representatives of the wage earners to take the same account of unemployment as they did before relief was provided.' (Final Report, p101)

This and the implacable opposition of organised workers, employed and unemployed, to public works at below fair wages were implicit but very significant features of the relationship between labour and the state in relation to unemployment and more generally. Organised labour was therefore a powerful element in the formulation and continuance of a maintenance based unemployment policy, though the system in practice fell well short of what the movement desired (non-contributory payments as of right).

One of the principal reasons for this shortfall was adherence to financial orthodoxy. This in effect demanded a maintenance system based so far as possible on the insurance principle, largely because this should normally have been self financing with less implications for general taxation. The abnormally high unemployment of the period put great strains on the insurance based system and the consequent pressure for unbalanced budgets to meet the shortfall in the unemployment fund was one of the major elements of the 1931 political crisis (R. Skidelsky 1967). But orthodoxy was of course a manifestation of the dominance of banking capital over most of the interwar period. Many accounts have alluded to direct and explicit pressure on the unemployment maintenance system from British and international banking, especially in 1931 (e.g. Longstreth, pp170-1; Mowat, p383). Strictly speaking it is difficult to justify this on the evidence, but there is no doubt that the general pressure exerted by bankers for government cuts indirectly had this effect (Williamson, pp126-7; Glynn and Oxborrow, p255).

Industrial capital shared many of the bankers' suspicions of unemployment maintenance. There was a general feeling amongst all capitalist interests that the system eroded individual responsibility and enterprise, a theme that virtually all official inquiries into the subject were consequently obliged to address. However industrialists derived more direct benefit from the system than other capitalist interests. In many ways it assisted industrial adjustment to cyclical and structural economic change by maintaining the workless as a labour reserve to be reabsorbed into employment when (and, in theory, where) necessary (Holman Gregory 1932, p102). In this sense unemployment pay further eroded what was left of any moral responsibility felt or economic advantage perceived by the industrialist to retain a workforce when trade was depressed. Some of the marked productivity increases identifiable in the older industries can presumably be attributed partly to the existence of an unemployment maintenance system, enabling a rather more rapid 'shake out' of labour than was hitherto practical (Glynn and Oxborrow, p93). Generally though there were continuing business fears that unemployment pay, especially off insurance payments, would hinder labour mobility, which businessmen of all kinds saw as an essential precondition of a 'natural' process of recovery (Balfour Report 1929, ppp131-5; PEP 1939, p16; Holman Gregory 1932, p100).

Overall therefore the dominant state policy towards unemployment reflected a continuing tension between the pressures of labour for a more generous non-contributory system, and capital which wanted as cheap a system as was consistent with social peace and one which would not hinder labour mobility. These underlying tensions made unemployment maintenance one of the most potent sources of interwar political controversy. By the 1930s though there were conscious moves to 'depoliticise' important aspects of the system and a tendency towards supposedly neutral managerialist administration was apparent. However as will be shown later in the chapter, the transition to a managerialist state in this most politically sensitive of areas was not an easy one.

The geography of unemployment maintenance

In Chapter 1 we examined the main features of the geography of unemployment, basically showing that in outer Britain unemployment was higher and more prolonged than in inner Britain. This feature reproduced itself in the geography of unemployment maintenance in several ways. To make sense of this we need to understand that there were three types of maintenance payments (R.C. Davison 1938). The first was unemployment insurance, which most workers received directly they lost their jobs. It was a contributory insurance scheme available to insured workers (numbering 11.75 million in 1920 when the scheme was introduced) provided they had sufficient contributions. A central assumption of the 1920 scheme was that total unemployment would be low and the individual's experience of it short. When these conditions consistently failed to materialise after 1921, some further initiatives were necessary. The gulf was filled by more discretionary centrally funded off-insurance maintenance payments known by a bewildering variety of official names, but commonly referred to throughout as the dole, which is the term we use here. Finally there was locally funded poor relief, known after 1930 as public assistance. This was the historic safety net and was given to those unemployed who were not entitled to other benefits or were refused them, or whose income was inadequate even with other state payments. In the long term it was being replaced by the central state unemployment scheme, a process which was finally completed in 1937 when public assistance payments to the able bodied unemployed were merged with the dole.

It is remarkably difficult to get comparable figures for all three types of payment. However in August 1932 when 2.86 million people were registered unemployed, 55% were receiving insurance payments, 40% receiving dole and only 5% receiving local public assistance (Holman Gregory 1932, p55). These figures however exclude the uninsured workers in receipt of public assistance on account of unemployment, which might well have doubled the proportion on public assistance. As recovery slowly took place however it was generally the short unemployed still on insurance benefits who re-entered employment first. Thus the figures, such as they are, show an increasing proportion of off-insurance payments by the later 1930s. By April 1937 (when public assistance for the able-bodied unemployed had been absorbed into the dole) 55% of unemployed males, though only 23% of females, received dole. These variations were also spatial as Table 6.1 indicates.

What is quite clear from this is that in older industrial areas, where experience of unemployment was more prolonged, proportionately more of the unemployed received the more tightly administered discretionary dole rather than insurance benefits that were available more nearly as of right. Within the broader categorisation there were of course regional and intra-regional differences that directly parallel the differences identified in Chapter 1. Comparable earlier figures are unfortunately unavailable though there is every reason to assume that these spatial distinctions were consistently apparent throughout the

TABLE 6.1: REGIONAL DISTRIBUTION OF RECIPIENTS OF UNEMPLOYMENT INSURANCE BENEFIT AND DOLE DECEMBER 1936

	% of Insured Workers 7/36	% of Recipients of Insurance Benefit 12/36	% of Recipients of Unemployment Assistance (Dole) 12/36
INNER BRITAIN			
London	21.3	15.2	5.2
South East	7.3	6.7	1.9
South West	7.4	7.4	3.3
Midlands	15.6	11.2	8.7
Inner Britain Total	51.6	40.7	19.2
OUTER BRITAIN			
North East	10.8	11.7	9.8
North West	16.1	10.4	20.6
Northern	6.0	7.1	16.4
Scotland	10.7	13.0	17.4
Wales	4.6	7.3	16.7
Outer Britain Total	48.2	59.3	80.8

Regional Boundaries as shown in Map 1.3

Discrepancies reflect rounding of original data

Source: Derived from Fogarty 1945, p14
Davison 1938, p123

period (Davison, p123; Holman Gregory, Interim Report 1931, p19, pp68-9). Moreover it was a pattern that, with certain variations, was echoed in the geography of poor relief/public assistance (PEP 1937, pp203-6). The main differences were apparent in east London and some other port districts, especially Liverpool, where local relief tended to be disproportionately high in relation to the level of unemployment and dole payments, and in northern textile towns where it tended to be disproportionately low. The main reasons for this divergence lay in the persistence of an irregular casual labour market in port areas and the typically low dependency ratios of textile areas which meant that unemployment rarely caused family destitution.

Much has been written about the social impacts of unemployment. Authoritative contemporary studies like that of the Pilgrim Trust (1938), more recent siftings of public records (e.g. Stevenson, A. Deacon 1976, 1977), committed accounts by unemployed leaders like Hannington, the social reportage of Orwell and Priestley and the creative writing of those with personal experience of unemployment like Greenwood (Love on the Dole), Brierley (The Means Test Man) and Garrett (Out of Liverpool) combine to create a powerful impression. All indicate the mixed sense of anger, shame, guilt and worthlessness associated with unemployment and the degradation and petty indignities which accompanied the 'futile and brutal ritual' of the 'genuinely seeking work' test (Deacon 1977, p20) or the hated household means test (Hannington, pp268-77), or more generally in being dependent on officialdom to give a little extra to permit visiting a wife in hospital or to replace bedding destroyed by the local sanitary department (B.B. Gilbert, p187). What is important spatially is that the pattern of unemployment, compounded by the disproportionate reliance of the unemployed in the older industrial areas on tested discretionary benefits produced a spatial concentration of such feelings. At times of particular frustration these would burst out and, though marches sometimes brought them to London, the main centres of unemployment-related disorder were in just such areas. In 1935 for example the proposed cuts in the dole that were to accompany the formation of the Unemployment Assistance Board (UAB) replacing local committees, produced a quite savage outburst of anger (Miller 1979; Hannington, pp298-320). Originating in the Rhondda, the movement against the UAB allowances soon spread to Merthyr Tydfil, West Cumberland, Scotland, Sheffield, Oldham, Manchester, Stoke (one of the most depressed parts of the midlands), Bolton and Blackburn. It was in such areas that the traditional strength of organised labour could be most effectively mobilised in support of the long unemployed, who remained an integrated part of the working class not, as they were increasingly in the south, an isolated and often virtually unemployable residue (Pilgrim Trust, pp324-32).

The UAB episode highlights another important dimension of the geography of unemployment maintenance, namely the role of the different agencies exercising discretion. The UAB was an attempt to create standardised treatment throughout the country, assuming a responsibility for the means testing that had been exercised since 1931 by local public assistance committees (even though they were determining a level of dole that was centrally funded) (J.D. Millett 1940; E. Briggs and A. Deacon 1973). Locally funded poor relief/public assistance was throughout locally determined, until its incorporation in the dole. However, despite close central supervision of both these aspects of local activity, the rather decentralised process of exercising discretion allowed major geographical variations in testing procedures and the levels of payments. Table 6.2 indicates something of the extent of variation in the operation of the means test during 1932. Generally there were less disallowances and more maximum payments in the depressed heavy industrial districts, especially where Labour was in a strong position. In part of course the variations reflected real differences in circumstances, especially between textile districts and the rest of outer Britain, but there were also strong central government suspicions of local softness. For their part many local authorities, Conservative as well as Labour, did not have the stomach to strictly apply a harsh test, particularly in areas of widespread long

TABLE 6.2: ANALYSIS OF APPLICATIONS TO CERTAIN PUBLIC ASSISTANCE COMMITTEES FOR TRANSITIONAL PAYMENTS (DOLE) 25.1.32-3.9.32

% Disallowances		% Maximum Payments	
Merthyr Tydfil	0.5	Merthyr Tydfil	98.9
Rotherham	0.6	Rotherham	98.7
Glamorgan	1.8	Glamorgan	93.0
Southampton	6.0	Barnsley	80.2
Sheffield	6.6	Southampton	71.0
Barnsley	8.0	Yorkshire (West Riding)	67.9
Liverpool	9.9	Sheffield	62.3
Yorkshire (West Riding)	14.6	Glasgow	58.4
Lanarkshire	15.9	London City and County	52.7
Glasgow	17.9	GB Average	50.8
GB Average	18.3	Manchester	48.9
Manchester	20.2	Leeds	45.8
Leeds	23.6	Halifax	32.5
Aberdeen	28.1	Birmingham	29.2
Bradford	28.8	Bradford	25.3
Oldham	30.3	Liverpool	20.2
London City and County	30.3	Lancashire	15.7
Lancashire	33.3	Oldham	11.8
Birmingham	34.8	Lanarkshire	11.4
Halifax	37.6	Aberdeen	11.2

Source: Holman Gregory, Final Report, p62

unemployment (Miller 1974, p171; A.J. Vinson 1980, pp196-202). There were repeated central interventions attempting to produce local compliance, including the direct superseding of Rotherham and County Durham public assistance committees (Briggs and Deacon, p56). However Miller (1974, 1976, 1979) argues that in effect central government allowed the strictly applied means test to lapse in 1932. Certainly huge local variations were still apparent when the UAB was created (UAB Report 1935, pp10-11, 82-289).

In many ways these had merely continued the pattern of poor relief administration in the 1920s, when the Ministry of Health under Neville Chamberlain had had repeated battles with 'soft' or rebellious Poor Law Guardians in east London, south Wales, Durham, south Yorkshire and Merseyside (P. Ryan 1976; Briggs and Deacon, pp44-8). Three Boards of Guardians were then superseded at West Ham, Bedwellty and Chester-le-Street and the battle with Poplar has become legendary (N. Branson 1979). In view of this it is rather surprising that local responsibilities were extended to the means test in the early 1930s. However the 1929 reforms had by then replaced the Guardians by county and county borough council public assistance committees and it was thought that the new local agencies would be more 'responsible', especially by the Ministry of Labour (Briggs and Deacon, pp48-53). Underlying all this was a strong desire by central government to avoid itself being too closely identified with the means test, which later manifested itself in the formation of the 'non-political' UAB (Millett, p233-4). When the local state asserted its autonomy, the managerial state form was created.

State intervention and labour mobility

We have already noted the business fears that the seemingly indefinite payment of centrally funded unemployment maintenance would inhibit the geographical and industrial mobility of labour. For some this issue was subsumed under a more fundamental question about whether unemployment maintenance actually sapped the will to work, and most authoritative inquiries were obliged to lay this ghost (e.g. Balfour Report 1929, pp131-5). Recently the argument has been revived by D.K. Benjamin and L.A. Kochin (1979,1982). They argue that interwar unemployment maintenance was higher relative to wages than at any time before or since and that consequently many of the unemployed were a 'volunteer army' (1979,p474). They do not explicitly consider the subsumed question about migration and the spatial pattern of demand for labour in any detail. However it is clear from what they do say that their theory relies partly on unemployment maintenance also being a disincentive to labour mobility out of older industries and declining areas (1979, p473). It is undeniable that there was only a small gap between wages and benefits for many, especially women, workers (e.g. UAB Report 1937, pp20-2, 81-2). However few, if any, historians have been convinced by their work (e.g. R. Cross 1982; M. Collins 1982; P.A. Ormerod and G.D.N. Worswick 1982; D. Metcalf, S. Nickell and N. Floros 1982). One of many objections is that they completely ignore the tremendous spatial variations in how the system operated, which we have outlined above (Glynn and Booth 1983, p346). Generally we follow the critics here and relegate benefit effects on unemployment levels to the margins.

If this is accepted then the mobility question stands on its own. Most expert interwar discussion assumed that there was a shortfall in long distance, interregional migration compared to earlier generations, believing that such migration had been very important in the nineteenth century (e.g. Report of Commissioner for S.A. in England and Wales 1937, p1). Unemployment maintenance seemed to be the only major new factor that could explain this. However, as Redford first showed in 1926, short, not long, distance migration had been the dominant pattern in the nineteenth century, a view which had not widely permeated expert thinking even by 1939. There were very good reasons why short distance migration was lower between the wars as the rural labour reserves dried up and improved transport permitted a daily journey to work to replace short distance migration (K.K. Liepmann 1944). Accordingly there is good cause to think that the whole phenomenon was misconceived, since the unemployed in all parts of the country, including depressed areas, did use bicycles and buses to widen their search for work (e.g. Liepmann, pp127-9; Belshaw 1955 p28; Ministry of Labour 1934, p133, pp199-200). However this could not solve the basic shortfall of jobs and labour surplus in much of outer Britain which, if it was to be resolved by 'natural' processes, required long distance interregional migration on a scale not formerly experienced. Blaming the unemployment maintenance system for inhibiting migration was not, in the circumstances, a particularly useful contribution to the search for some means of stimulating such a movement. It meant that efforts to encourage migration focussed on the dole system and employment exchanges and neglected other key factors like housing.

The industrial (i.e. labour) transference scheme was introduced in

1927-8. An experimental scheme was applied to some depressed mining districts and the Cabinet was impressed by the scheme (D.E. Pitfield 1978, p429). Accordingly it authorised the establishment of the Industrial Transference Board (ITB) to report on the question. Their report, issued in 1928, rested on the assumption that migration was a 'natural' solution to uneven development. Much emphasis was placed on 'the realisation by the unemployed persons themselves of the stark realities of the situation and upon their resolution to try a fresh start elsewhere' and 'natural economic development'. The role of the state was conceived as secondary to these, mainly 'to ensure free play for the forces making for transfer' (all p55). It firmly rejected publicly funded relief works in the depressed areas as unsound arguing that 'nothing shall be done which might tend to anchor men in their home district by holding out an illusory prospect of employment' (p18). Not specified but implicit was that transference would be a cheap policy as indeed it was, each transferee costing only £10 (Dennison, p118).

Most of the main elements of the policy adopted derived from the ITB report, though some of the emphases differed. The key elements of the policy in practice were financial assistance to transferees, training schemes and transfer relief works (Pitfield 1978). The first involved the payment of travelling and lodging espenses during the transfer process. The exact details of this varied over time according to the problems which became apparent. The principal innovations were the household removal scheme introduced in late 1928 and the family removal scheme in 1933 to facilitate the transfer of whole families. The greatest development was apparent in training schemes which had originally been established to assist the readjustment of ex-soldiers and female war workers. The Government Training Centres which gave intensive six month courses intended to fully develop new skills were greatly expanded both for internal transference and overseas migration, though the latter soon had to be run down as demand for migrants dried up (Ministry of Labour Reports 1929, pp33-40; 1930, p32). Although some centres were in the depressed areas, most were deliberately located in more prosperous areas such as Park Royal, Slough and Watford, all opened in 1929 (Labour Report 1929, p33). Here the skills being developed were all in demand and transference actually preceded training. Generally these training centres were relatively popular because they offered substantial training and restricted their intakes to the numbers they could place in employment. However throughput was small; by 1933 only 43,195 had taken such courses, including many non-transferees. In 1936 just over a quarter of transferees had been on a training course (A.D.K. Owen 1937, p339).

Rather different were the Transfer Instructional Centres introduced in 1929 (Labour Report 1929, pp37-40). Transference had rested more heavily on grant aided public relief works than had been envisaged by the ITB which had favoured a much larger role for private firms. In keeping with the philosophy of transference though, such works were deliberately located in prosperous areas where unemployment relief grants were available on more favourable terms than elsewhere, provided a large proportion of transferees were used (J.H. Burton 1934, p210). By August 1932 over 80% of transferees were working on relief schemes (D.E. Pitfield 1973, p195). However it had soon become apparent that many transferees had lost physical fitness during prolonged unemployment and could not do the heavy manual work that unemployment relief schemes normally involved. The Transfer Instructional Centres were introduced to provide twelve week courses to meet this problem. Like the Training Centres they were mainly located outside the depressed areas but in most other respects they differed. They were very unpopular with the unemployed because coercion by way of threats to future dole payments was sometimes used to force attendance, because there was little real training, because permanent job prospects on successful completion were very poor and because they involved using the unemployed as unpaid labour for local authority schemes in prosperous areas like Blackpool, Carshalton or Poole or for the Forestry Commission. In 1932 their direct link with transference was severed as unemployment relief grants were axed (Labour Report 1932, pp30-3). They continued, as Instructional Centres, reaching new heights of unpopularity (Davison, p118; W. Hannington 1937, pp92-114). Generally one of their main effects when directly linked to transference had been to increase its unpopularity.

The impact of transference

Table 6.3 shows the best available information about the extent of official transference over time. Two peaks are apparent, in 1929-30 and 1936-7, preceding and following the worst years of depression. It proved very difficult to operate transference between these peaks. There was much opposition in receiving areas when local unemployment increased, even if it was still well below that in the exporting areas (Labour Report 1932, p23; Pitfield 1973, p169).

TABLE 6.3: ASSISTED LABOUR TRANSFERENCE 1928-38

	Total Individual Transfers: All Schemes	Households and Family Removals
1928	7,300*	-
1929	43,698	2,850
1930	33,031	2,100
1931	23,374	1,680
1932	14,140	990
1933	13,443	605
1934	16,421	1,308
1935	30,679	3,718
1936	49,545	10,025
1937	43,177	7,673
1938	29,627	4,000

* part year only

Source: Derived from Pitfield 1978, p431

Moreover the cutbacks in relief works had a direct effect. Spatially the effects are indicated in Table 6.4 and Maps 6.3 and 6.4. These show how outer Britain contained most of the losing areas and inner Britain most of the gaining ones. However there was a significant amount of transference within outer Britain, particularly moves of females from mining areas into domestic service comparatively near their homes (Pitfield 1978, p430).

Overall though the numbers of official transferees (about 300,000 individuals and 25,000 families) were not large compared either to the total level of interregional migration from the depressed areas (see Table 1.4), the level of unemployment or the normal inter-area employment placing work of the employment exchanges. Thus in 1933 alone nearly 387,000 people were placed in employment outside the area of the exchange at which they registered, though most of these were of course very short distance placings (Labour Report 1933, p20). It was estimated that transference accounted for about a quarter of all migration from the depressed areas (Dennison, p118). It is difficult to be precise because an unknown number of transferees failed to settle and returned home as transfer relief work ended or older industries

TABLE 6.4: ORIGINS AND DESTINATIONS OF ADULT TRANSFEREES 1932-JUNE 1937

Origins	%	Destinations	%
Northumberland and Durham	36.24	London	8.26
South Wales	29.56	South East	30.74
Cumberland	4.43	South West	17.47
Lancashire and Cheshire	14.89	Midlands	10.74
Scotland	7.64	Other	32.80
Other	7.24		
Total	100.00 (94,293)		100.00 (94,293)

Source: Dennison, cited from Pitfield 1978, p432

revived or for personal reasons. By 1937 the Ministry of Labour estimated this wastage at 27% of adults and 35% of juveniles (Owen, p338), though other estimates are higher (Pitfield 1978, p433). Moreover much of the discussion about impacts has not concentrated specifically on official transference but has focussed on labour migration generally. This seems justified in that the policy aimed merely at 'oiling the wheels' of what was perceived as a natural process, so that unofficial transference was widely taken as indicating a greater measure of success than if all migration had been under the official scheme.

Discussing both official and unofficial movement, Owen has given the fullest account of the impact of labour migration. He (and other studies of about the same time) emphasised the age and skill selectivity apparent in migration, depleting the exporting areas of their best workers, leaving higher than average proportions of unskilled, disabled, unhealthy, retired and in other ways dependent populations. He also showed how migrants, particularly the Welsh, were often resented by resident workers in the receiving areas particularly as an influence depressing wage levels (pp346-8). Exell (1981) writing as a Welsh migrant to Oxford has confirmed this from personal experience: 'The Oxford people didn't want the Welsh, because the Welsh were undercutting the English' (p2). Many employers certainly saw transferees as a source of cheap labour, particularly the women and

MAP 6.3

LABOUR TRANSFERENCE : SCHEDULED AREAS 1929

MAP 6.4

LABOUR TRANSFERENCE : CHANGES IN SCHEDULED AREAS 1934 AND 1938

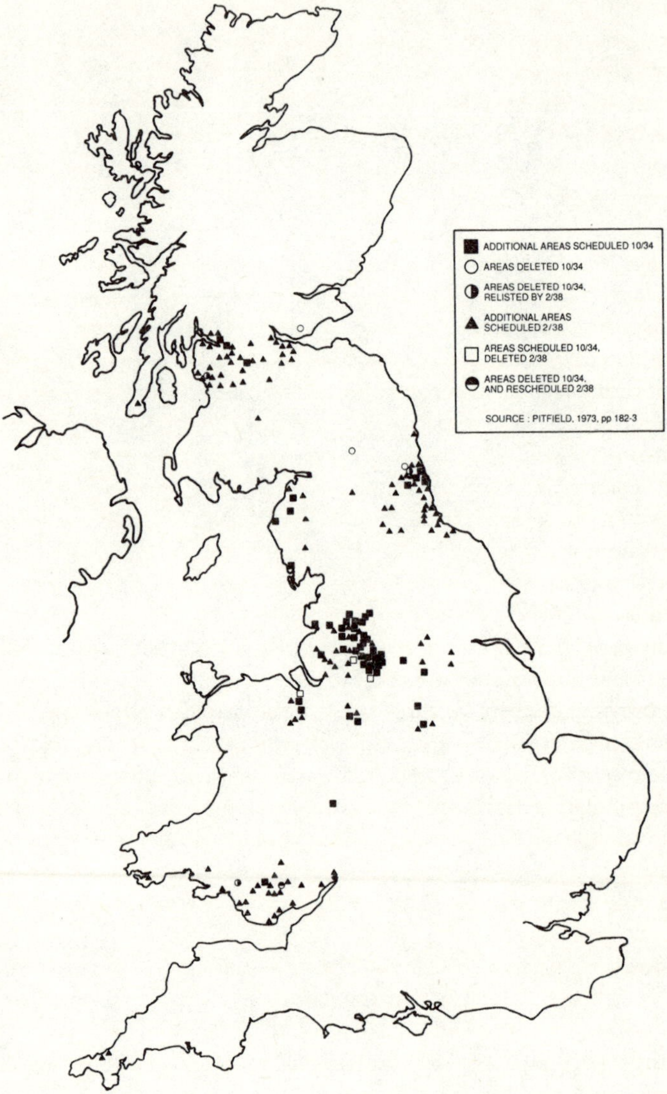

girls who entered domestic service, juveniles generally and the ex-miners who were retrained as waiters for London hotels (Davison, p116). However this should be set in perspective. One of the reasons why official transference was relatively unpopular was that many unemployed workers from the depressed areas were aware of this question. Quite aside from their genuine and considerable attachments to their home areas, they were reluctant to work for the low wages offered to transferees by many private employers (Pilgrim Trust, pp226- 7). It is also significant that many of those foremost in pushing union organisation in the new industries were migrants from the depressed areas (Owen, p347; Exell generally, especially pp14-17; 49- 50).

For most potential transferees the choice, such as it was, was between living below the poverty line and working in a strange environment and living below the poverty line and not working in a familiar environment. The continued payment of dole was of course an important factor in providing this element of choice. Housing circumstances were also important. Thus possession of a controlled rent private tenancy or freehold ownership of a house or tenure of a tied colliery house (which usually outlasted the pits) or, very occasionally, a council house, were all powerful disincentives to move (Dennison, pp188-9). Costs of living were also rather higher in the receiving areas (G.H. Daniel 1939, pp379-80). The severance from friends and relatives produced an acute sense of isolation amongst many lone transferees. Large scale assisted migration from a single old location to a new one was virtually unknown except at Corby, noted in the previous chapter. Clearly though the postwar experience of new town and overspill policies suggests that outstandingly successful large scale migration policies, admittedly mainly on an intraregional basis, were possible with higher expenditure and coherent attempts by the state to control and co-ordinate the spatial pattern of employment, housing growth and migration. As we will see in Chapter 9, this point was only just beginning to be recognised in the later 1930s.

Labour, unemployment and uneven development: conclusions

Transference, like the rest of interwar unemployment (and indeed labour) policies, rested fundamentally on the assumption that there were self righting mechanisms within the capitalist economy and that the role of the state was to lubricate these mechanisms, use a judicious mixture of coercion and concession to maintain the social stability and dominance of capitalist values that would allow them to operate, and stand back until they did. The ability of the interwar state to base policies on such assumptions derived from the successful containment of organised labour in the early 1920s, allowing the relatively unchallenged re-establishment of what were seen, incorrectly, as the preconditions of successful capitalist accumulation on the pre-1914 model. The main state concessions to labour in this were in the sphere of social policy, including unemployment maintenance payments which, at best, reduced some of the distributional side effects of the capitalist development process. There was no real attempt in state policy to modify the process of capitalist development to reduce unevenness at its source, that is within the system of production.

In the case of population distribution, it is possible to argue, as many interwar studies effectively did, that the payment of centrally funded dole reduced unevenness by maintaining populations in the depressed areas. Under a purely insurance based or locally funded relief system the long unemployed would, so the argument goes, be obliged to quit the most depressed districts. However as we have shown this was partly counteracted by the presumption of migration as a natural solution that permeated many state policies as well as the specific transference schemes. Such policies, far from producing a perceptibly more even distribution of unemployment, tended simply to denude the most depressed districts of their most able inhabitants, increasing the proportion of dependent and vulnerable groups. Moreover the dole system itself reproduced unevenness in new ways. Large numbers of people in outer Britain were rendered dole dependent for long periods and thus subject to a degree of state intrusion into their lives that was barely present in the more buoyant areas with few long term unemployed. It is arguable whether such reproduction in new forms was itself an intensification of unevenness, but the case for viewing it as such, at least as regards the perceived and experienced quality of life, is a strong one. In turn the defeat of attempts by local agencies, usually under Labour control, to humanise administration of relief tended to intensify this experience, even though delocalisation was amply justified on grounds of financial equity. However the outcome for relief administration was an extreme one. In the next chapters we examine more fully the role and importance of the local state.

7

Local State Intervention: Patterns and Processes

Introduction

Thus far this book has been structured largely around aspects of state intervention. To some extent these were reproduced in the agencies of intervention so that chapter 4 was largely about the armed service ministries, chapter 6 about the Ministry of Labour, etc. However, in this and the next chapter the approach is reversed. Thus the agency becomes the structuring principle, even though we are primarily concerned with three specific aspects of intervention undertaken by the local state: housing, highways and parks. The justification for this reversal rests on the distinct characteristics and relative autonomy of the local state as a network of multipurpose state agencies with locally accountable jurisdictions operating within an increasingly complex framework of relationships with the central state. Thus although highways and more especially housing were major and expanding areas of state intervention in their own right, they are partly chosen, with parks, to illustrate different aspects of local state activity.

Other aspects have already been considered in the previous two chapters in the wider context of central policies for electricity supply and the relief of the unemployed. However, though important, these were not entirely typical of local government as a whole because responsibility for them was substantially delocalised during the interwar period. Thus although a greater central initiative in policy making and financial responsibility was apparent across a whole field of local state functions, there was no complete subversion of local initiative and responsibility. As Hennock has pointed out, the interwar period was a crucial intermediate stage in central:local governmental relations (1982, pp44-8). Before 1914 and especially in the nineteenth century there was the Victorian municipality locally determining its own policies and actions. Since 1945, when local government has been stripped of many of its pre-1939 responsibilities, it has increasingly become just an implementer of central policy. The interwar period was then a plateau of municipal power, yet by 1939 major erosion had already taken place.

The description, explanation and interpretation of spatial variations in local state intervention therefore assumes a greater complexity than in fields where central agencies acted directly. The basic alternative interpretations outlined in chapter 3 therefore need some specific elaboration. Thus, reflecting the considerable autonomy of the local state, it becomes possible to envisage a local balance of class forces or managerial interests rather different to those embodied in central policies. For example a municipality might well have been particularly sensitive to the interests of the working class or a particular fraction of capital or a particular set of official or professional preoccupations. Such a locally dominant grouping of interest might display congruence with or divergence from centrally dominant configurations of interest. Shifts in these configurations might be expected over time, though not necessarily at the same pace or in the same direction locally and centrally, so that the cumulative impacts would be even more complex. Since every local authority would, at least theoretically, display its own unique mix of characteristics, a spatial pattern of great complexity can be envisaged.

To make sense of this therefore it is clearly necessary to proceed first from an examination of the patterns of intervention. The processes underlying these patterns must then be addressed by embracing both the major features of the centrally defined system of local government and central:local relations, and some sampling of local uniqueness in case studies. This chapter investigates patterns and major institutional processes while the next examines four case study towns. First however it is necessary to place some limits on what is to be explained.

Which patterns of what intervention?

For the purposes of these two chapters we make several assumptions to place the task within reasonable bounds. First, intervention is represented by per capita capital expenditure. The use of per capita expenditure itself is not unusual and a considerable literature has developed in geography and adjacent disciplines (R.J. Bennett 1980). The emphasis on capital expenditure is less common though not unknown (K. Hoggart 1984). Its chief attractiveness is that it effectively embraces the widest possible range of expenditure influences, since it includes all the factors operating on current spending plus others specific to borrowing and investment. It is also important in that interwar municipal investment was a more potent influence on long term spatial patterning than current spending. However, important qualifications are that there were certainly rather greater interwar disparities in capital spending than in current spending amongst the same authorities and that the process owed rather more to central influences.

Second, we concentrate on the county boroughs (CBs). These were single tier authorities formed in 1889 which became fully comprehensive local authorities after the abolition of the School Boards in 1902 and the Poor Law Guardians in 1929 (H. Finer 1950, pp57-69). Outside London they were the typical local authority in the larger urban centres, notionally over 50,000 (or 75,000 after the 1926 revisions of procedure) but there were quite a number below these thresholds (Finer 1950, pp70-3). In total they accounted for about a third of the population of England Wales throughout the interwar period. In spending terms the CBs in general were more active on trading services and housing than other authorities, but there were many individual overlaps (pp33-9).

A major problem though was that they were underrepresented in the buoyant regions of Britain. This was partly because of the unique position of London where the three county boroughs (West and East Ham and Croydon) were islands of single tier administration in a sea of two tier administration within and outside the London county (W. Robson 1939, pp322-87). However it also reflected the mounting county resistance to new CBs or extensions of existing CBs which became more active from the early 1920s (e.g. J.M. Lee 1963, pp109-19). Thus only one new CB, Doncaster, was created between the wars. By 1939 many non CB authorities in growth areas such as Luton, Cambridge, Cheltenham, Torquay-Paignton, Poole, Slough and Solihull had passed the original CB threshold but retained a lower status. There were a few towns in less favoured areas in a similar position (e.g. Rhondda, Stockton and Chesterfield) but in general this was a feature of the buoyant areas. It meant of course that the CBs were skewed spatially toward outer Britain.

The third qualification has already been mentioned, namely the limitation to three municipal functions: housing, highways and parks. Together they represented 41.8% of the gross CB loan debt outstanding in March 1936, compared to 38.1% on trading services. The remainder comprised other rate fund services such as education and public health. However the attractions of the chosen three are that they were undertaken by all authorities and represented a cross-section in scale and type of intervention.

Housing was, on average, the largest area of CB capital spending, accounting for 32.4% of the gross loan debt outstanding in 1936. It was an important item of social welfare provision, supplying, in state subsidised form, something which was also provided privately. It was also subject to a high degree of central policy guidance and financial assistance. Highways, which accounted for 9% of the 1936 CB loan debt, was an item of infrastructure provision, a 'public good' provided locally, but with a very high degree of central policy guidance and assistance, at least for major roads. Parks, by contrast, were a minor item of amenity provision (0.4% of the 1936 loan debt), provided without central financial assistance and very little policy guidance. Together these three areas reflected a cross section of central and local initiatives, generating pressures from a variety of sources for and against spending. It seems unlikely that any fundamental differences in the processes shaping spending could be found in the other rate fund services. However trading services are an important exclusion that can only be justified on grounds of space. Finer's (1941) classic 431-page study does however provide much of what we cannot cover here and well illustrates the great complexity of the subject. By comparison the geography of intervention in housing, highways and parks was almost straightforward.

Patterns of Intervention

Housing: It was the scale rather than the fact of municipal housing provision which was new to the interwar period. Though the pre-1914 municipal housing schemes were qualitatively important in the definition of a new tenure form, they were quantitatively insignificant. Thus in 1909-10 housing had accounted for only 2% of the gross loan debt of all local authorities (Finer 1950, p401). The reasons for this transformation and the course of interwar housing policy have been well described elsewhere and can be shortly summarised here (M. Daunton (ed) 1984; M. Bowley 1945; J. Melling (ed) 1980; CDP 1976; M. Swenarton 1981). In the long term there was the increasing obsolescence of the urban housing stock and a decline in the profitability of private speculative working class housing. This was in turn related to the low wages of the urban working classes, municipal regulation of housing standards, the reduction in the supply of cheap housing by commercial expansion in central business districts and the discriminatory taxation of investment in housing. In the short term the peculiar circumstances of the first world war disrupted normal housing supply mechanisms and heightened the political bargaining power of the working classes which, with the tacit approval of industrial capital, brought state regulation of the housing market by pegging rents at prewar levels and setting even higher standards of working class housing provision.

The combined consequences of these two sets of factors were dramatic. From 1919 central government gave annual housing subsidies to local authorities to meet a part, usually the larger part, of the deficits on council house rents and in the 1920s capitalised lump sum subsidies to private builders via local authorities. There was only one serious attempt by central government to completely retreat from the housing market, in 1922, though this was short lived. Instead of the open-ended subsidies of the 1919 (Addison) Act were replaced by fixed subsidies under the Conservative 1923 (Chamberlain) and Labour 1924 (Wheatley) Acts. Both these, like the Addison Act, were focussed on general needs housing (i.e. filled from a general waiting list).

In the event most local authority housing was built under the more generous 1924 Act subsidy which was ended in 1933, when the emphasis of state assistance was decisively shifted to slum clearance and later the abatement of overcrowding under the 1930 (Greenwood) and 1935 (Hilton- Young) Acts. Throughout the period unsubsidised municipal housing was also built, usually under the 1925 Housing Act, to replace housing removed for non-housing purposes, typically roads schemes, or in the later 1930s to meet the growing shortfall of general needs housing. By 1937 about 4% of the gross CB loan debt on housing was represented by such schemes.

The trend of per capita capital spending on housing in the CBs is shown in figure 7.1. This shows the three clear peaks of activity; 'homes for heroes' in the early postwar period, the late 1920s/early 1930s Wheatley peak and the late 1930s slum clearance peak. These spending figures were paralleled closely by housebuilding activity, after allowance is made for the higher building costs of the early postwar period.

The spatial pattern is compiled by aggregating the yearly per capita capital spending of each CB (excluding the 1921-2 figures which, for economy reasons, were never compiled) and then expressing them as an index of the CB average, itself corrected to exclude the missing year. This is of course a rather crude indicator, which makes no allowance for temporal variations in building costs. However there are considerable practical and conceptual difficulties in applying the

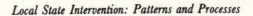

FIGURE 7.1 : HOUSING EXPENDITURE
Per Capita spending in the County Boroughs 1919–1939

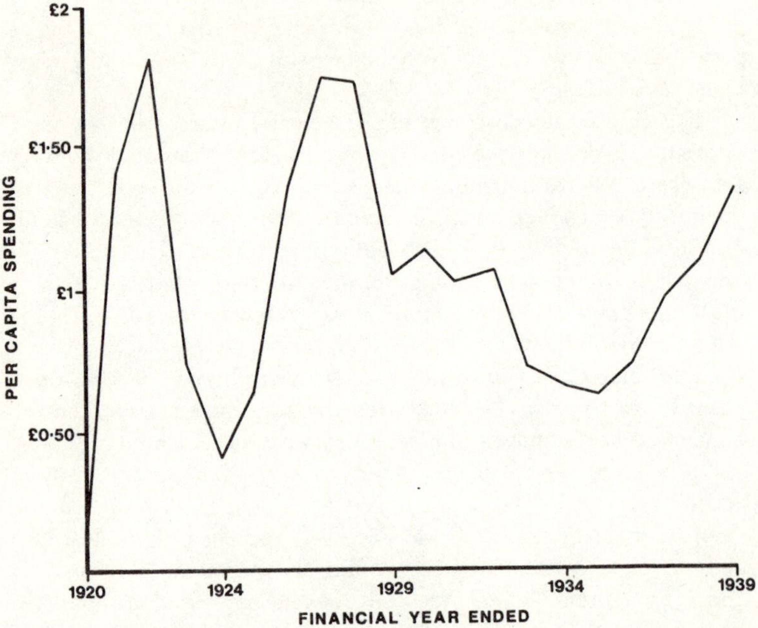

standard national index of building costs compiled by Maiwald from local data to municipal housing expenditure which included land and estate development costs as well as just building costs (K. Maiwald, cited from Richardson and Aldcroft, pp75-7). In any case, after the early postwar period, building costs were rather stable, especially by post-1945 standards, and the accidental absence of the 1921-2 figures is a correcting factor. Overall it is very doubtful how far building cost variations do distort the local spending index. The absence of any indication of varying levels of individual CB activity over the period is of course a problem but this is partly rectified in the next chapter's case studies.

Table 7.1 shows the spatial pattern. A very wide range of variation was evident from about a seventh of the average in West Ham to two and a quarter times the average in Wakefield. Types of towns which tended to low spending were the generally buoyant and prosperous seaside resorts and substantially residential towns (e.g. Southend, Bournemouth, Croydon), towns with predominantly inner conurbation characteristics (e.g. West Ham, East Ham, Salford), and

TABLE 7.1: LOCAL VARIATIONS IN COUNTY BOROUGH CAPITAL EXPENDITURE ON HOUSING PER CAPITA 1919-39 EXPRESSED AS INDEX OF CB AVERAGE (£18.37)

Rank	County Borough	Index	Rank	County Borough	Index
82	West Ham	14	38	Bury	95
81	East Ham	16	37	South Shields	95
80	Southend	21	36	Reading	95
79	Salford	25	35	Huddersfield	98
78	Bournemouth	26			
77	Grimsby	27		COUNTY BOROUGH AVERAGE	100
76	Barrow	29			
75	Merthyr Tydfil	30	34	Tynemouth	102
74	Portsmouth	36	33	Dewsbury	103
73	Hastings	42	32	Rochdale	105
72	Southport	44	31	Worcester	105
71	Blackburn	44	30	Gloucester	109
70	Oldham	45	29	Manchester	111
69	Stockport	46	28	Oxford	111
68	Darlington	49	27	Coventry	112
67	West Hartlepool	53	26	Lincoln	113
66	Blackpool	55	25	Bristol	116
65	Croydon	56	24	Chester	117
64	Gateshead	59	23	Leicester	117
63	Newport	59	22	Newcastle	123
62	Wigan	62	21	Leeds	125
61	Great Yarmouth	64	20	Warrington	125
60	Bath	64	19	Sheffield	127
59	Burton	66	18	Bootle	131
58	Burnley	66	17	Barnsley	133
57	Preston	67	16	Ipswich	135
56	Sunderland	69	15	Northampton	138
55	Plymouth	70	14	Liverpool	139
54	Wallasey	71	13	Birmingham	144
53	Cardiff	72	12	Derby	145
52	Stoke	74	11	Nottingham	148
51	Halifax	74	10	Smethwick	150
50	Southampton	74	9	Rotherham	160
49	Eastbourne	76	8	West Bromwich	161
48	Birkenhead	83	7	York	164
47	Bradford	83	6	Walsall	170
46	Middlesbrough	84	5	Norwich	177
45	Canterbury	87	4	Carlisle	179
44	Brighton	88	3	Wolverhampton	181
43	Bolton	88	2	Dudley	206
42	St Helens	93	1	Wakefield	226
41	Swansea	94			
40	Exeter	94			
39	Hull	94			

Source: see text

in severely depressed and declining areas (e.g. Merthyr Tydfil, Barrow, Blackburn, Gateshead).

Conversely CBs tending to high spending were the more buoyant industrial towns of the midlands and the north (e.g. Wakefield, Carlisle, Wolverhampton, Derby) and the big English cities (e.g. Nottingham, Birmingham, Liverpool, Sheffield, Leeds). In between came towns displaying mixes of these characteristics, for example seaside and residential towns with slum problems (e.g. Brighton, Exeter, Canterbury), towns which were moderately 'depressed' (e.g. Cardiff, Bolton, Middlesbrough, Halifax, Stoke, Dewsbury), and buoyant industrial towns with a great deal of private housebuilding (e.g. Coventry, Oxford, Reading).

Highways and Bridges: Local authority capital expenditure on highways and bridges did not increase between the wars as dramatically as housing. In fact it actually declined in relative importance from 14% of the total local authority loan debt in 1889-90 to below 7% in 1937 (Finer 1950, p401). While we should not make too much of this relative shift, it is clear that the interwar period was not the break from previous highways policies that was apparent for housing. Rather the interwar period figures in a longer term evolution of highways and in many respects the most dramatic shifts occurred pre-1914 and post-1945. Thus the late nineteenth century saw an emerging state policy for roads with the winding up of the private Turnpike Trusts after 1862 Highways Act, and the beginnings of central government maintenance grants (Finer 1950, pp147-51; 458).

The increasing importance of urban traffic by the beginning of the twentieth century stimulated further central action, notably with the establishment of the Road Board in 1909 and a more formalised system of grants to local authorities (W. Plowden 1973, pp73-87; C.M. Buchanan 1970, pp13-7). From this time new road construction began to become a priority, following an initial concern with surface improvements, though few schemes had passed beyond the planning stage by 1919, when the Road Board was incorporated in the Ministry of Transport. The new Ministry further refined the grant structure, using the road classification scheme completed in 1920. The resultant grant system was a combination of annual road maintenance revenue grants and variable (usually between 50% and 75%) capital grants for new or substantially new major schemes.

The long term trend was an increase in central capital funding, but this did not progress very far in the interwar period, being equivalent to just under 18% of CB capital expenditure in 1922-3 and just over

FIGURE 7.2 : HIGHWAYS AND BRIDGES EXPENDITURE
Per Capita Spending in the County Boroughs 1919–1939

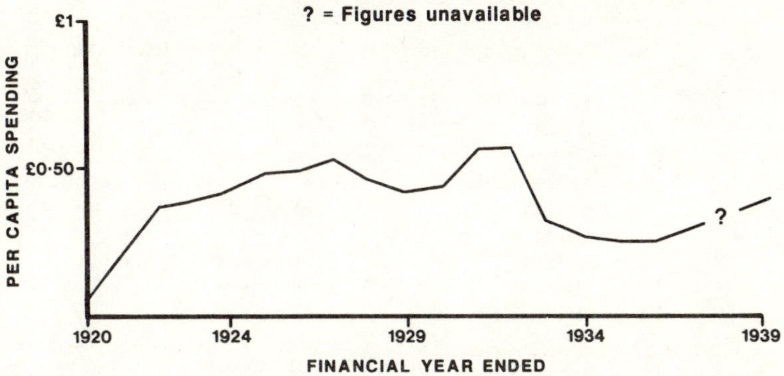

22% in 1936-7. Some assistance for non-classified roads was also available as unemployment relief grants paid as annual subsidies under specified employment conditions (J.H. Burton 1934, pp208-11). Finally we should note that outside the CBs an important change was effected under the 1936 Trunk Roads Act, which transferred 4500 miles of 26 major national routes to direct central responsibility (Finer 1950, p151). This had an indirect effect on the CBs since only minor road schemes were contained within the boundaries. The same delocalisation of trunk routes in the CBs did not occur until 1946. The trend of per capita capital spending for highways and bridges is shown in figure 7.2. The omission of the 1937-8 figure is because the figures were never published and the relevant tabulation sheet is missing from the Public Record Office. However the basic trends are clear. A sharp rise in the early 1920s was followed by a more gradual increase in 1927, followed by a slight decline to 1929, moving then to an interwar peak in 1930-2, a sharp drop in 1932-3, gradually declining to 1936, with a final rise to 1939. Overall the yearly fluctuations were rather less than for housing and the aggregate per capita expenditure, £7.20, after allowing for the probable level of the missing year, was a little over a third of that for housing. It is difficult to introduce cross checking on cost fluctuation because of the non-standard nature of the schemes, but the modest scale of spending during the early postwar inflation suggests that this can safely be ignored.

Table 7.2 shows the local pattern in relation to the modified CB average (minus the 1921-2 local figures) of £6.83 per capita. A slightly smaller spread than for housing is evident, from East Ham at a little under a fifth of the average and Blackpool over two and a half times

TABLE 7.2: LOCAL VARIATIONS IN COUNTY BOROUGH CAPITAL EXPENDITURE ON HIGHWAYS PER CAPITA 1919-39 EXPRESSED AS INDEX OF CB AVERAGE (£6.83)

Rank	County Borough	Index	Rank	County Borough	Index
82	East Ham	18	38	Swansea	95
81	Oldham	22	37	Wakefield	100
80	Canterbury	27	36	Worcester	100
79	Merthyr Tydfil	35			
78	Salford	35	COUNTY BOROUGH AVERAGE		100
77	Barrow	37			
76	Gateshead	37	35	Huddersfield	101
75	Wigan	37	34	Warrington	102
74	West Hartlepool	51	33	Exeter	102
73	York	53	32	Reading	103
72	Stockport	54	31	Wolverhampton	104
71	West Bromwich	55	30	Cardiff	105
70	Stoke	55	29	Oxford	108
69	Sheffield	58	28	Carlisle	110
68	Grimsby	58	27	Ipswich	111
67	Bath	58	26	Chester	112
66	Birkenhead	59	25	Nottingham	112
65	Rochdale	62	24	Dudley	113
64	Norwich	65	23	Bristol	115
63	Smethwick	65	22	Newcastle	115
62	Eastbourne	66	21	Liverpool	118
61	Blackburn	68	20	Dewsbury	118
60	Manchester	69	19	Tynemouth	120
59	St Helens	70	18	Coventry	122
58	Middlesbrough	70	17	West Ham	126
57	Lincoln	70	16	Leicester	127
56	Bootle	76	15	Plymouth	127
55	Preston	76	14	Halifax	128
54	Southampton	77	13	Hull	135
53	Derby	79	12	Newport	135
52	Darlington	81	11	Bolton	138
51	South Shields	81	10	Gloucester	144
50	Barnsley	84	9	Southend	152
49	Bury	84	8	Leeds	156
48	Burton	85	7	Northampton	157
47	Birmingham	87	6	Croydon	158
46	Portsmouth	88	5	Rotherham	159
45	Sunderland	88	4	Bradford	160
44	Bournemouth	88	3	Hastings	204
43	Great Yarmouth	89	2	Brighton	252
42	Burnley	94	1	Blackpool	265
41	Walsall	95			
40	Southport	96			
39	Wallasey	98			

Source: see text

this figure. Some expenditure tendencies can be readily identified though they are much more confused than for housing. Broadly though low spenders tended to be somewhat depressed or inner conurbation areas (e.g. East Ham. Oldham, Merthyr Tydfil, Salford, Barrow). However some rather more buoyant areas were also low spenders (e.g. Canterbury, York, West Bromwich, Bath, Eastbourne) reflecting perhaps lower priorities or necessities for roads expenditure.

Conversely, tending to higher expenditure were several seaside resorts and generally more buoyant areas (e.g. Blackpool, Hastings, Brighton, Southend, Croydon, Coventry), though with some conspicuous exceptions (e.g. Bradford, Bolton, Newport, Halifax, West Ham, Dewsbury). Again therefore the impression is that specific local priorities or necessities may have been important. It also seems likely that the longer term evolution of municipal highways responsibilities may have contributed to a pattern less clearcut than that for housing. Thus the exact local circumstances regarding highways and bridges would reflect past maintenance and construction regimes as well as immediate interwar circumstances. By contrast the sudden dramatic emergence of a fully fledged municipal housing function in virtually all areas would mean that the immediate local circumstances of the interwar period impinged more directly on spending.

Parks, Pleasure Grounds and Open Spaces: Parks and open spaces also exhibited this longer term evolution. However it was never a major item of spending and grew a little slower in the long term than local government spending as a whole. Essentially the legal framework remained that defined under the Public Health Acts from 1875 onwards, together with the 1906 Open Spaces Act (H. Finer, 1950, p193; T. Adams 1932, p257). No grants were paid by central government for parks or open spaces as such, though unemployment relief grants were commonly used for parks purposes. However these are not itemised in local government statistics so that it is not possible to indicate their importance.

Probably more important were private initiatives modifying the extent of municipal capital, though not usually annual, spending commitments. Three types of action are identifiable. These were private gifts of land or sales on favourable terms specifically for open space purposes; local collective public action to preserve open spaces; and financial assistance by national bodies like the National Playing Fields Association, Carnegie Trustees and the Pilgrim Trust.

FIGURE 7.3 : PARKS, PLEASURE GROUNDS AND OPEN SPACES EXPENDITURE

Per Capita Capital Expenditure in the County Boroughs 1919–1939

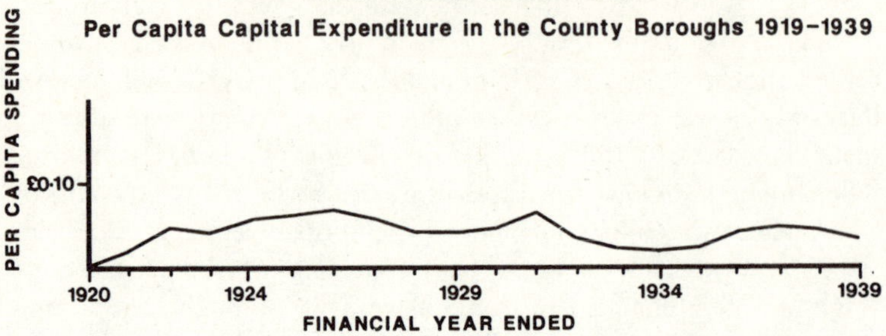

Generally there was an interwar shift, encouraged by the national bodies, away from the formal park in favour of provision for active recreation (A. Howkins and J. Lowerson 1979, pp49-50).

As Figure 7.3 shows per capita spending followed roughly similar trends to those for highways except that expenditure fell back in the later 1930s. In aggregate interwar parks spending **added up to** £0.82 per capita and, as with highways, it is difficult to make allowance for cost variations over time, though there is no reason to suppose that it was a major distorting factor. Table 7.3 shows the local variations about the adjusted average (£0.77). The most striking feature was the very wide spread from less than one sixteenth of the average in West Ham to nearly eight and a half times the average in Blackpool.

The tendency for seaside resorts to be high spenders is very striking and moreover evident not just in the obvious examples of Blackpool, Bournemouth, Eastbourne, Great Yarmouth etc., but also in the lesser resorts of South Shields, West Hartlepool, Portsmouth and Tynemouth. There do not seem to be any real exceptions to the seaside resort pattern, though the inland resort of Bath did not conform. However beyond this no readily discernible tendencies are evident. Again the longer term evolution of parks provision, reinforced by the absence of any consistent national policy advice, guidance or formal financial assistance probably accounted for the rather confused and disparate pattern when viewed systematically.

The overall pattern

Aggregating the per capita spending for the three items for each CB enables some crude sorting of intervention patterns. Map 7.1 shows the spatial distribution by quartiles of the resultant 'urban development' spending figure. To make full sense of this though it is necessary to

TABLE 7.3: LOCAL VARIATIONS IN COUNTY BOROUGH CAPITAL EXPENDITURE ON PARKS AND OPEN SPACES PER CAPITA 1919-39 EXPRESSED AS INDEX OF CB AVERAGE (£0.77)

Rank	County Borough	Index	Rank	County Borough	Index
82	West Ham	6	38	Leicester	87
81	Rochdale	14	37	Rotherham	88
80	Canterbury	17	36	Salford	89
79	Chester	18	35	Dewsbury	89
78	Liverpool	22	34	Middlesbrough	89
77	Stoke	22	33	Leeds	92
76	Ipswich	29	32	Warrington	95
75	Burton	32	31	Barrow	95
74	Wolverhampton	32	30	Preston	96
73	Cardiff	33	29	Norwich	98
72	Sheffield	36			
71	Grimsby	37	COUNTY BOROUGH AVERAGE		100
70	Newport	37			
69	St Helens	38	28	Oxford	105
68	Barnsley	40	27	Northampton	108
67	Gloucester	43	26	Gateshead	109
66	Merthyr Tydfil	43	25	West Bromwich	110
65	Sunderland	44	24	Darlington	112
64	Halifax	45	23	Swansea	122
63	Bury	48	22	Croydon	146
62	Reading	52	21	Plymouth	152
61	Carlisle	54	20	Birkenhead	158
60	Dudley	55	19	Tynemouth	160
59	Bath	56	18	Southampton	169
58	Wigan	57	17	Derby	170
57	East Ham	58	16	Bootle	174
56	Nottingham	60	15	Portsmouth	175
55	Stockport	64	14	Exeter	188
54	Lincoln	66	13	Worcester	191
53	Newcastle	66	12	York	197
52	Coventry	67	11	Wallasey	217
51	Huddersfield	67	10	West Hartlepool	219
50	Birmingham	67	9	Brighton	231
49	Oldham	67	8	Hastings	255
48	Blackburn	71	7	South Shields	270
47	Smethwick	74	6	Southend	282
46	Burnley	74	5	Southport	309
45	Bradford	74	4	Great Yarmouth	451
44	Hull	75	3	Eastbourne	666
43	Bristol	81	2	Bournemouth	792
42	Bolton	83	1	Blackpool	848
41	Manchester	83			
40	Wakefield	85			
39	Walsall	85			

Source: see text

appreciate the spending mix. Only seven of the 82 CBs examined did not spend most on housing. The exceptions were Blackpool, Brighton, Hastings, Croydon, Southend, Bournemouth and West Ham. However in some other towns highways and parks spending, though not dominant, was sufficiently important to significantly modify the usual dominance of housing.

What is particularly striking about Map 7.1 and the expenditure mixes which underlie it is the patterning by spatial and functional proximity which is evident, suggesting considerable similarities in the factors shaping expenditure patterns in different local jurisdictions. The particular distribution of spending also strongly suggests an association with the process of change in the interwar space economy. The general picture is an apparent reinforcement of the buoyancy of the midlands and parts of the north and south by high municipal spending, with generally lower spending in the less buoyant areas of the north and south Wales and the very buoyant south east. The detailed picture is of course very much more complex, but there is still a remarkable consistency across boroughs with common economic experiences.

In the midlands for example the major exceptions to a fairly consistent pattern of high housing-led spending were towns like Stoke and Burton with regionally untypical local economies. In Yorkshire the relatively buoyant eastern fringes of the West Riding were characterised by consistently high housing-led spending. Lower spending was apparent in the less buoyant towns further west. Clear housing-led patterns were apparent in Sheffield and Barnsley, but with a much stronger roads emphasis in the woollen towns. Across the Pennines there is also this strong impression of spending reflecting buoyancy, though not always in the same mix. The still fairly buoyant big city economies of Liverpool (despite its high unemployment) and Manchester were associated with high or fairly high housing-led spending, especially in the former. The very fast growing Blackpool by contrast exhibited very high spending in a typical resort spending mix dominated by roads and parks. And among the industrial towns of the north west, though none were very favoured, the very low spending of, for example, Salford, Oldham, Blackburn, Wigan and Barrow, mirrors their serious economic problems. Conversely Bolton, Rochdale, Burnley, St Helens, Birkenhead or Warrington did better economically and were higher spenders. An interesting feature is the strength of roads spending in many cotton towns, compared to the more typical, housing- led pattern of the coal and heavy industrial

MAP 7.1

COUNTY BOROUGH CAPITAL SPENDING ON URBAN DEVELOPMENT
1919-1939

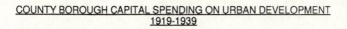

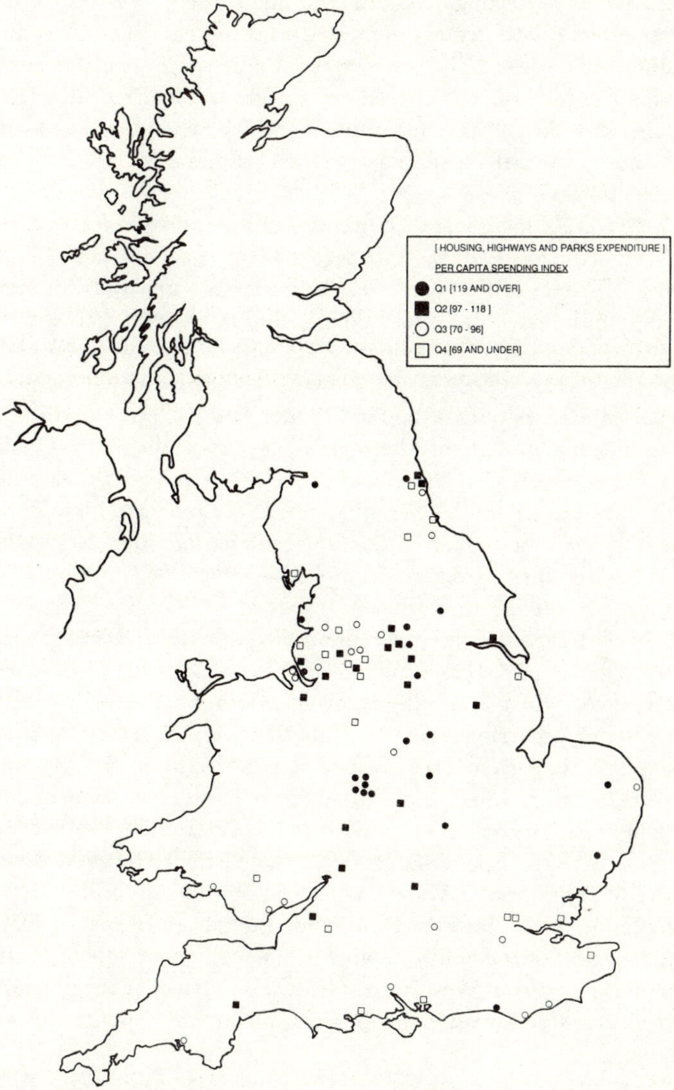

areas. This distinction in spending mix was not universally present, but it is similar in some respects to the textile/heavy industrial contrast apparent in Yorkshire.

The absence of higher spenders in the most depressed area, south Wales, is very striking. Within the area there was a further correspondence with acutely depressed Merthyr showing a very low spending regime while the less severely depressed coastal boroughs were higher, but still below median, spenders. Their spending mix moreover showed a clear roads emphasis, which, when combined with their more general spending patterns, amounted to a clear infrastructural emphasis.

There were some general similarities on the north east coast, the most acutely depressed English region. However the more acute housing problems of that area were reflected in a generally stronger housing emphasis, while resort type spending patterns boosted the expenditure regimes in Tynemouth and South Shields and, to a lesser extent, West Hartlepool. Only Newcastle, the relatively buoyant regional capital, exhibited the kind of spending pattern found in the midlands or the buoyant northern areas, or parts of the south. Finally we should note that Darlington was untypical, relatively buoyant but very low spending and does not appear to fit the generally identifiable trend. This serves to remind us that any explanations must be capable of accommodating greater complexity than a mere simple determinism deriving from growth trends.

The very buoyant south east reinforces this. With a few exceptions, strong roads or parks emphases were present in spending patterns. Only Oxford, which was experiencing an industrial growth process similar to that occurring in some west midlands towns, showed a strong housing spending element. However it was Brighton, the dynamic centre of a burgeoning south coast resort/residential conurbation, which provided the region's only high aggregate spending, with a very strong, resort type, spending regime, boosted by a relatively active housing programme. The low spending of declining inner metropolitan West and East Ham obviously had different origins to Southend or Bournemouth, and had most in common with the depressed regions, but West Ham at least was touched by the pressures for roads spending generated by the very buoyant metropolitan area as a whole.

Other parts of the south showed spending patterns that contained northern and south eastern-type elements. Norwich and Ipswich were housing led high spending regimes typical of the buoyant north and midlands. Bristol and Gloucester showed similar tendencies, though other parts of both regions were more typically southern.

Municipal spending and the interwar space economy

Overall therefore the general picture is of highest urban development spending in 'middle' Britain - i.e. the most favoured parts of outer Britain and the more peripheral parts of inner Britain. The most buoyant and most depressed parts of Britain (at least on the experience of England and Wales) seem to have been the areas of low spending. As we noted in chapter 1, localities did not necessarily reflect the growth performance of wider regions, though such economic divergences were usually manifest in spending patterns. Certain kinds of towns, particularly the big provincial cities and holiday resorts, exhibited important spending similarities wherever they were, often subordinating any similarities of spatial proximity. Again though these can normally be understood in terms of local economic processes.

We are left then with a strong impression that there was some sort of association between patterns of municipal spending and the changing space economy of the interwar period. It must be said at once that there is no neat statistical relationship between spending and such obvious and readily derivable indicators of growth as population or rateable value change. A relationship of population growth:spending is discernible, and was identified by Bretherton et al in their contemporary study of public investment. But it was not clearcut and many partial or occasionally complete exceptions are noticeable.

A whole series of confounding factors can be identified. Thus boundaries were not adjusted at equal rates in all areas; many towns in the older industrial areas found it easier to secure large increases while those in the more buoyant south sometimes remained very constrained. The environmental legacy left by the pre-1914 period had been particularly characterised by the persistence of strong regional and local patterns of housing and was not equal in all areas. As we saw in chapter 1, the north was predominantly a landscape of small dwellings, the south one of larger ones.

More fundamentally, local and regional population changes were not perfect indicators of economic changes. Quite apart from the migrational lags, noted in chapter 6, the birthrate varied very substantially, as we saw in chapter 1. Some depressed coal mining and heavy industrial areas retained rather higher birth rates than elsewhere, while in the more buoyant and rather affluent south, rather lower birth rates were typical. To complicate matters further, the very low birth rates normal in textile, especially cotton, areas meant that population decline often exaggerated the impact of the economic problems that were apparent in such areas. Religious and related cultural factors also maintained abnormally high birth rates in some areas, notably Merseyside.

Some of the problem is also statistical. Thus the absence of a 1941 Census and the lack of any consistent correspondence between employment exchange areas and local government areas mean that what might otherwise be the best indicators, showing growth in jobs and workers, are not obtainable. But even if the perfect indicators were derivable, it seems unlikely that a clearcut simple linear relationship could be isolated. Thus the political nature of local government generated some degree of choice or discretion. Choices might be heavily loaded both by local economic and demographic pressures or by institutional constraints or priorities arising within the system of local government expenditure as defined by central government. However some conscious decision making between different items of spending would always have been present to introduce a degree of variation between towns that was substantially independent of either economic or institutional factors. Much work on local expenditure determinants in more recent years has tended to emphasise this political dimension (e.g. L.J. Sharpe and K. Newton 1984). There is no reason to suppose that it does not apply to the interwar period. The question is to what extent?

Our inability to isolate and systematically demonstrate a clear relationship between local economic change and local state spending patterns as if it were a clearcut scientific equation does not mean that important linkages are not present. Indeed, in the statistical sense, the independence of the two variables under examination is doubtful since municipal capital spending directly created jobs, many of them local ones (Bretherton et al, p203) enhanced rateable value and undoubtedly played a part in the attraction or maintenance of local populations and local non-municipal employment. It is perhaps useful to conceive of it as relationship which occurred in ways that, while structured by certain general processes or tendencies, was never exactly the same in any two areas. The structural, the institutional and the local political process all clearly played their parts, but the exact local mix was always unique, at least in its final detailing. What this points to is the necessity of local case studies, but first we need to examine the institutional processes of the local government system.

This was a key intermediate stage between the structural dimension of economic change and demographic readjustment and the local political process.

Institutional processes and spatial effects I: List Q

There was never any explicit central state plan to determine or guide the spatial distribution of municipal investment. However there was an implicit scheme embedded in the whole centrally created system of local government finance and administered by the Ministry of Health policy that discriminated between the spending aspirations of different local authorities and can certainly be claimed to have shaped some of the main spatial features of interwar municipal spending. While it would be wrong to see the operation of this implicit scheme as being wholly dependent on one aspect of central:local relationships, the key role of the loan sanction and the associated central guidelines about its application is undeniable. The loan sanction was (and is) primarily a mechanism of central control over particular schemes. However a Ministry of Health policy intended to use the loan sanction to influence levels of local capital investments and expressed in a series of secret blacklists was first formalised during 1922 by a small Ministry Committee of officials on the indebtedness of local authorities (PRO HLG52/1343). The direct source of this initiative was internal to the Ministry of Health and it was largely framed by a then Assistant Secretary, destined to become a key figure in interwar central:local relations, I. Gwilwym Gibbon (Ward 1986).

Its real origins though were wider. Essentially it marked an adaptation by the new Ministry, created only in 1919 in the postwar mood of optimism to oversee the homes for heroes programme and other health reforms. Thus the changed economic, political and financial climate of 1921-2 saw a reassertion of the power of banking capital and, as we noted in chapter 2, a re-establishment of financial orthodoxy by the Treasury and a presumption of expenditure cuts (G.C. Peden 1983, pp378-80). No overt Treasury pressure was evident on the Committee but it is clear that, in such circumstances, the Ministry of Health, particularly its officials, felt vulnerable. To survive and retain any vestige of independence, they needed to show that the Ministry was capable of internalising Treasury orthodoxy and translating it into the field of local government. It was moreover an opportunity for the Ministry to assert and more firmly establish its consolidatory role in central:local relations over other central agencies, like the Board of Education, Ministry of Transport and Electricity Commissioners, which had dealings with local government.

Thus the larger scale structural changes in the balance of economic power were focussed by more purely managerial factors into specific mechanisms. When the first blacklists were compiled in August 1922 there were two separate lists 'A' and 'B', but from November 1925 they were consolidated as List Q (PRO HLG 52/1344). Regular updates continued, especially in the 1920s and early 1930s as the economic position worsened, and the Treasury view of financial orthodoxy secured complete ascendancy (PRO HLG 52/1345). The number of blacklisted authorities grew rapidly from 73 in 1922 to 159 in 1927, peaking at 314 in 1932, including 49 of the 83 CBs (Ward 1986, pp7-15). However by the later 1930s a considerable slackening was apparent.

The exact criteria used in blacklisting varied over time, but the kind of indicators used included high rate poundages, falls in rateable value, sharp increases in poor relief, severe and/or prolonged unemployment, reliance on bank overdrafts, heavy existing loan debt in relation to rateable value, unexercised borrowing powers already sanctioned and financial irregularities (Ward 1984a, pp349-50). The categories defined also varied, reflecting both the seriousness and, in some cases, the sources of blacklisting.

Overall two concerns, not always explicitly stated, predominated in the listings. The most consistent, invariably associated with the more serious categories, was the problem of the heavily depressed authorities experiencing structural economic decline, prolonged unemployment, faced with stagnating or declining rate bases, rate recovery problems and huge poor relief bills often comprising 40% or more of rateborne spending (Ministry of Labour 1934, p122, pp166-8, and chapter 8). Typically such authorities had very high rates in the pound, though because of weak rate bases, rateborne spending, especially for non-poor relief purposes, was usually low (Ward 1982a, pp98-9). Thus the listings were in effect indicating an intention to limit capital spending more severely in such depressed areas than elsewhere.

The Ministry of Health firmly adhered to this line and resisted Ministry of Transport and Board of Education pressure for leniency over works associated with unemployment relief grants and to maintain standards in the early 1920s (PRO HLG 52/1344. 13.10.22; 6.1.23). Later the Ministry of Labour's transference policy examined in chapter 6 added a more formal reinforcement to this approach, but the Ministry already clearly understood and actively sought the inevitable impact of such a loan sanction policy on the depressed areas. As Sir Arthur Robinson, the Permanent Secretary, advised his Minister Neville Chamberlain, in August 1925:

> '...it seems to me that we and the other departments should not agree to additions to the capital liabilities in these areas. One wants in effect to discourage people from sticking to them and to drive them into shifting for themselves by going elsewhere.' (PRO HLG 52/1344. Minute 6.8.25).

By contrast the other main concern of the blacklists, with high debt spending authorities, was distinctly secondary. In the 1930s for example high debt alone qualified only 'C' categorisation, which was more a warning light rather than adequate grounds for outright refusal as applied to classes 'A' and 'B' (PRO HLG 52/1345. 7.32 List, p1). In the 1920s high debt alone was not a listing criterion.

Overall therefore the blacklists are important as a statement of central priorities for the geography of local state investment, above and beyond any actual operational significance in determining actual spending levels. They were a direct link between the Treasury view of public spending orthodoxy and the town hall. Essentially they incorporate a view of local state investment as something which should spatially reinforce the capitalist-led development process. Thus where private capital was disinvesting, there should municipal investment be most limited. Conversely no central loan sanction restraints were placed on municipal spending in growing areas where this could be managed without high indebtedness which, significantly, was not defined per capita but in relation to rateable value. However even if a high debt listing occurred, it was not taken as seriously as a decline related/financial weakness listing. The local state in such circumstances was not to be centrally denied the borrowing powers to service the social, infrastructural and other demands generated by capitalist-led growth; rather it was the sounding of a cautionary note.

In many respects this scheme was reflected in actual spending patterns. Thus low spending depressed or declining areas like Merthyr Tydfil, Gateshead, Barrow, West Ham and Wigan were heavily blacklisted in the most serious categories for long periods (Ward 1984a, p352). High spending high debt areas like Leeds, Wakefield, Rotherham, Norwich, Birmingham, West Bromwich, Derby, Coventry etc. were listed for shorter periods and in less serious categories. And the affluent and often faster growing towns like the holiday resorts, where substantial private housebuilding .eased the pressure for expensive municipal programmes, were unlisted.

However association is not causation. Several depressed or declining areas which showed low or fairly low spending were not seriously blacklisted (e.g. West Hartlepool, Oldham, Salford) or, in the case of Burnley, simply not blacklisted at all. And in most of those low spenders which were seriously blacklisted, loan sanction refusals seem to have occurred very rarely. Both these suggest rather more subtlety in the institutional process than the simple operation of a control mechanism. This is confirmed by Ministry of Health evidence to the Select Committee on Estimates in 1932, indicating its desire that local authorities, who of course knew nothing about the blacklisting themselves, should internalise the principles of 'sound' public finance on which List Q was based and exert financial responsibility and self restraint (PRO HLG 52/182; Select Committee on Estimates 1932, Minutes of Evidence 11.5.32).

Typically hints were given to listed authorities at the pre-application stage to the effect that any requests for sanction would have to be carefully scrutinised in the light of the local financial situation. Sooner or later most authorities took the hint, which meant that local sanction refusals were relatively uncommon. Municipal persistence with capital spending proposals in the face of Ministry hints and earlier refusals was regarded as highly 'unsound' by the financial division, and tended to bring more serious blacklisting. Officers were often blamed for failing to restrain their (invariably Labour) councils. Thus Merthyr Tydfil's persistence in the face of loan sanction refusals earned the comment 'badly served by officials' in List Q. But for every persistent municipality there were many more which followed the approved line and did not challenge orthodoxy.

A few authorities, most notably West Ham, which had particularly bad relationships with central government, seriously attempted non-loan strategies using pay-as-you-go revenue funding of capital spending, thus circumventing the loan sanction procedure (Harris, p213). However this was very difficult to manage without large rate fluctuations unless spending was kept fairly low, which is was in West Ham's case. It also had the disadvantage that central subsidies were unavailable because their receipt was conditional on raising loans for capital projects. This also applied to the local Act, which was the traditional mechanism of sanctioning loan-based local spending. Moreover this was also expensive and subject to the same central financial orthodoxy that underpinned List Q, though it was necessarily expressed more openly in parliamentary committee (e.g. Finer 1941, p89). In fact these alternatives to the loan sanction were less available to the financially weak or relatively overcommitted authorities, that made up List Q, than to the richer and less financially stretched municipalities, the group of authorities least likely to be blacklisted.

II: The subsidy system

Most blacklisted authorities were then 'locked in' to the loan sanction system, principally by the need to maximise their subsidy take-up, necessitated by their financial stress. Yet the subsidy system itself arguably operated to the disadvantage of the financially weak authorities, because, with four notable exceptions, all interwar central-local subsidies were calculated on the percentage principle (Finer 1950, pp478-82; Burton, pp200-5). This involved paying a specified proportion of approved expenditure, leaving the remainder to be paid for locally. Such a system inherently discriminated against poor authorities with a structurally weak revenue position. The main point of such a subsidy system is that the actual costs of similar schemes were reduced equally for all local authorities, but that the local revenue burdens necessary to meet that residual cost continued to vary inversely with the local revenue base. Thus a per capita expenditure of £0.12 that in 1927-8 required an £0.01 rate in Oxford would require an £0.033 rate in Merthyr Tydfil. Similarly a £0.23 per capita expenditure in Blackpool needed an £0.02 rate compared to an £0.056 rate in Gateshead.

The main exception of long standing was for elementary education (paralleling the softer line of the Board of Education on the loan sanction noted earlier). Highly rated (i.e. low rateable value) areas received a discretionary extra payment, though set at a lower percentage than the main grant, so that it only partially overcame financial disadvantage (Burton, pp62-5). Moreover its direct impact was confined to education though it obviously had an indirect effect on the more general financial position of poorer districts.

More directly relevant to the spending items we are examining was the 1919 Housing Act, which gave an open-ended subsidy that limited the local rate contribution to a maximum of one (old) penny (1d) in the pound. Alone of all the interwar subsidies it eliminated local revenue differentials from decisions about housing spending. However the lack of any upper limit on central contributions in a period of inflated building costs soon made it the target of expenditure cuts and it ceased to be available for new building after 1921, to be replaced by percentage subsidies (L. Orbach 1977, pp126-40; Swenarton, pp129-35). Any impact it had therefore was shortlived.

More important in the longer term were the block grant introduced under the 1929 Local Government Act and the selective assistance given to some areas under Special Areas Acts after 1934. At the time the block grant was heralded, with other reforms of 1929, as the solution to the problems of what, in the 1920s, were termed the 'necessitous areas'. Essentially the grant was the first step towards a national rate support grant, which replaced several specified percentage grants, including roads maintenance, but excluding housing, education and major roads, and provided a central contribution to offset the loss of rate income incurred by 75% industrial derating (Finer 1950, pp485-94; Burton, pp188-96).

What made it significant in the present context was that it included a crude needs/resources formula based for the CBs on child population, percentage unemployment and low rateable value. (In addition a sparsity factor applied to county areas.) This was supposed to cope with the problems of the Merthyr Tydfils and the Gatesheads, though in practice the financial advantage to such areas did not become dramatic until after 1937 when an unemployment superweighting was introduced. Block grant calculations for earlier grant periods were dominated by the other purposes of the grant. Former low percentage grant take up was initially reproduced with only slight modification in the new block grant. Many buoyant high spending towns received bigger block grants than the least favoured low spenders.

The Special Areas included only seven CBs (Newcastle, Gateshead, South Shields, Tynemouth, Sunderland, West Hartlepool and Merthyr Tydfil). However these areas benefited by extra spending from the Special Areas Commissioner, sometimes given in the form of 100% grants, unavailable outside the Special Areas. As we will see in the next two chapters though, the potential impact of this on local government spending was subject to legal restrictions and other, non-local, agencies were often the main beneficiaries.

Overall therefore all the exceptions were limited in their effects. Certainly they did not counteract the dominant spatial effect of subsidies which was to reinforce the uneveness between the financially weak (i.e. depressed and poor) areas and the financially strong and buoyant areas. However it is very difficult to isolate the exact role of sudsidies as opposed to the loan sanction. They were both integral parts of a system of central:local financial relations so that it would be futile to separate their individual effects. It is though instructive to briefly glance sideways at Scotland where there were significant differences in the institutional framework of central relations, but with broadly similar spending patterns to those apparent in England and Wales. In fact the loan sanction was often not necessary to enable Scottish authorities to proceed with a loan-based scheme of spending, provided two-thirds of the local council supported the scheme (Select Committee on Estimates, 30.5.32). However the Board of Health argued that their power to grant or withold subsidies, combined with a stronger tradition of audit and inspection in Scotland gave them a control at least as strong as that in England and Wales. There is no reason to question their conclusion, so that we are again drawn back to this picture of a central financial orthodoxy of local state spending capable of being enforced in various ways. In England and Wales it rested on a loan sanction-subsidy system; in Scotland on subsidy-audit.

It would not be difficult to extend this list of institutional effects, but none of the others were comparable in importance to those we have identified. Explicit and decisive central policy shifts as from general needs to slum clearance housing in 1933 produced some signs of a revival in spending in some depressed areas, where obsolescence was a major problem, and a decline in spending in some buoyant areas, where it was not. However this was not to the extent that many commentators have suggested (e.g. R. Ryder 1984, p46; Richardson and Aldcroft, pp103-7). Shifts in roads policies also benefited some areas at the expense of others, but again the effects were very limited and not comparable to the fundamental and systematic impacts that arose from the nature of the central:local state financial relationship.

Conclusions

This chapter has shown that patterns of local state investment in a cross section of social welfare, infrastructure and amenity provision demonstrated some association with the changing space economy of interwar Britain. Crudely, areas of economic decline or stagnation exhibited lower spending and areas of moderate-high growth high spending. However areas experiencing greatest growth showed only middling or low spending, largely because the extreme buoyancy of private housebuilding in such areas was associated with rather low municipal housing expenditure.

Obviously such a pattern might arise in a variety of ways. This chapter has investigated the impact of the institutional processes arising from the workings of the local government system. In particular we have argued that the loan sanction and subsidy systems would tend to produce lower spending in areas of economic decline than in buoyant areas. The loan sanction blacklist was particularly expressive of a philosophy underpinning central decisions that influenced the spatial patterning of municipal investment. In effect it showed that municipal spending was expected to reinforce the capitalist-led development process. Specifically it was curtailed most completely in those areas which private capital was abandoning.

This view of state intervention derived directly from Treasury financial orthodoxy and ultimately from the dominance of banking capital in the interwar economy. Yet to suggest a purely structuralist, capital-logic, explanation is misleading. List Q was not directly drawn up by a committee of bankers. It was rather a view that was internalised within the central state by civil servants, who in turn sought and usually achieved its further internalisation within the local state, often through the agency of local officials, professionally trained to accept and operate the principles of sound public finance. In a real sense therefore it was a managerialist code, indirectly expressive of the interwar dominance of banking capital, rather than being a more instrumentalist manifestation of, for example, the attitude of money markets to local authorities seeking to raise loans. The key institutional impact on the geography of local state investment was then a managerial refinement of financial orthodoxy acting to constrain and, sometimes to a substantial extent, define what was possible.

However the structuring of the local state by such forces was not complete. What happened in most authorities still owed a great deal to the local dimension. The exact quantity of spending on particular items were the product of local circumstances and the local configuration of interests and pressures, arising from various fractions of capital, local civil society which often incorporated ratepayerist as well as Labour movement sentiments, and the internalised priorities of the local state itself. In the next chapter we show how local experiences of growth and decline could operate in widely varying ways to produce different quantities and mixes of municipal spending and intervention.

8

Case Studies of Local State Intervention

Introduction: the four towns

In this chapter we briefly examine the patterns and processes of local state intervention in Gateshead, Burnley, Croydon and Wakefield (Ward 1983, pp166-443 gives a fuller treatment). Their significance in the context of this book is that they represent virtually the full range of interwar local experience. Thus Gateshead was a poor and badly depressed Tyneside town (F.W.D. Manders 1973). Its population, 125,142 in 1921, had fallen to 116,400 in 1939 on account of substantial outmigration more than cancelling out the effects of continuing high birth rates (see Table 1.5). Traditionally Tyneside's 'dormitory for the working class' (Priestley, p303; 1921 Census, 1925b, p48), interwar Gateshead became also a dormitory for the unemployed. Its remaining local industries of coal, chemicals and railway engineering collapsed and Tyneside generally was depressed. Accordingly Gateshead had one of the most acute unemployment problems of any large British town, averaging 44.6% of insured workers unemployed in 1932 (cf. Map 1.2). Large families, low female activity rates and low wages for those in work combined with traditionally low housing standards to create the worst overcrowding and slum problems outside Scotland (see Map 1.5). All the other social and health indicators reinforced an impression of Gateshead as a classic depressed town.

Burnley, a cotton weaving town in north east Lancashire was also badly affected by depression (W. Bennett IV 1951, pp95-116). Insured unemployment averaged 36.7% in 1931, the worst depression year. Its population also fell from 103,186 in 1921 to 87,310 in 1939. However the main components of this change were low birth rates (and by the later 1930s an excess of deaths over births) which combined with more modest outmigration to produce a rather greater percentage decline than in Gateshead. Linked with these demographic features, economic activity rates were traditionally very high and there were many fewer dependents per worker than average or more especially in Gateshead.

This and a good record of attracting new industries (see chapter 9) meant that, despite generally low wages, Burnley survived high unemployment without the acute and widespread poverty of Gateshead. Visually though its blackened stone terraces, mills and weaving sheds presented a grim appearance to visitors (Nockolds 1978, p26). It took a seasoned observer of the north, like Priestley (pp278-9), to realise that cotton towns like Burnley stood up to depression remarkably well.

If Gateshead and Burnley were two different faces of depressed Britain, Croydon and Wakefield were even more sharply contrasting areas of growth. Croydon, in metropolitan Surrey, grew from 190,877 in 1921 to 243,900 by 1939, making it one of the fastest growing county boroughs in interwar Britain. Its growth was still primarily fuelled, as pre-1914, by private residential growth for the affluent workers and business people of London (J.B. Gent (ed) 1977). Increasingly though this was underpinned by substantial growth in local employment in new lighter industries and services. Demographically it combined the rather low natural increase typical of the affluent south with large migrational gains from inner London and elsewhere. Its problems were those of coming to terms with growth, the complete antithesis of Gateshead.

The small west Yorkshire city of Wakefield grew more modestly from 52,891 in 1921 to 59,040 in 1939, reflecting moderate natural increase modified slightly by migration, inwards in the 1920s, outwards in the 1930s (Ward 1983, pp395-428). This small increase was sufficient to make Wakefield one of the fastest growing non-resort county boroughs in outer Britain. However, underlying employment growth was rather greater than population growth alone suggested (cf. 1921 Census 1925b, p150 and C. Moser and W. Scott 1961, pp148-9). Moreover its employment structure was remarkably diversified compared to other small northern centres, including coal mining, woollen textiles, engineering, retailing, public services and transport. While it was a mix that was not immune to economic problems, local unemployment was generally below average, though there were some juvenile unemployment problems by the late 1930s (Fogarty 1945, pp22-3). But despite its relatively healthy local economy, Wakefield had the environment of a northern industrial town with blackened buildings, back-to-back housing and a congested and cluttered core. This mismatch explains much about its interwar municipal intervention regime.

Analysis of spending patterns

As we saw in Table 7.1, Wakefield was a very high spending housing authority, while maintaining a substantial investment programme in highways (Table 7.2) and other aspects of infrastructure. However its spending on parks and open spaces (Table 7.3) was rather more modest. Overall it was the typical spending profile of a buoyant industrial town. Croydon, by contrast, showed a classic residential/resort town spending pattern with low housing spending and high spending on roads and parks. Burnley and Gateshead both showed patterns typical, in their own ways, of depressed towns. Burnley was the higher spender with moderately low spending on housing and middling spending on roads and parks. Gateshead, by contrast, showed low housing spending, very low roads spending and moderately high spending on the cheapest item, parks.

Table 8.1 shows something of the relative housing spending of the four authorities over time. In each case there was a slight lag before these spending trends were closely reflected in housing completions. Some elements of the pattern are expected. Thus the rapid growth town of Croydon was relatively most active in the general needs phase, especially in the first quinquennium when private housebuilding was most dislocated. Thereafter spending progressively diminished and was lowest in the last, slum clearance, phase. Wakefield was also most

TABLE 8.1: QUINQUENNIAL ANALYSIS OF HOUSING EXPENDITURE

Financial Years	Total CB per capita Capital Expenditure	Individual CB Spending as % of CB Total			
		Wakefield	Croydon	Gateshead	Burnley
1919-24*	£ 2.71	126	118	35	78
1924-29	£ 6.45	315	62	78	50
1929-34	£ 4.53	194	43	61	46
1934-39	£ 4.69	192	24	44	102
1919-39*	£18.37	226	56	59	66

* excludes 1921-2 figures (not compiled)

Source: As Table 7.1

active in the general needs phase, but activity was heavily concentrated in the second quinquennium when housing expenditure and completions reached quite astonishing levels (£17.83 per capita in the three financial years 1925-28). Thereafter in the later general needs and slum clearance phases expenditure was merely very high. Gateshead though showed a less expected pattern, with remarkably low spending on slum clearance and later (cheaper) general needs housing in 1929-39. Like Wakefield, it peaked in the 1924-29 period with two years of great activity 1925-27 under the Wheatley general needs programme. Burnley though showed a more expected pattern for a declining town with a minor peak in the first quinquennium, followed by relatively low activity, but then peaking in the final slum clearance phase.

Table 8.2 treats highways and bridges expenditure similarly, again showing considerable differences between authorities. Thus Croydon, though displaying high spending throughout, peaked in the first two quinquennia, especially 1922-6. Wakefield by contrast showed little activity in the 1920s but then exhibited a great surge of spending in the third quinquennium, especially 1929-33. The last quinquennium also showed relatively high spending largely on account of a single peak in 1938-9. Burnley's major activity was concentrated in the two middle quinquennia, with two peaks in 1925-8 and 1931-3. Gatehead showed a minor peak in 1922-4 in an otherwise low spending quinquennium.

TABLE 8.2: QUINQUENNIAL ANALYSIS OF HIGHWAYS EXPENDITURE

Financial Years	Total CB per capita Capital Expenditure	Individual CB Spending as % of CB Total			
		Wakefield	Croydon	Gateshead	Burnley
1919-24*	£ 1.10	35	230	78	57
1924-29	£ 2.42	39	135	27	104
1929-34	£ 2.16	157	133	25	130
1934-39*	£ 1.15	181	189	40	69
1919-39*	£ 6.84	100	158	37	94

* excludes 1921-2 figures (not compiled) and 1937-8 figures (missing)

Source: As Table 7.2

Thereafter spending was consistently low.

Finally Table 8.3 shows the pattern for parks and open spaces. The patterns here are extremely erratic for the growing towns, but more consistent in the declining towns. Thus Croydon showed very little activity in the first quinquennium, a little more in the second, but then great surges of activity especially in 1930-1, 1936-7 and 1938-9. In Wakefield the surge came in the first quinquennium, especially 1919-20 and 1923-4 with hardly any spending 1927-34 but more activity in the last quinquennium. In contrast Gateshead showed moderately high activity in the first quinquennium, consistently low activity until 1931, but then a marked jump in 1932-4, partly sustained in the last quinquennium. Burnley was least erratic, especially in the 1920s when a consistent yearly trend was apparent. However the higher spending of the last two quinquennia reflected a less consistent course with occasional peaks, especially 1930-2, punctuated by troughs.

Overall therefore we have some sense of the detailed spending patterns that underlay the spatial pattern considered in the previous chapter. With this combination of temporal and spatial data we can now begin to consider the sources of the different spending patterns of each of the four towns. At the immediate, empirical, level we can envisage explanations based on:

1. Financial capacity to undertake spending.
2. System and central:local institutional pressures.

TABLE 8.3: QUINQUENNIAL ANALYSIS OF PARKS EXPENDITURE

Financial Years	Total CB per capita Capital Expenditure	Individual CB Spending as % of CB Total			
		Wakefield	Croydon	Gateshead	Burnley
1919-24	£ 0.13*	250	6	108	65
1924-29	£ 0.27	60	42	28	55
1929-34	£ 0.18	10	235	211	111
1934-39	£ 0.19	83	297	128	72
1919-39	£ 0.77*	85	146	109	74

* excludes 1921-2 figures (not compiled)

Source: As Table 7.3

3. Local demand pressures.
4. Local political processes.

We therefore examine each of these before relating them back to the theoretical perspectives of state action identified in chapter 3.

Financial capacity

As Table 8.4 shows, Croydon was by far the strongest financially of the four towns on account of its growth and predominantly affluent population (Financial News, 24.6.38). Rateable value per capita and rateable value growth were both well above average. Rates in the pound were below the CB average except in 1925-6, essentially reflecting the impact of a modest expenditure regime on a strong rate base. A general financial strategy was also followed that, where possible, favoured user payments instead of general taxation and this further helped keep rates down. Thus Croydon's council house rents were set relatively high, accounting for 73.5% of housing revenue in 1936-7, compared to a 57.2% average (Housing Revenue Account 1936-7 in Ministry of Health, Local Government Financial Statistics). Such strategies were however a manifestation of political decisions and

TABLE 8.4: SELECTED FINANCIAL INDICATORS
Rankings (of 83 CBs) indicated in brackets

	Wakefield	Croydon	Gateshead	Burnley	CB median
Rateable value per capita, April 1929	£ 6.65 (41)	£ 8.40 (15)	£ 4.65 (76)	£ 6.35 (51)	£ 6.65
Rates in the £ as % of CB average, 1929-30	125 (15)	73 (75)	141 (5)	91 (55)	101
1938 Rateable Value as % of 1919 Rateable Value	164 (46)	205 (11)	139 (72)	140 (71)	169
Poor Rate as % of Total Rates 1929-30	20.7 (39)	23.1 (25)	47.3 (1)	18.1 (48)	19.8
Gross Outstanding Loan Debt per capita 1935-6	£73.69 (1)	£29.76 (64)	£16.54 (80)	£32.27 (45)	£38.41

Source: All indicators derived from Ministry of Health, Local Taxation Returns/ Local Government Financial Statistics

a highly developed local political culture of ratepayerism rather than of some inherent financial capacity to undertake spending. If that had been an important determinant of Croydon's spending, then its very strong local financial base, built on growth and affluence, would have made it a very much higher spender than it was.

Similarly Wakefield would not have been such a high spender. Table 8.4 indicates rateable value per capita at only the CB median level and only middling interwar growth in rateable value. Combined with an expansive capital expenditure programme, sufficient to give Wakefield the highest loan debt per capita of any CB by the early 1930s, and an active programme of current rateborne spending, this meant rates in the pound were well above the CB average in all but one year (1922-3). Conversely Burnley, despite its economic problems, had the financial capacity to spend more than it did. In March 1930, for example, the Chairman of its Finance Committee could remark (with some feeling, since he was also a leading cotton manufacturer), 'I only wish that the industry on which we depend was in as healthy condition financially as the municipality' (*Burnley Express and Advertiser* (BE & A), 22.3.30). Thus apart from the early 1920s, rates were consistently below average. Partly this reflected conscious political decisions to use trading service profits as rate relief. Mainly though it was because modest spending had a corresponding impact on a ratebase that, though not very strong, was not entirely without resilience.

Only in Gateshead does financial capacity appear as an active determinant of spending. As the indicators collected in Table 8.4 show, the town exhibited classic symptoms of financial weakness exacerbated by a heavy poor relief burden and lack of trading services to offset rates and ease cash flow. In some respects indeed, largely because of a mini-building boom in the late 1930s, some of these indicators actually underestimate the acuteness of financial problems at particular times. Thus in 1925-7 during the worst period of industrial decline, rateable value actually fell, while the poor rate simultaneously moved from a modest 18.3p in the pound in 1924-5 to 55p in the pound in 1926-7. There is a clear link between the onset of acute financial difficulty and capital spending which also declined, not only for expensive programmes, like housing, but also on the cheapest item of parks. The council found that even with unemployment relief grants and charitable assistance it could only meet the small residual costs of playing field schemes with difficulty (e.g. Gateshead Council Minutes (GCM) 83, 1928-9, pp319, 376-7, 407). However financial weakness does not explain everything. The poor performance of Gateshead under the particularly generously subsidised 1919 Addison Act housing programme in the early postwar period suggests that other non-financial factors were involved. Similarly housing spending experienced a counter trend decline in 1936-8 at a time when the town's financial position was improving with economic recovery. Overall though financial weakness was an important part of the explanation of Gateshead's low spending regime. This was in sharp contrast to the other towns where financial capacity in an objective sense was important only as a permissive factor.

Institutional and system influences

That local financial weakness was such an important factor in Gateshead was in part a comment on the system of local government finance. As noted in chapter 7, the main system of central subsidy assistance discriminated against towns like Gateshead because of inability to meet the residual local contributions of percentage grants. By January 1929 for example it had used only £145 per mile of classified road grants compared to £3967 by its richer neighbour, Newcastle (GCM, 83, 1928-9, p123). However the most serious institutional effect on Gateshead was blacklisting. The town was added to the List Q loan sanction blacklist in April 1927. Despite pursuing a local policy of financial responsibility and challenging orthodoxy with nothing more threatening than municipal deputations to the Ministry, it continued to be listed in the moderately serious B(2) and B categories until 1939 (Ward 1984a, 1986). This ruled out any ambitious programmes, even though the council found no problems in floating municipal stock issues on money markets, even at times of great economic difficulty, as in 1929 and 1932 (GCM 83, 1928-9, p499; 2, New Series (NS), 1931-2, p266).

Central policy thus kept Gateshead to a steady and rather low spending course in the later 1920s and 1930s, even though the block grant from 1930 and later special area assistance began to provide extra funding to manage the local fiscal crisis, especially after 1937. The council though was very much a 'model prisoner' of central orthodoxy and internalised its logic. Rather than pushing for higher spending it cut the rates, which, though remaining above average, were subsequently below those of Wakefield (for example) for much of the 1930s. Local responses were also important in the decision to co-operate with the new North Eastern Housing Association (NEHA) set up in 1935 by central initiative as a non-local state funded regional housing agency for the Durham and Tyneside Special Area (GCM,6, NS, 1935-6, pp56-8, 238). It was this which produced the counter trend decline in Gateshead's housing spending in the late 1930s. But while other nearby authorities like Jarrow and Stanley resisted, Gateshead led the way in co-operating with the new body (PRO HLG 101/824; 826). Again therefore local reaction to institutional and system effects was important.

By comparison with Gateshead, the other authorities were relatively unconstrained by institutional and system effects. Wakefield was blacklisted in September 1929 in category B (2) and remained so until July 1937 when it was reclassified in the less serious category C. The principal concern was the huge loan debt increase associated with the massive housing programme and other schemes in the later 1920s (PRO HLG 52/1345, List of 7/32, p35). However a secondary concern appeared simultaneously with the first listing. It involved Clarence Hatry, a financier who handled the flotation of municipal stock, and, finding himself short of cash in a complex scheme to reconstruct the finances of the United Steel Companies (see chapter 5), fraudulently issued £300,000 of Wakefield Corporation stock (*Wakefield Express* (WE), 21.9.29; 28.9.29). This saddled the city with a unique debt and, though no local culpability or negligence was suggested, reinforced central perceptions of the need for caution. What is remarkable though is that, in contrast to Gateshead, this central concern did not lead to any very substantial curtailment of Wakefield's capital spending. This bears out the contrast, referred to in chapter 7, between the listed declining towns where financial weakness reflected a declining economic base, and growing towns where high municipal investment and associated high debt was usually part of the growth process, meeting demands which were created by growth itself. This last was in essence the argument which Wakefield used when combating central pressures for cuts in October 1930 (PRO HLG 48/245, Note of Meeting 6.10.30). It was, in large part, accepted.

Neither Croydon nor Burnley were blacklisted, though Burnley's highly unorthodox approach to its local industrial promotion scheme in 1936-7 (see chapter 9) meant that it was seriously considered for inclusion (PRO HLG 52/1345, Note of 6.5.38). Neither were they discriminated against by the subsidy structure in the same way as Gateshead. Burnley council no doubt would have used more general central grants to spend more. However, since it was operating well within its financial capacity and following a spending course that hardly demonstrated grant maximisation tendencies, it would be difficult to claim any implicit system effects at work. Both towns on occasions pursued policy lines that diverged markedly from those encouraged centrally. However richer Croydon was better placed to do this. Not infrequently its council deliberately chose low or non-subsidy policy options to keep local control. Thus in 1932 it arbitrarily redefined 1322 council houses built under the more generous Wheatley subsidy to have been built under the lower Chamberlain subsidy so that the high rents already charged (and deemed illegal under the Wheatley scheme) could continue to be charged (Croydon Council Minutes (CCM), L, Pt I, 1931-2, pp1049- 57). And there were many other examples. None of the other towns were able to achieve such local independence, though only financially weak Gateshead was seriously constrained by centrally created institutional and system effects.

Local demand pressures: housing

In both the growing towns the requirement for housing was brisk. However the huge importance of private housebuilding in the growth of Croydon (see Table 8.5) meant that the pressures on the municipality were not commensurate with the scale of population increase. Relatively low overcrowding and a comparatively new housing stock also further depressed the need and demand for municipal housing. However demand, if not need, was further squeezed deliberately by the high rent policies and extraordinarily strict residential qualifications, which required ten years continuous residence for most municipal housing (CCM, XLVII, Pt I, 1928-9, pp1398-9). This was clearly intended to discourage less affluent people moving to the borough simply to secure municipal housing. However, such local political attitudes were inconsistent with the new growth of manufacturing and commercial employment in the borough itself, which generated local sources of demand for cheaper housing that were less easy to ignore. The early postwar schemes failed totally to address the scale of the housing shortage for such groups (CCM, XXXVII, Pt I, 1918-9, pp1546-52; XXXVIII, Pt I, 1919-20, pp204-5). They housed the lower middle classes whose housing opportunities were temporarily thwarted by the wartime disruption of private housing construction (CCM, XXXIX, Pt I, 1920-1, p803).

Schemes in the mid/late 1920s reflected demands arising from factory workers (and those displaced by central area street improvement schemes), but there was a marked reaction against this in the 1930s. The hope was that private builders would now cater for this wider mass market. Thus a major new 4500 dwelling low rent scheme at New Addington was initiated (but never completed) in 1934 by the First National Housing Trust, a subsidiary of the Henry Boot building group, with the active encouragement of Croydon Corporation (e.g. *Croydon Advertiser*, 29.1.34). However the rents were not as low as promised and proposals for a large scale revival in municipal building had re-emerged by 1938, significantly at the same time as further commercial and industrial developments were under active consideration in several parts of the borough (CCM, LVI, Pt I, 1937-8, pp1079, 1083). These moves were thwarted until post-1939 by an outbreak of ultra-ratepayerism

The pattern of demand was entirely different in Wakefield as Table 8.5 shows. The combination of growth, serious overcrowding and a major obsolescence problem in the older core of the city generated a demand for municipal housing well in excess of that in the other towns. An important point that differentiated Wakefield from Croydon and many other growing towns was that its housing market did not encourage much private housebuilding. Municipal housing accounted for a massive 71.9% of interwar completions (1 per 11.9 of the 1939 population). This compared with only 14.3% in Croydon (1:65.0), 32.6% in Gateshead (1:47.9) and 55.6% in Burnley (1:36.9). Wakefield's rather low private output probably reflected the local preponderance of employment in mining and manufacturing, and the fact that it was a small and still rather discrete housing market. In this it showed housebuilding characteristics similar to those in other small and moderately buoyant CBs outside the south, e.g. Carlisle (PRO HLG 52/801). Of course it could be suggested that demand for private housing was simply squeezed out by Wakefield's massive municipal programme. However the evidence for this is not strong. Thus there were periodic lulls in municipal activity which produced no sustained upturn in private building. More importantly the Ministry of Health, given its growing worries about Wakefield's housing debt, would certainly have refused approvals if they felt real 'poaching', as they termed it, was occurring (e.g. PRO HLG 48/245, Note of Meeting 18.9.29). The question regularly came up at central-local meetings and the council had to defend itself against sceptical civil servants. That their defence was successful strongly suggests that no-one really believed that Wakefield's demand for housing could be met by the private sector.

But if Wakefield was not a Croydon neither was it a Gateshead.

TABLE 8.5: SELECTED NEED/DEMAND INDICATORS
Rankings (of 83 CBs) indicated in brackets

	Wakefield	Croydon	Gateshead	Burnley	CB median
Population Growth 1921-38 (a)	+9% (15)	+27% (7)	-9% (74)	-16% (80)	+2%
Rooms per dwelling 1921 (b)	4.15(73)	5.75(15)	3.44(81)	4.23(70)	4.97
Average family size 1921 (b)	4.25(37)	4.03(57)	4.43(16)	3.96(66)	4.19
Population at or more than 2 persons per room 1921 (c)	14.0%(18)	4.7%(64)	37.0%(1)	5.6%(55)	8.6%
Increase in family numbers 1921-31 (d)	25.5%(15)	35.3%(8)	9.3%(68)	6.5%(77)	14.9%
New private enterprise houses completed 1919-39: 1939 Population (e)	1:30.5(na)	1:10.8(na)	1:28.3(na)	1:46.3(na)	na-National average 1:14.0
Peak housing waiting list applications: population (f)	1:22 (na) (Apr 1923)	1:32 (na) (Jul 1929)	1:50 (na) (Apr 1933)	1:85 (na) (Oct 1932)	na
Licensed Motor Cars per thousand population 1929 (g)	15.7 (56)	31.8 (8)	7.6 (81)	13.6 (63)	17.9
Licensed Mechanically Propelled Road Vehicles per thousand population 1929 (g)	41.8 (44)	61.0 (9)	21.5 (80)	31.2 (67)	43.1
Acres of public open space per thousand population 1919 (h)	1.1*(na)	2.0 (na)	0.5 (na)	1.7 (na)	na

* 1922 figures

Sources:

(a) 1931 Census, General Report, 1950, Table XXII, pp49-51
Fogarty 1945, pp26-9

(b) 1921 Census, General Tables 1925, Table 30

(c) Ibid and General Report 1927s, Table XXVII

(d) 1931 Census, Housing Report and Tables 1935, Table 5

(e) City of Wakefield, Number of Houses Erected During Years 1878-1950
CB Croydon 1951, p5; CCM, LVI, 1937-8, Pt II, pp1353-7; LVII, 1938-9, Pt I, p1518
Gateshead CB, Public Health Department Report for 1939 1940, p35
Burnley: derived from annual Medical Officer of Health Reports and NE Lancashire Jt TP Advisory Committee 1929, p36

(f) WE, 14.4.23; CCM, XLVII, 1928-9, Pt I, p1141, 1342;
GCM, 3, New Series 1932-3, p315; BE and A, 8.10.32

(g) Ministry of Transport 1930

(h) G.L. Pepler 1923, pp19-20; W.C. Berwick-Sayers 1938; Manders 1973, pp241-2; Burnley CB The Official Handbook 1938, pp32-6

Although the housing requirements of Wakefield's population did not constitute an effective demand sufficiently strong to call forth a more active response from private housebuilders, neither was it such a weak demand that a wide section of its population could not afford municipal rents (which were neither particularly high nor low). Rent arrears were only a problem in the aftermath of the 1926 strike. Unemployment was normally below average and poverty was not serious. Accordingly the waiting list for municipal housing was always buoyant, especially in the early 1920s. It was greatly reinforced by replacement demands in the 1930s. As we have implied, such things were rather different in Gateshead, where local economic problems not only weakened the capacity of the local state to invest in housing, they also seriously weakened the ability of local populations to afford the rents.

Table 8.5 shows that Gateshead demonstrated acute housing needs, though interwar surveys did not always reflect this, because of local and central fears of the costs of meeting such needs (e.g. PRO HLG 4/3167, Appendix J; GCM, 71, 1920, pp42, 89-90). Nor were they manifest in waiting list applications because rents in most 1920s and many later schemes were too high for the great majority of those in housing need. This 'rental effect' was graphically demonstrated in 1928 when some low rent, low standard council houses were developed as an experiment. There were 'well over a 1000' applicants for the first such scheme of 68 dwellings (GCM, 83, 1928-9, p84). More such schemes followed and these circumstances produced the peak waiting lists in the early 1930s. However even very low rent council housing could only be afforded with difficulty by many tenants. A survey in another depressed north east coast town, Stockton on Tees, showed that death rates amongst very poor tenants were higher on council estates than in older housing because rents ate into food budgets (G.C. M'Gonigle, cited in Priestley, pp347-8). There is good reason to suppose this also applied to Gateshead (e.g. GCM, 83, 1928-9, p123).

Gateshead therefore showed high housing need but rather weak demand during the worst depression period. However it is doubtful whether weak demand was the main part of the explanation of Gateshead's low housing spending. Thus the low rent schemes developed after 1928 did clearly generate considerable demand even from the very poor, despite the kind of impact on household economies referred to above. Moreover as recovery occurred there was a mini-private building boom from 1935, providing for the bottom end of the market and showing that housing demand was not totally depressed.

Accordingly we are drawn back to the town's weak financial position and system constraints as more critical determinants. In the final analysis the council was unable to sustain the level of building necessary to service the effective demand for municipal low rent housing that it had uncovered in the late 1920s. Low demand, especially pre-1928, was a factor but financial and system constraints were crucial.

Burnley, without the demographic pressures or acute poverty of Gateshead, was different. Here low demand was an important determinant, with an ageing population, low rates of household formation, low overcrowding, and a housing stock that was old-fashioned but solidly built. Moreover, as Gittins suggests (1982, p185), the fact that married women normally expected to work probably delayed the development of a strong ideology of female domesticity, thereby reducing the popular desire for modern dwellings and affecting demand for both private and municipal housing. Nor did the generally low incomes of employed and unemployed workers in Burnley do anything to encourage housing demand. Thus despite traditionally high owner occupation and a highly developed local building society movement, private housebuilding was very low (Swenarton and Taylor 1985, pp387-9). But, unlike Wakefield, there was little demand pressure evident on the municipal side either. Need indicators and municipal waiting lists were in accord. Even the longest waiting list in Autumn 1932 was two thirds made up of already housed old age pensioners seeking bungalows (BE & A, 8.10.32). Ordinary applicants were very much a minority. Gradually time and new fashions underlined the obsolescence of older housing. Replacement demand accordingly became a progressively larger factor in the later 1930s, underpinning the higher housing expenditure of that period. Similar pressures were also apparent in Wakefield and Gateshead, though in the latter the local state's role had been ceded to NEHA.

Overall therefore in Burnley, as in Wakefield and Croydon, demand was an important factor shaping local state housing expenditure. Gateshead exhibited generally low demand alongside high need, but its financial position and system constraints remained crucial in understanding its spending regime. We must now consider how far the same tendencies were apparent for highways and parks.

Local demand pressures: highways and parks

Gateshead's highways spending was entirely consistent with the crude demand indicators derived from vehicle registrations. However these took no account of the considerable through traffic problems. Gateshead's position at the Tyne's lowest bridging point funnelled movement both north-south along the Great North Road and from eastern Tyneside and Sunderland. Thus the South Tyneside Regional Town Planning Report in 1928 proposed extensive road building to relieve congestion and three or four new bridge crossings (pp22-6). One new crossing, the Tyne Bridge (financed mainly by Newcastle Corporation and central government), was simultaneously nearing completion and became (until 1937) the only toll free high level crossing. Soon it too was badly congested. The other bridges were not built and by the late 1930s there were increasing complaints about resultant central congestion in Gateshead (e.g. *Gateshead Weekly Pictorial Post*, 17.3.39, p16). While such problems were less serious during the worst depression years, there were alternative 'demand' pressures for road building that arose from high unemployment. In 1929 for example the regional planning consultant reported that road building was particularly suitable for generating large scale employment for the many unemployed miners in Gateshead and district (Gateshead Town Improvement Committee Minutes, 1928-31, pp84-5). Finally we should note the increasing appeal of the road as a potent symbol of modernity in the 1930s. This had a particular relevance in a town where over- dependence on railways and railway engineering was a major source of its interwar decline. Local road planners were directly influenced by ideas of modernism in relation to road planning (e.g. GCM, 9, NS, 1938-9, p238). The local town planning scheme, approved in 1938, was dominated by ambitious road schemes (PRO HLG 4/3172).

Overall therefore Gateshead exhibited a demand for roads well in excess of that suggested by basic indicators and spending levels. In Burnley however a demand based explanation is more plausible. Again there was the major problem of through traffic, which was growing very rapidly on the important trans-Pennine route through the town (North East Lancashire Joint Town Planning Advisory Committee, 1929, p54). Also, as in Gateshead, traditional transport media remained to haunt interwar roads policy. In Burnley though they impinged in an altogether different way when a major aqueduct bearing the Leeds-Liverpool Canal over a main central street threatened imminent collapse in 1924, necessitating complete rebuilding at municipal expense (Burnley Improvement Department 1927, pp6-7). The town had never relied on railways as heavily as

Gateshead, and it was the paucity of rail links which animated debates about roads policy (E.D. Smithies 1974, pp56-7).

Less prominent were the employment generation demand effects that were so important in Gateshead. In Burnley heavy manual roadmaking work was less appropriate for the female weavers who were the main unemployed group. Overall though there was considerable consistency between demand pressures and actual spending, and the main objects of expenditure corresponded closely with the specific demands that were identified.

Wakefield and Croydon also showed a strong association between demand indicators and highways spending. In Wakefield there was a close rank correlation between vehicle registrations per thousand and spending level, though a rather weaker one for motor cars alone. This suggests a greater sensitivity to business generated spending demands that is entirely consistent with other evidence. Thus one of the most potent elements in the interwar growth of Wakefield was the creation from the early 1920s of a complex network of bus services by the large private West Riding company based in the city. It was itself a significant local employer but its main importance was that it enlarged the growth potential of the city by extending its labour market and retailing hinterland into the surrounding rather straggling mining and industrial districts in a way that earlier tramways and railways had never done. This in turn meant that Wakefield's interwar growth was particularly dependent on road transport and there was no lack of awareness of this amongst the local business community (e.g. WE 14.4.23). Local business had also enthusiastically backed Wakefield's campaign for county borough status in 1913-5 which had laid great emphasis on highway problems under county administration (WE 8.3.13). A particular concern was the central bottleneck of the old Wakefield bridge. It is therefore significant that the building of a new bridge in 1932-3 was the main single item of interwar highways spending, and a major contribution to the efficient functioning of the central area. More generally, as in Gateshead, there was an awareness of roads as a tangible symbol of a progressive city (City of Wakefield 1932, pp4-6). But whereas Gateshead could not fulfil its ambitions, Wakefield could and, to a large extent, did.

In Croydon the demands for road building were much more broadly based. Thus before 1914 central government had recognised a metropolitan need for a Croydon by-pass road to ease movement between the south and London (C.M. Buchanan 1970, pp11-4). This had been met with suspicion by the local Chamber of Commerce which feared it would damage Croydon's retailing and central service functions (PRO MT 38/36). It was from this lobby that the demand to widen and improve central Croydon's narrow streets originated. Both proposals were very important components of interwar spending, especially the latter which at times created great local controversy (e.g. RIBA Art Standing Committee et al 1923; G.F. Carter 1925, p181). Meanwhile the scale of private residential and other development was itself generating pressures for a road infrastructure to be provided. These were accordingly a continuing item of spending, implementing the proposals of the town planning schemes (Carter generally). The specific pressures to provide particular roads normally came from housing developers (e.g. CCM, LIII, Pt I, 1934-5, pp1073-4). However it is significant that private car ownership was rather high in Croydon so that some domestic ratepayer pressure for roads spending and parking provision was also evident by the late 1930s. Roads were never a target for economies.

The same ratepayer attitudes applied to parks, and more deputations lobbied Croydon council on open space questions than on any other issue. Much of this was a reaction to the rapid building over of former farmland. However many of the larger private developers operating in the borough, such as the locally based Wates Brothers, soon realised that open space provision on their estates was a popular amenity, and they provided land for this purpose either free or on favourable terms (e.g. CCM, XLVIII, Pt I, 1929-30, pp1505-6). Moreover from 1935 the London County Council's proposals for a green belt were embraced enthusiastically by Croydon council which set up an Open Space Acquisition Committee specifically to purchase suitable land (CCM, LIII, Pt I, 1934-5, pp658-60). Given this build up of popular and developer demand pressure, the generally high parks spending, particularly in the later 1930s, is entirely understandable.

For rather different reasons, demand pressures were also high in Gateshead. Thus in 1919 it was one of the CBs worst provided with public open space, and the newly formed National Playing Fields Association identified it as a 'blackspot' in 1927 (PRO HLG 4/1035, Notes 18.3.27, 27.4.27). Moreover, as for roads, there was an employment generation demand effect reinforcing purely environmental demands. Undoubtedly therefore high demand was a key factor shaping Gateshead's above average parks spending. And the low cost of parks projects meant that they were less susceptible to local financial problems than more expensive items like housing and highways. The immunity was only partial, as the poor spending performance 1924-9 suggests, but it was still important.

Burnley shared some of the demand features of Gateshead, so that its high densities and lack of gardens in working class areas had already attracted the interest of national lobbies before 1919 (e.g. NHTPC 1910). However spending was rather lower than in Gateshead. The sources of this would seem to be partly that Burnley was already better provided in 1919 and that local philanthropy was active so that a complete park was provided by this means in 1925-7 (Burnley CB 1929, p34). More importantly Burnley's spending was mainly on land acquisition. There was less concern for employment generation on parks schemes than in Gateshead. Overall therefore Burnley secured more open space for less expenditure.

Wakefield lacked most of the active demand features which characterised the other towns and helped make Croydon and Gateshead into high spenders. Though not particularly well provided, there was neither active local lobbies, nor national pressure group interest. Significantly local planning proposals adopted a local standard of 2.5 acres per thousand population, well below the accepted professional standard of 5 acres per thousand and that adopted in nearby towns (G.L. Pepler 1923, p19). Given this demand background it is perhaps surprising that spending was as high as it was. Part of the explanation is that one large public open space was originally purchased in 1919 for housing and only used as parkland when its unsuitability, on account of undermining had been established. It was a kind of unintentional parks spending that was not uncommon in other very high spending authorities.

Overall though the experience of highways and parks demand had generally reinforced the picture established for housing, that demand was an important determinant where financial weakness and system constraints were not present. Therefore we can identify the crude determinants of spending levels in the four towns and, by extension, all CBs in these terms. However to leave explanation there at the economic/structural level, is to overlook the significance of the political process, which is both the means by which things happen and an important influence in its own right. We have already hinted repeatedly at the significance of the political process in shaping responses to financial, system and demand pressures. We now examine it in more detail.

Local political processes

As noted in chapter 2, the main party political feature of interwar Britain was the partial emergence of Labour as a major force. This was apparent in all four towns even though Labour never came near taking control of Croydon from the Ratepayer-led (in effect Conservative) grouping that dominated the council throughout. The others all experienced Labour administration for the first time. Gateshead was controlled longest by Labour from 1923-6 and, by a rather slender majority, after 1935. Wakefield had Labour councils 1929-30 and 1934-8. In Burnley the Labour breakthrough came in 1934 and lasted until 1938. However neither Labour nor its opponents, invariably Conservative dominated groupings, though not always so labelled, behaved identically in all towns. Greatest variety was evident amongst non-Labour groupings. In Burnley especially, and Wakefield, to a lesser extent, political culture was traditionally dominated by Liberalism and this persisted in municipal forms, political practices and, more pervasively, in a local moral and ideological hegemony. In practical terms it meant that there was no strong municipal political tradition in the two towns that opposed expenditure and intervention as such. Major local economic interests especially of industrialists were still directly represented on both councils in the 1920s and in Burnley (Smithies, p330) throughout. Thus the idea of an active progressive, reformist municipality serving the locality, especially the business community, by wise intervention was well developed before Labour appeared. Consistent with traditional Liberal principles, party rule was not very rigid and experienced Labour members were incorporated into positions of responsibility even before Labour took control.

Gateshead had a very different political tradition (Manders, pp48-50, 266-85). Municipal liberal reformism was very underdeveloped and local industrialists and major employers were no longer resident in the town and had not been directly represented on the council since well before 1914. The anti-Labour grouping was long dominated by small businessmen and private landlords who consistently took an anti-interventionist stance, favouring low rates rather than a progressive interventionist municipality. In these circumstances Labour was not incorporated into municipal institutions as readily as in the other towns. Croydon contained elements of both the Burnley-Wakefield and the Gateshead patterns. Thus although it lacked the industrial traditions that sustained northern municipal Liberalism,

Croydon had a sophisticated local political culture, beyond mere dormitory politics (Ward 1983, pp166-70, 230-8). Municipal institutions and practices were highly developed and the commercial and professional interests, mainly central Croydon based, who usually dominated council affairs, had different views to the anti-interventionist shopkeepers and landlords of Gateshead. However the emergence of a fully fledged business-led interventionist and liberal reformist municipality was thwarted politically by the strength of domestic ratepayerism, reflecting the predominantly residential character of the town. Actual municipal policy therefore was normally a balancing act between these two anti- Labour elements. Both were represented on the main Ratepayers Association political organisations. Normally domestic ratepayerism was something to be appeased rather than allowed to dominate policy in any active sense. Periodically though the dominant business grouping misjudged ratepayer feeling on some issues, provoking, in extreme cases, outbreaks of fundamentalist ratepayerism. This occurred most notably in 1937 when the formation of the Croydon Vigilance Association marked a clear split. Normally though policy just, in the words of Labour critics, 'wobbled'.

There was greater consistency between towns as regards the character and policy of municipal Labourism. However some significant differences were apparent. In Gateshead for example the Labour movement before 1932 was essentially an alliance between a radical and active Independent Labour Party (ILP) and railway dominated trades unionism. The ILP split from Labour was particularly damaging locally and it left a local Labour party dominated by moderate trade unionists, described by a disgruntled Labour parliamentary candidate as 'a lot of fossils' (M. Callcott 1980, p225; Manders, p283). In Croydon Labour had a more middle class, intellectual and romantic 'back to the land' character than the northern boroughs, where trades unionism was more prominent. Where trades unionism was important its character naturally tended to reflect local industrial structure and labour relations traditions. Thus in Burnley the weavers and miners were very prominent; in Wakefield the miners and railwaymen, even though the more diversified local employment structure diluted their influence. All these industries experienced great tensions in the 1920s and early 1930s, but it is remarkable how little this spilled over into the political arena. Workplace battles were not, in general, refought in the council chamber though in Gateshead, where there was greater pre-existing political animosity than elsewhere, the wider class tensions of 1926 did little to diminish it.

The political process generally added both a texture and a fine tuning to the economic and structural 'messages' sent to the local state via pressures for spending institutional constraints and the local rate base. However it also had its own specific impacts on actual spending. In Gateshead particularly the course of housing spending makes much more sense when the political level is included. Thus the failure to make much use of the generous Addison subsidy reflected continuing apathy from the landlords who consistently voted against proposals, swimming against the national tide (e.g. Manders, p172; GCM, 69, 1918-9, pp362-3). The sudden surge in 1925-7 reflected the ambitious housing programme of the first Labour council, abruptly truncated by financial problems, institutional constraints and the political shift to the Moderates in 1926. Byrne has argued that the main reason for Gateshead's poor interwar housing performance lay within the local political process (D. Byrne 1982a, 1982b). However this is not consistent with the evidence of structural and system constraints, nor with the shifts in the character of the Moderates after 1926 (Ward, 1982b). Thus landlords increasingly gave way to builders and related small business interests who saw municipal activity in a different light, as something not automatically competitive with their interests. A Labour council in the late 1920s/early 1930s might have challenged financial orthodoxy more vigorously but ultimately it could not have substantially increased the spending of a severely depressed town. It was trapped in a system controlled by the central state and in such circumstances Labour control at the local level was virtually irrelevant for capital spending, as the experience of the Labour stronghold of Merthyr Tydfil graphically illustrated. When Labour finally regained control in Gateshead in 1935 its character too had changed. Shorn of its radicalism it collaborated with NEHA, going against the party line in neighbouring districts so that economic recovery saw less rather than more spending.

The different political traditions of Burnley and Wakefield meant that the swing to Labour marked a less decisive shift in the political agenda of the local state than in Gateshead. Labour in Burnley reinforced the slum clearance programme and played a part in producing the highest spending on housing in the late 1930s. However in other respects they perpetuated traditional municipal concerns with spending focussing on public utilities, infrastructure and other items of direct concern to business. Significantly they retained the previous incumbent, a Liberal cotton manufacturer, as the Finance Committee chairman, despite a clear majority. In Wakefield too great continuity was apparent. Thus the peak period of housing spending occurred before Labour actually controlled the council. The chairman of the Housing Committee during this key period was a leading Labour councillor who seems to have played a critical role in persuading business opinion that high housing spending was in their interests as well as simply in the interests of the working class.

The door to high housing and other spending had already been partly opened during the prewar campaign for CB status which was underpinned by a widespread business commitment to a progressive and vigorous local authority helping transform the city's growth prospects (e.g. WE, 8.3.13). In April 1923 the Liberal Mayor, a leading local woollen manufacturer, launched a Chamber of Commerce initiative to promote Wakefield (WE, 14.4.23). During this he referred explicitly to the deterrent effect of present housing conditions on industrial development and underlined the need for municipal action given the failure of private initiatives. Significantly the new Labour Housing Committee Chairman was one of the speakers at this initiative. This mood continued, even when the Hatry scandal broke, and business voices were remarkably restrained in calling for expenditure cuts, and did not target the big spending field of housing (WE, 28.9.29). However, industrial derating, also introduced in 1929, was certainly a key factor defusing this issue for industrialists, if not all businessmen, enabling high spending to coexist with low industrial rates. And when the Corporation launched its own industrial promotion campaign in 1932, municipal spending on housing and other items was catalogued with pride. On housing the message was clear. The municipality had greatly assisted

> 'the solution of a social service problem which is of paramount importance to industry, realising that well housed workers make happy and contented employees.' (City of Wakefield 1932, p7).

Such business-oriented thinking existed in Croydon but was less well developed and was not proclaimed so loudly because of the strength of local domestic ratepayerism and the weakness of Labour. Dominant ratepayer sentiments were appeased only by high rent housing provision and a highly segregated spatial pattern of council housing development in the west where industrial growth was concentrated. However in the late 1930s a more comprehensive drive to provide for new employment growth in central and outer Croydon in conjunction with a municipal satellite town and other municipal spending brought out the Croydon Vigilantes (*Croydon Times*, 27.8.38) in force. As we have already noted, roads and parks spending were part of the area of political agreement between the business and ratepayer interests. Housing was not and although business interests wanting local economic growth favoured municipal provision, the weakness of the local Labour movement denied such moves the enthusiasm and wider commitment that was present in Wakefield.

Overall therefore local politics was important in the articulation of demand pressures and the perception of financial and other constraints to spending. Local officials were also important in this process, occasionally in clearly visible ways. Thus in Wakefield the Medical Officer of Health was a powerful voice pushing the cause for more housing spending in the 1920s, while the Clerk and Treasurer advocated a steadying in the late 1920s/early 1930s (e.g. Medical Officer's Report for 1922, p53). On one occasion the Treasurer secretly advised the Ministry of Health to refuse further loan sanctions on housing (PRO HLG 48/245, 6.10.30). In Gateshead the Treasurer played an important role in the 'internalising' of financial orthodoxy in the late 1920s/early 1930s. Generally the main importance of officials was in reinforcing institutional and system effects. Thus local official views increasingly reflected those of central officials more closely than those of local politicians. In a city like Wakefield the enthusiasm for spending of the Medical Officer and Chief Housing Architect and the growing misgivings of the Treasurer reflected exactly the attitudes of different divisions of the Ministry in its dealings with the city (e.g. PRO HLG 48/245. 22.1.29). The growing importance of local officials in the interwar period was probably therefore decreasing the effect of the local political process and increasing the impact of other more structural and system factors. We must now return to these and the deeper sources of local state action that underlay them.

Local states and uneven development: immediate processes and broad perspectives

All the case studies were unique places. The exact conjunction of processes which operated to shape their local state intervention regimes were not repeated elsewhere. However we might also reasonably assume that they were broadly representative of different types of local circumstance. Gateshead was the classic poor depressed town where capitalist production declined rather more than the processes of social reproduction. This created what neo-Marxist theorists would identify as two simultaneous crises of legitimisation and accumulation. The local state was faced with competing demands to maintain social stability, in circumstances of a very unstable decline process, and to restore conditions favourable for capital accumulation. At the same time decline was eroding an already weak local tax base and generating contradictory spending pressures that were unmanageable at the local level without central financial assistance. Until the late 1930s central state intervention was almost completely to enforce a spending orthodoxy that did nothing to resolve these crises and in effect reinforced the decline process. In such highly constrained circumstances the local state adopted social spending strategies that partly defused the crisis of legitimisation and avoided a complete breakdown of social stability, but did very little to resolve the crisis of accumulation.

In none of the other towns was there such a real sense of a crisis of the local state as in Gateshead. Burnley was undergoing a decline process which was more pronounced in reproduction than production. While there were long term problems associated with this, in the short-medium term this reduced the pressures for social spending, whether to maintain social stability or to service labour force reproduction. This permitted greater concentration on spending that directly serviced production, manifest here in roads spending. Wakefield differed from Burnley principally on account of its growth record, though it shared a common ascendancy of production over reproduction processes. In such circumstances there were pressures from both capital and labour to enhance labour reproduction and, more directly, production. Finally Croydon was a town dominated by a privatised process of social reproduction that created suburban dormitory characteristics. However this identity was increasingly challenged by production and employment growth. These competing identities created different sets of pressures for local state intervention, reconcilable for some expenditure items but conflicting in areas of social, labour-reproductive spending.

Summarised thus it is easy to detect a 'logic of capital' explanation of much local state spending, with the immediate processes being surface manifestations of a deeper dynamic. The expression of such priorities in local state policy recognisably occurred in the several ways identified in neo-Marxist theory. Thus there was the directly instrumentalist representation of local businessmen on the local council, especially in the production dominated centres of Burnley and Wakefield in the 1920s. However the changing structure of capital, particularly the delocalisation of its control to banking or finance capital was everywhere undermining this dimension. In Gateshead large scale capital was entirely absent as a local political force. The instrumentalism of small capital was supplemented and increasingly superseded by structural effects expressed and ultimately enforced institutionally and managerially within central:local financial relations. The traditional local parsimony of private landlords gave way to system effects that advanced the orthodox logic of banking capital within the local state.

However local business instrumentalism was also undermined by the increasingly mass democratic nature of local politics. Labour became a significant force in all the case studies, especially the three northern towns. Thus a class dimension entered the political arena and played an important role in shifting the agenda of the local state. However even where it gained control, Labour's success in securing its own project for the local state was clearly dependent on how far it also corresponded to the priorities of capital. Thus high housing spending occurred where Labour and the capitalist development process demanded it, but not where Labour alone wanted it. Structural and institutional constraints were sufficient to contain local socialist ambition. Thus the original Labour project of challenging capitalism was replaced by one of securing a kind of local welfare state under a capitalism that inevitably therefore had to be fairly healthy. This Labourist project grew most easily in Wakefield and Burnley where the direct servicing of the demands of both capital and the working class by the local state were not obviously conflicting aims. They were also towns where liberal reformist hegemony, embracing ideologies that travelled part way on the same road, was most highly developed. However in Gateshead and similar heavily depressed towns, the contradictions of municipal Labourism were cruelly expressed. The essential paradox was that the strength of Labourism was dependent on the strength of capitalism.

This compression of municipal politics into a Marxist 'balance of class forces' mould is rather less credible for Croydon. Thus consumption issues not obviously related to the means of production were the staples of political discourse. A highly developed domestic ratepayer movement, formed the main effective political opposition to the instrumentally expressed local business ambitions of capitalist- led growth in Croydon. As Saunders has pointed out, this suggests a conception of class based more on Weber than on Marx and one which emphasises the role of the domestic sphere in urban politics. Such a pattern of local politics was rather less developed in the other towns. However interwar Croydon was indicative of what was increasingly occurring as the buoyant parts of Britain entered the mass consumption era. In that sense perhaps it was a glimpse of what was increasingly to occur nearly everywhere from the 1950s.

Overall though this chapter has broadly confirmed that the changing priorities of capital and, more specifically, the changing geography of capital accumulation were the source of the principal forces animating local state capital expenditure regimes. The local political process brought in other forces that shifted local spending outcomes from a purely capital serving focus. But as we have identified in so many other aspects of state action, local state investment in urban development broadly reflected and in important respects reinforced capitalist-led uneven development. Local political fine-tuning notwithstanding, local state investment essentially serviced the priorities of local capital accumulation activities. The legitimacy of this process of uneven development led by capital and locally state serviced as necessary did not begin to be questioned until the later 1930s, as we will see in the next chapter.

9

Towards Spatial Planning?

Introduction

In the earlier chapters of this book we have observed that state intervention, whether by local, central or corporate agencies was not spatially neutral and in varying degrees reinforced the unevenness created by the changing geography of capitalist accumulation. By the later 1930s the view was growing across a widening political and economic front that this uneveness was, for varying reasons, damaging. To the longstanding pleas for state support from the captains of the depressed industries and the representatives of the communities dependent on these industries were now added the strategic arguments noted in chapter 4, a more widespread public sympathy about unemployment and a shift in business opinion recognising the production and market disadvantages of allowing outer Britain, especially the depressed areas, to languish. At the same time there was also a widening awareness of the potential role of the state in consciously and deliberately influencing or even managing the workings of the capitalist economy. Much has been written about the macro- aspects of this shift, broadly towards Keynesian policies in the later 1930s (Winch, pp198-218; Middleton 1985). However in this chapter we concentrate on the spatial aspects, which linked Keynesian thinking with a wide range of other considerations to bring the beginnings of regional policy in the last years of peace.

This early regional policy was marked by the granting of special assistance or preferential treatment to organisations in particular specified areas of the country that were badly affected by depression. Initially the beneficiaries were local state or non-profit making organisations, but from 1936 private firms trading for profit and located in these areas began to receive assistance provided or administered by central state agencies. The scale of the shift remained small before 1939, but nonetheless it was an important precedent, intended partly to offset widely perceived disadvantages but increasingly from 1936 to directly stimulate the capitalist development process in centrally specified locations.

Local economic initiatives to 1934

Viewed from the perspective of the central state, as it usually is, this explicitly spatial policy was an entirely new role for the state. However we suggest here that it was rather the gradual assumption by the central state of an area of intervention that had existed previously, albeit in a somewhat unsystematic and semi-covert form within the local state. The circumstances which led to centralisation were not simply the economic problems and their social and political implications, but a combination of the manifest failure of localities, financially weakened by depression, to solve their own problems, and a growing recognition of the potential dangers of leaving local authorities to act unilaterally. As will be shown though the advocates of centralist regional policy had by no means eliminated local initiatives by 1939.

Such initiatives seem to have originated in the early twentieth century, when a generally slackening economic growth rate combined with a cyclical downturn to produce quite serious economic problems in many areas. At least some of these areas began publicity initiatives to attract new industries, using methods of 'place-promotion' that had been pioneered during the nineteenth century by railway companies, private housing developers and some resort municipalities, most notably Blackpool. Brochures aimed at industrialists and businessmen were produced, some in French and German as well as English, indicating a recognition of the potential importance of foreign investors. These would set out the industrial advantages of local areas, and in some cases specify or hint at other municipal incentives. Site provision, favourable premises valuation for rating purposes, 'flexibility' over application of local regulatory codes and supply of municipal electricity on favourable terms were offered by ambitious schemes like that of West Ham (W. Powell 1973, p78; J.E. Martin 1966, p21). In other areas there was less interest in general publicity, but local development committees would attempt specific approaches to industrialists. The corporation for example played an important role, mainly related to land and electricity supply, in attracting the Rolls Royce to Derby in 1908, a location the company had not originally considered (G. Bloomfield 1978, pp130-2; I. Lloyd 1978, p24).

After world war I the problems first of readjustment to peacetime conditions and then the onset of recession in many areas signalled a much greater municipal interest in stimulating local economic development. By this stage though the balance of initiative in central-local relations had shifted decisively to the centre and local authorities found the Ministry of Health distinctively unhelpful in approving or encouraging such promotional activity. Although resort publicity ventures were formally legalised under the Health Resorts and Watering Places Act 1921, publicity designed to stimulate industrial development was consistently discouraged. Amongst towns seeking, but failing, to get local powers to promote their interests by publicity were Sheffield (1920), Wigan (1921), Bristol (1922), Hull (1924), Newport (1925), Accrington (1928), Birkenhead (1930), West Hartlepool and Southampton (1931) (PRO HLG 57/357; 52/1392). However lack of powers did not prevent a good deal of promotional work continuing. Sheffield and its neighbour Rotherham were both active just after world war I and in the 1920s (H.K. Hawson, pp152-3; M.P. Fogarty 1947, p29). A common device was to conceal municipal financial involvement behind the facade of a local development association/board/conference structure, which would normally include local business organisations and (very occasionally) trade unions as well as municipal authorities. By 1930 such bodies existed for Tyneside (1926), Bristol (1928), Glasgow and District and Teeside (both 1930) (Ward 1984b). However municipal financial contributions to such bodies were still technically illegal as any local authority which made the mistake of asking the Ministry of Health invariably discovered (PRO HLG 57/357). The Ministry's policy was that competitive local promotion of all kinds was wasteful, yet they were not able to enforce a ban on such local initiatives, because, as yet, they did not possess general audit powers over all authorities. They could force small urban districts to desist but not most county boroughs, unless their ratepayers objected, which was unlikely because promotion was cheap and locally popular.

Additionally other central ministries took a different view. The Board of Trade tended to encourage local initiatives, especially where they were aggregated into regional bodies. Thus it was with their blessing that such bodies were founded for Lancashire (1930), Scotland (1931), Wales (1932) and serious but unsuccessful attempts were made to overcome local rivalries to create a North Eastern Board (also 1932) (BT 104/1). According to Fogarty such Board of Trade enthusiasm for local initiative was merely 'a face-saving expedient for covering up their own inaction' (1947, p5). Certainly such a view was plausible in the early 1930s as unemployment peaked. While the Ministry of Health continued, whenever it got the opportunity, to deny legal authority to local promotional schemes, as at Merthyr Tydfil in October 1934 (PRO HLG 57/252), a more general softening of central views on promotion, especially publicity, was apparent.

The most obvious symptom of this was the Local Authorities (Civic Publicity) Act 1931, a private member's bill with government backing, promoted by the Travel Association of Great Britain and Ireland, a body which handled overseas promotion of tourism. Shortly afterwards it was renamed the Travel and Industrial Development Association (TIDA). The Act legalised only overseas publicity of local areas and stipulated that all publicity should be channelled through TIDA. Both these conditions were very widely ignored and most authorities simply took the measure as government approval for promotional schemes. Local brochures proliferated. Titles were either snappily alliterative, sometimes unfortunately so, like 'Do It At Dundee' and 'Barrow in Furness Commercially Considered' (both 1931), 'Wakefield Commercially Considered' (1932) and 'Burnley Means Business' (1935), or they counterposed the name of the town against some striking motto signifying its enterprise and prime location. 'Birmingham: The Hub of Industrial England' (1932) and 'Leeds: The Industrial Centre of the North' (1934) were good examples. Some authorities attempted more targeted publicity ventures instead of, or in addition to, the general brochure and the received impression is that these were more successful in stimulating industrialist interest (e.g. Fogarty 1947, pp227-8).

However publicity alone was not enough. Ambitious schemes based solely on advertising usually disappointed local expectations. It was what the town could offer after industrialist interest had been stimulated that mattered and local state action to enhance the attractiveness of the business environment was obviously important. This tended to favour higher spending authorities, especially where the objects of spending directly benefited industry. Some municipalities continued to offer concessionary electricity explicitly for industrial promotion purposes (and sometimes water and gas). However the standardisation of generation practice and the narrowing of local price differentials after 1919 made it doubtful how significant such initiatives were (Ward 1984b, 1985). Municipal docks and aerodromes were also utilised for promotional purposes, but increasingly the emphasis shifted during the 1920s and especially the 1930s towards land and buildings provision as the major incentive. The increasing scale of municipal land dealings by the interwar period offered many opportunities for site provision. Many of the largest municipal authorities had by the 1930s secured local powers to acquire land by negotiation without having to specify its use in advance, while surplus lands from housing, sewerage, electricity, gas, docks or aerodrome schemes were often well suited for industrial development (Ward 1986, p7). Initially this process occurred incrementally, but gradually more conscious planning ideals of industrial estates began to appear. Particularly significant was Manchester's Wythenshawe satellite town commenced in the late 1920s which included municipal development of industrial sites and factory building (Barlow Report 1940, p282). However other authorities, notably Liverpool, were also beginning to use town planning as a gradual way of improving the quality of environment and infrastructure in factory areas in conjunction with more ambitious promotional initiatives. These tendencies were to intensify by 1939.

It remains very difficult to assess the effectiveness of local initiatives. But it is perhaps significant that central government intervened most decisively in areas where local government was financially weak and prevented by the vicious circle of List Q from mounting expensive spending programmes within which municipal promotion schemes could develop. By contrast a quite severely depressed area like Lancashire was characterised by vigorous municipal traditions and very active policies, especially for the trading services and infrastructure projects, and certainly witnessed the most complete development of local promotional initiatives in the 1930s. Doubtless this was partly a result of the failure of 1930s regional policies to fully embrace Lancashire, but it is at least arguable that it was also one of its causes. Rather more speculatively we might ask also whether the extent of promotional activity in Yorkshire and more prosperous areas was a factor in explaining why such areas withstood the interwar depression so comparatively successfully. Current work on local initiatives does not permit us yet to attempt answers to these kinds of question, and clearly it is unlikely that local action was ever anything more than a contributory factor, but even being able to pose such questions makes us reconsider the inevitability of centralist regional policy for the depressed areas.

Special and depressed areas 1934-6

As we noted in chapter 6 the dole and reliance on spontaneous recovery formed the basis of central policy towards unemployment and the depressed areas during the worst years of the depression. The first shifts in this orthodoxy did not occur until 1934. By this time the economy as a whole was in recovery but, as noted in chapter 1, this was least apparent in outer Britain. Opinion within and outside parliament was shifting in favour of more intervention, and a series of *Times* articles in spring 1934 were particularly important in precipitating the immediate events that led to the 1934 Special Areas Act (Pitfield 1978, pp434-5). In April, investigators were appointed to report on conditions in four heavily depressed areas of south Wales, industrial Scotland, Tyneside and Durham and west Cumberland and make policy suggestions in the light of their findings. As Booth has shown, this was not the move of a government committed to a re-evaluation of its policy; it was a conscious and cynical attempt to secure an authoritative statement that nothing could be done (A. Booth 1978, pp143-4). Thus the areas in question had all been painstakingly surveyed in 1932 for the Board of Trade; there was no lack of knowledge. Furthermore the instructions given them by Cabinet discouraged their recommendation of any major policy shifts. What government wanted was a restatement of the transference and retraining policies, a few social palliatives to improve the lot of those unable to move and little else. In three of the four reports they got broadly what they wanted (Ministry of Labour 1934). The exception was Euan Wallace's report on Durham and Tyneside which advocated national action on the location of industry, raising of the school leaving age, earlier retirement pensions, together with more specific local and regional initiatives including local government reform (pp68-116). All this was very close to Labour party policy for the depressed areas, though it also reflected views that were becoming accepted by a widening section of business opinion.

This support for national intervention was acquiring momentum during 1934 and the cautious tone of all the other reports was now perceived by the government as a potential embarrassment. A Cabinet committee acknowledged in October 1934 that actions based on their recommendations were 'unlikely to satisfy the expectations which had been created in all quarters by the appointment of investigators' (PRO CAB 24/251, CP 227 (34), p1). In these circumstances the Cabinet, recognising widespread concern, but still believing that they could and should do nothing substantial, proposed the dramatic gesture of appointing two Depressed Area Commissioners (for England and Wales, and Scotland) to oversee the four areas investigated, but excluding the large urban areas of Glasgow, Cardiff, Swansea and Newport (Map 9.1). A House of Lords amendment later renamed

MAP 9.1

THE SPECIAL AREAS

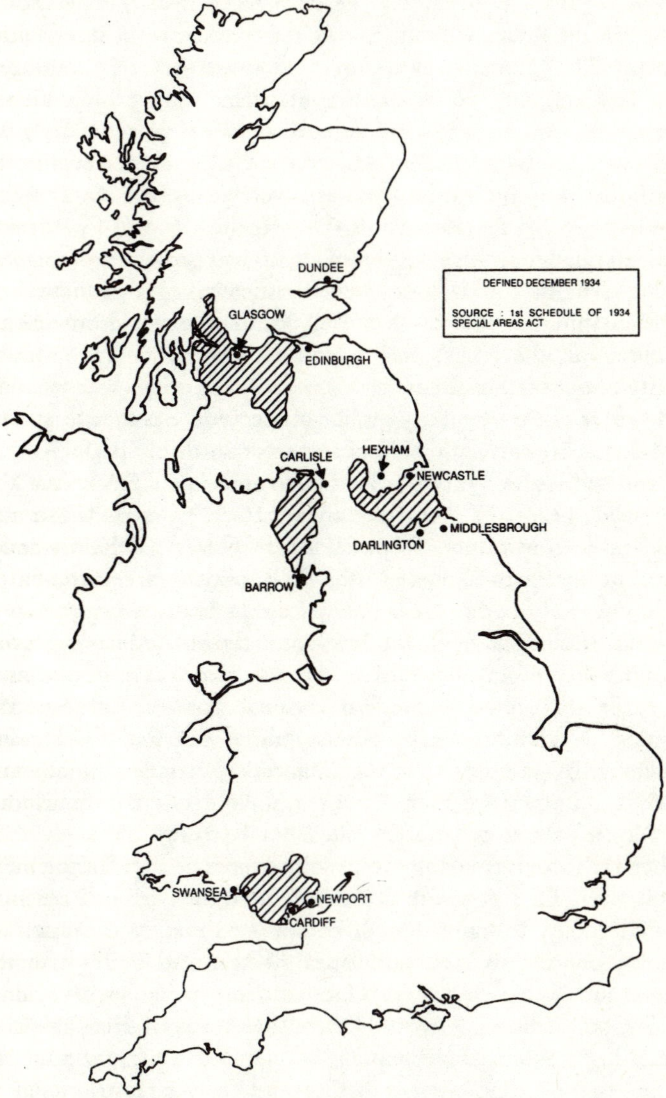

these the Special Areas. The stated intention was that the whole initiative should be seen as experimental, with the commissioners relatively free of detailed supervision and able to take unconventional actions intended to improve the areas. In practice however the main purpose of this was to enable the state more readily to withdraw support in the future without having set precedents for intervention (pp4-5). The actual powers granted were severely curtailed, precluding assistance to private organisations trading for profit and 'topping up' assistance to local authorities for services already grant aided (except land settlement and allotments). No central Ministry relinquished any pre-existing powers over the Special Areas to the commissioners, so that the Ministry of Health's List Q for example remained unaltered. Most serious of all, no real provisions were made for long term finance. Despite characteristically vague promises from the prime minister, Ramsay MacDonald, that he would honour any commitments, the reality was a fund of only £2 million, with no security about further funds.

However one particularly significant decision was that to appoint Sir Malcolm Stewart as the commissioner for the three Special Areas in England and Wales. While the Scottish commissioner, Sir Arthur Rose (who had been the Scottish investigator) worked within the considerable constraints of Special Areas powers (R.H. Campbell 1979), Stewart pressed these to the limit, playing a key role in the development of Special Areas policy from its hesitant beginnings. A successful businessman, in the brick and cement industry, Stewart personified the progressive business opinion that was so important in the 1930s shift towards modern regional policies and economic planning. His ambitious proposals quickly fell foul of Treasury orthodoxy. By January 1935 the Chancellor, Neville Chamberlain, noted: 'I am afraid we have made a mistake with our commissioner and I anticipate more trouble' (cited Booth, p149).

Stewart's troublemaking successfully overcame some of the major limitations of the Act and in doing so created the basis of a centralist regional policy. Initially though he operated mainly through local organisations, mainly local authorities, giving grants for improvement schemes such as clearing derelict land and improving health facilities (1st Report of Special Areas Commissioner 1935). His interest in stimulating economic development was manifest in the grants he gave to the regional development bodies and he was instrumental in overcoming local jealousies and finally securing the successful establishment of the North Eastern Development Board in 1934 (PRO

BT 104/1). However the main point was that initially there was, in effect, a partnership between central and local agencies. While aspects of this partnership continued, things began to change during 1935 and new corporate style agencies, not directly accountable to local electorates began to appear. The first was the North Eastern Housing Association (noted in chapter 8) created in 1935 as a mechanism for sidestepping the Ministry of Health's monopoly of financial relations with local government and intended to accelerate subsidised housebuilding in the hard pressed areas of Durham and Tyneside (PRO HLG 52/823-4; HLG 101/286). As noted earlier though, its apparent delocalisation of subsidised housebuilding was met with great suspicion in many areas, limiting its initial impact.

More important was the introduction of the trading estates during 1935-6, which began to turn the Special Areas programme into a centralist regional policy concerned with industrial development and location. During 1935 several local authority clearance schemes were under way in the Special Areas and it became increasingly clear that the most appropriate re-use of the sites was for industry (PRO BT 104/23, Memo Tribe-Forbes Adam, 29.7.35). At the same time Stewart was exerting direct and indirect pressure on the government to allow him to proceed with a trading estate experiment providing serviced industrial estates in the Special Areas. With an election approaching the National Government felt vulnerable in the many parts of depressed outer Britain which had returned MPs supporting it in 1931. Unemployment was obviously going to be a key issue at the forthcoming election and some more solid gesture towards the recovery of the Special Areas was therefore felt to be expedient. Accordingly a definite commitment to the trading estates was included in the 1935 election manifesto (PRO BT 104/27, Note 12.3.37; Booth, p150).

Organisationally though the Special Areas office had already decided that local partnership was inappropriate for such ventures and by August 1935 was firmly committed to the idea of new agencies permitting more direct control and management with local authority co- operation but no organic links (PRO BT 104/23, Memos of 6.8.35, 12.8.35). It was though recognised that it might be difficult to dislodge the local authorities from the sites they had themselves cleared and some exceptional schemes might therefore involve them more fully. However when the new trading estate companies were created for all the Special Areas (except west Cumberland where the North Eastern body operated) enthusiasm for such local schemes had further diminished. These new bodies were publicly funded private companies charged with estate and advance factory development and management functions. Their directors, appointed by the Special Areas commissioners, were composed primarily of industrialists and businessmen, most with strong regional links, usually with a token trades union representative (e.g. PRO BT 104/30). A small official staff was also appointed.

During 1936 decisions were being made about implementing the trading estates proposals. The government wanted very large and visible estates with maximum publicity value, even though this might not be the best solution to alleviate local unemployment. The type of estate was also discussed extensively. Eventually the Slough model of a light industrial estate was preferred (PRO BT 104/31). This option had always been favoured by Stewart, as the misleading label 'trading estate' (Slough's title) used throughout the discussions, indicated. He wanted to encourage the new lighter industries to develop in the depressed areas, but regional opinion, especially on the north east coast, continued to think in terms of heavy industry and looked to a development more on the lines of Trafford Park, Manchester. However Stewart's view prevailed and the first three estates at Team Valley (Gateshead), Treforest (Pontypridd) and Hillington (Glasgow) were all on the Slough model. All were under way by the end of 1936, but none had yet made any appreciable contribution to employment creation. Their principal significance at this time was as symbols of a qualitative change in state intervention.

Another symptom of this was the schedule of depressed areas to which, other things being equal, preference in government contracting should be given. This originated at virtually the same time as the Special Areas policy. Thus Cabinet was discussing ways of using naval contracts to divert work to heavily depressed areas in Autumn 1934 (see chapter 4), and in December 1934 it was announced that contracting departments were prepared to give special consideration to tenders submitted by firms in employment exchange areas suffering from prolonged and severe depression (296 HC Deb 55, 1934-5, c1309-10). No detailed schedule was published until March 1936, by which time extensive additions had been made, as indicated in Map 9.2. Broadly the original schedule included the newly defined Special Areas, together with some immediately adjacent centres like Cardiff, Newport and Swansea, much of industrial Lancashire (though not Manchester or Merseyside) together with smaller areas, mainly in Yorkshire, Cornwall, Flintshire and Staffordshire.

In February 1936 substantial additions were made to the schedule (309 HC Deb 5s, 1935-6, c1535-7). The basis of the extended schedule was the Special Areas plus all places where male unemployment had averaged 25% over the previous twelve months or cotton areas where female unemployment averaged over 15%. The results were an inclusion of large urban centres like Liverpool, Birkenhead, Glasgow, Leith, Dundee and Middlesbrough, large parts of mid, north and west Wales, the Highlands of Scotland and smaller additions in Yorkshire, the midlands, south west and east Anglia.

This schedule evidently remained in operation until 1939 and was given in evidence to the Barlow Commission in February 1938 (Fogarty 1945, pp22-5). It remains very doubtful though how effective such contracting preference was since all other things were rarely equal. Clearly there were many firms (notably shipbuilding) in such areas that were heavily dependent on government contracting, as noted in chapter 4. They had suffered when the volume of naval expenditure diminished in the 1920s and early 1930s, particularly since the Royal Dockyards in the south were preferred. However as rearmament occurred the private yards, predominantly in the north and Scotland, benefited. In general, despite occasional specific interventions, the shift seems to have occurred quite independently of the contracting preference scheme. It was more a case of rearmament and recovery re- emphasising the importance of the basic industries of outer Britain, rather than contracts consciously being directed there rather than elsewhere. The shift was important, so that in the 18 months ended November 1936 some £41 millions worth of contracts had been placed in the depressed areas, including £24 millions in the Special Areas (Pitfield 1978, p440). But it was not to any great extent the result of contracting preference.

In fact because of the highly regionalised space economy, the main opportunities for the exercise of true contracting preference tended to be limited to lower value items. Moreover it was often difficult for firms not accustomed to government contracting to break into the field, especially in times of economic stress. Unfamiliarity with tendering opportunities and procedures, problems with working to exact and often unfamiliar specifications and tolerances and difficulties in integrating larger contracts with other work were apparently quite common (PRO BT 104/16). Such factors tended to undermine the intentions of preference. Essentially to work in the way such a policy appeared to promise, it had actually to give preference even when all others things were not equal. There were of course major obstacles to implementing such a policy.

There were two other governmental actions at this time that had a bearing on national policies towards spatial development. We have considered them in chapters 4 and 5 and need only emphasise their relevance here. The first was the Air Ministry's air safety zonal classification of 1934, something which reinforced many though not all the developing proposals to assist the depressed areas. It provided further arguments for locating strategically important production in depressed outer Britain, except Durham and Tyneside, and had begun to have some impacts especially for the new Royal Ordnance factories announced for Lancashire and south Wales during 1935. However the major impacts of this zoning came later, particularly for aircraft production. The other case was the very public debate during 1935-6 about the location of the Richard Thomas steel strip mill. Though the eventual decision to locate at Ebbw Vale in preference to the Scunthorpe location originally preferred is capable of bearing several interpretations, growing state sensitivity to the depressed area issue, especially in the run up to the 1935 election, was clearly an important factor, and was perceived in this light at the time.

Special and depressed area policies 1936-9

The Special Areas Reconstruction Agreement Act 1936 and the Special Areas (Amendment) Act 1937 significantly extended the scope of policy. In principle they enlarged and made explicit the assistance to private industry that was implied in the trading estate schemes. However since this was moving beyond orthodoxy, the moves were very tentative. The immediate source of both measures were the suggestions of Sir Malcolm Stewart in his annual reports, issued as command publications and taken very seriously by Cabinet. In his first report he echoed a widespread feeling within the older industrial areas and called for special finance to assist industrial development (1935, pp16-8). The government's reluctant response from October 1935 was to prod an equally reluctant Bank of England into forming the Special Areas Reconstruction Association (SARA). This was supposed to achieve the contradictory objective of giving special loan assistance to small firms in the Special Areas while operating on commercial lines (C.E. Heim 1984). There were clearly great misgivings within government and the Bank as to whether such a 'gap' in finance existed. The Bank warned of 'the risk of a fiasco' and the Treasury thought the whole proposal was 'pretty horrible' (Heim, 1984, pp537-8). However the government view was that the costs of being seen to do nothing outweighed the risks of failure.

All SARA's £1 million capital was privately subscribed with a Treasury guarantee. By the time of its flotation it had been incorporated into orthodoxy as a charitable gesture, intended to show that major financial institutions could act with social responsibility. By adopting this particular route to meeting Stewart's demands it was hoped that general criticisms of the financial system could be diminished and faith in market mechanisms reinforced, thus defusing pressures for any more interventionist responses. However SARA's impact was too limited to be successful in this. £1 million was simply inadequate to make any impression, particularly given the limitation to making small loans (£10,000 or less) to small firms on commercial criteria. Heim attributes these weaknesses to the Bank of England and the general climate of reluctant intervention within which SARA was conceived.

From December 1936 SARA was complemented by the Nuffield Trust, an entirely private foundation established through a gift of £2 millions from the motor manufacturer Lord Nuffield (P.W.S. Andrews and E. Brunner 1955, pp276-80). This body worked very closely with SARA but was less tightly circumscribed by orthodoxy and was generally more successful (Heim 1984, p548). Finally in March 1937 the third special finance organisation, the Treasury Fund, was established. This £2 millions fund was one of the main provisions of the 1937 Act and was important as the first direct, non-surrogate, involvement of government in providing capital for industrial expansion in the 'certified' depressed areas (not just the Special Areas) (Pitfield 1978, p440). It was intended to meet the perceived inadequacies of SARA and was more specifically targeted on 'larger' firms (of ten or more employees). However it shared some of SARA's weaknesses and lack of flexibility and was equally dependent on complementary funding from Nuffield.

The impacts of all three organisations was very limited. Maximum estimates of employment created by the actions of all three did not exceed 20-25,000, which compared unfavourably with the 290,877 unemployed in the Special Areas in December 1937 (Heim 1984, p533). Table 9.1 shows the main spatial features of this funding. Several key points are apparent. Thus south Wales proportionately relied least on special finance and was the only area where most capital for expansion in firms considered for assistance came from elsewhere. West Cumberland by contrast was least attractive to ordinary capital.

TABLE 9.1: FUNDING OF NEW INDUSTRIAL INVESTMENT IN SPECIAL AREAS 1936-8

% Contributions	South Wales	Durham and Tyneside	West Cumberland	Scotland
Nuffield	23.6	29.8	49.7	31.2
Treasury	15.6	21.6		5.1
SARA	7.7	11.1	18.5	23.9
Other capital	53.0	37.5	31.8	39.8
	100	100	100	100
	(£2,840,000)	(£2,360,041)	(£474,150)	(£582,500)

Source: PRO T187/37. Return of 30.9.38

Generally Nuffield was the main source of special finance in all areas, especially west Cumberland. SARA was most important relative to other sources in Scotland and west Cumberland. Treasury funding, strictly the only direct state funding, was most important on the north east coast, though it was also significant in south Wales. The clear impression therefore is that south Wales and Durham and Tyneside, particularly the latter, received most benefit from special finance organisations. This is broadly confirmed by contemporary employment estimates, though these appear optimistic compared to later figures. However they do appear to indicate that job provision was more costly in these two areas than in west Cumberland and Scotland. This was probably because more male employment in metal working and engineering trades was created in the first two areas, more female employment in lighter industries in the last two (PRO T 187/61).

The impact of the extension of Treasury assistance to certified areas outside the Special Areas under the 1937 Act marked the tentative beginnings of the principle of graduated assistance. In part this was simply a compromise with pressures to extend the Special Areas (Campbell, p176ff; Pitfield 1978, p440). No schedule of certified areas was ever published but it would probably have looked very similar to Map 9.2. The main beneficiary of this extension was Lancashire and

MAP 9.2

GOVERNMENT CONTRACTING PREFERENCE : SCHEDULED AREAS

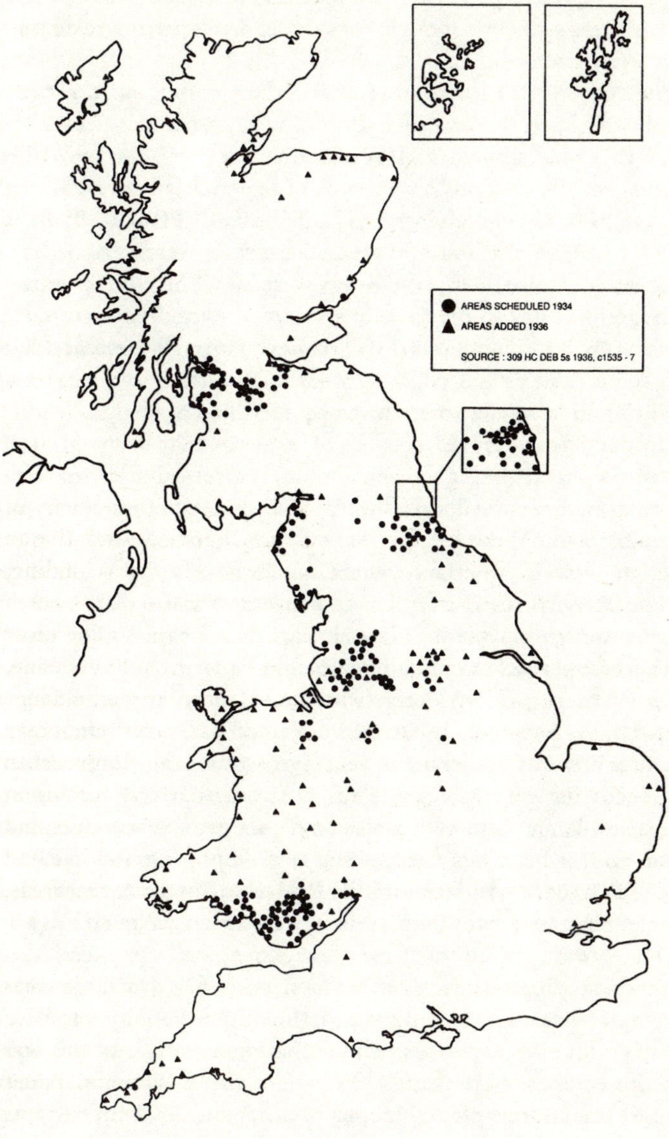

an industrial site company was formed in 1937 to take advantage of government financial assistance. Little direct use was made of the facilities but certainly it acted as a 'bait' to attract several firms (Fogarty 1945, p206). The reasons for the absence of significant action in other areas is unclear though Fogarty reports local apathy in the far south west peninsula (1945, pp387-8).

The 1937 Act also permitted financial contributions to approved firms in the Special Areas in respect of rates, rents and taxes. These were rather small amounts but represented the first instances of direct subsidies to private firms on account of regional policy. By Autumn 1939 125 firms were receiving such contributions (PRO T 187/61, DA 569/8). Most were in south Wales, where rates were very high, and least in west Cumberland, where they were low. The indirect subsidies to private industry in the form of serviced sites and advance factory provision by the trading estate companies continued to expand in the later 1930s. The initial concentration on the three big estates was modified and from 1937 there was a proliferation of smaller sites. This had initially been resisted because of concerns that it would detract from the impact of the big schemes, but their success diluted these fears. Accordingly more smaller sites were created in localities of very high unemployment. However this policy had been followed from the outset in west Cumberland where no large estate was developed (Barlow Report 1940, p287). Table 9.2 shows the distribution of factories and employment in late spring 1939. Team Valley was the most successful single location in employment terms but overall south Wales was more successful, largely because of more large employers on isolated sites. As yet there were few examples of such larger mobile industries present in other areas, though some dramatic improvements were occurring during 1939. Thus west Cumberland had secured several new labour intensive firms making service uniforms, berets etc. by the end of September, including one employing 1020 (PRO T 187/61, DA 569/8). In Scotland the Rolls Royce aero engine factory, noted in chapter 4, was by then under construction at Hillington.

The prime cause of this quickening was the accelerating rearmament programme. The Munich crisis of 1938 indicated an immediate threat of war that underlined the validity of the Air Ministry vulnerability zones, while inflationary boom conditions in the south emphasised the need to look for further production increases amongst the underexploited labour resources of the depressed areas. While new extra capacity and part process branch factories were being established in depressed outer Britain, primarily for government

TABLE 9.2: FACTORIES AND EMPLOYMENT ON TRADING ESTATES AND OTHER SITES IN SPECIAL AREAS TO 31.5.39

	Completed factories		
Estates/Sites	Number	Square feet	Employment
DURHAM AND TYNESIDE	107	837,942	3114
Team Valley	99	740,142	2525
Pallion	4	49,200	262
St Helen Auckland	3	40,600	238
Tynemouth	1	8,000	89
SOUTH WALES	53	893,428	3548
Treforest	46	598,829	1868
Dowlais	2	28,000	218
Cwmbran	1	36,984	189
Ynyswen	1	66,000	706
Llantarnan	1	75,000	528
Porth	1	16,615	29
Cyfarthfa	1	72,000	5*
WEST CUMBERLAND	5	120,168	288
Maryport	1	6,000	25
Cleator Mills	2	41,768	148
Hensingham	1	21,000	56
Millom	1	51,400	59
SCOTLAND**	96	n.a.	1718
Hillington	88	n.a.	1501
Barrhead	1	n.a.	60
Alexandria	1	n.a.	29
Kirkintilloch	1	n.a.	7
Airdrie	1	n.a.	62
Chapelhall	2	n.a.	59
Larkhall	1	n.a.	-*
Carfin	1	n.a.	-*

* just starting
** Scottish figures relate to 30.6.39

Source: PRO T187/61, DA815/55 and DA569/8

contracting purposes, there was also a renewal of attempts to strengthen the contracting preference scheme. Stewart's successor, Sir George Gillett, took the matter to the key official body, the Contracts Co-ordinating Committee in late 1938. He secured their agreement to discriminate positively in favour of Special Area firms by assisting them with contracting procedure and allowing them to undertake short production runs to gain experience of manufacturing to government specifications and tolerances (PRO BT 104/16). This was not merely a charitable gesture, but was entirely consistent with the policies then being followed in relation to defence contracting. Thus as the threat of war grew it became imperative to re-engage the idle parts of the economy in the rearmament machine; 'educational' uneconomic orders were an essential part of that process.

This reintegration was increasingly in conflict with transference policy. Potential conflicts had been identified from the outset of Special Areas policy, but the immediate effect was a strengthening of transference, as we saw in chapter 6. However after the shift in 1936-7 towards encouraging industrial development in such areas, the potential conflicts became more apparent. This was evident first in England and Wales. Thus Stewart in his third and final report wanted transference used only for the 'no-hope' areas (1936, pp3-4). The following year Gillett foresaw 'a diminishing need for transference' (1937, pp31-2). However the shift was slower in Scotland; even by 1937 transference was still seen as relevant for several years (Scottish Report 1937, p54). In the event Gillett's perception was correct. The most significant new development in transference after 1937 was focussed on intra-regional migration, proposing to reintegrate the unemployed workforces of 'no-hope' districts in parts of the wider region where employment was reviving. This occurred spontaneously in areas like west Cumberland where there were moves to the rearmament boom town of Barrow (see chapter 4). However on the north east coast there were moves towards a more planned strategy. Thus by 1938-9 NEHA was proposing that slums cleared in areas of pit exhaustion in west Durham should be replaced in areas where long term employment prospects were better such as near the Team Valley estate or in the colliery districts of east Durham (PRO HLG 52/826). Like many Special Area initiatives it was quantitatively insignificant, but qualitatively it set important precedents of state intervention. Essentially it represented the seeds of spatial planning ideas that germinated in the postwar period, specifically under the 1946 New Towns Act and the settlement restructuring policies of County

Durham.

This small episode was typical of a general tendency apparent within some sections of central government by the end of the 1930s whereby a more coherent approach to spatial development was being attempted. Together the developing concerns of the depressed areas and the mounting spatial and other pressures of a rearmament driven boom economy seemed to demand a more explicit role for the central state in supervising and even spatially directing the processes of capitalist development. But though the Special Areas had laid down markets for such a centralist policy, many obstacles remained. One was the continued vitality of local intervention.

The local state and industrial location policies 1934-9

Paradoxically the very Special Area initiatives that were laying the basis of centralist industrial location policy also served to further encourage local initiative. Thus the narrowness of the scheduled areas, excluding so many areas that were badly depressed or at risk of being so, was a powerful spur to the perpetuation and extension of local action. Within the Special Areas the very limited spatial impact of the major industrial estates created resentment in those districts where sites were not selected. This sense was intensified because the early period of partnership between the Special Areas Commissioners and local government often encouraged and focussed local interests which were then disappointed as new, non-local, organisations with different priorities were created. More generally the trading estate initiatives and other aspects of industrial development policy in the Special Areas provided models for local emulation. Finally we should note that the increasing pressure from the commissioners for some brake on development in the buoyant parts of the country as part of a national policy began to push local authorities in such areas into positions of resistance.

There was much local promotional activity in Lancashire. Liverpool secured legal powers in a 1936 local act for the most ambitious industrial promotion scheme undertaken by any interwar local authority. Amongst other things it involved powers to directly develop land at Speke, Knowsley and Fazakerley for factory purposes, to erect factories and advance money to occupiers (PRO HLG 54/265). By 1939 some 7000 jobs had been provided in these areas, mainly in the shadow airframe factory relocated to Speke in 1937 (Barlow Report, pp282-3). However most other firms had merely relocated from elsewhere in the city (Fogarty 1945, p238). Another significant Lancashire scheme was at Burnley (Ward 1984b, 1985). After receiving many inquiries from its 1935 publicity campaign, the council began reconditioning old mills and weaving sheds and letting them to new industries. Most of the new occupants were foreign firms in light industries requiring cheap female labour. However one contact was from a major Chicago hardware firm wishing to open a British branch plant which involved heavy investment in machinery and a diverse range of labour requirements. None of the existing premises were suitable so the council built a modern single storey factory for rent to the company, Platers and Stampers (later Prestige). A considerable rateborne subsidy was involved in all the rentals, especially for the new factory. However some 4000 jobs were created and the scheme was locally popular.

Central reaction to both these schemes was surprisingly muted. This was probably because of Ministry of Labour sympathy for Lancashire's case to be given central assistance. However the Ministry of Health had great misgivings about Burnley, which had no legal authority for its actions and had broken all the rules about subsidising private industry from the rates. Reluctantly it gave retrospective recognition, but it was warned not to repeat the exercise and, despite its generally sound finances, was being seriously considered for blacklisting in 1938 (PRO HLG 52/1345, Note of 6.5.38). There were no such worries about Liverpool until central ambitions to control industrial location had developed further, when the potential conflicts were clearly recognised by the Special Areas Office.

The case of Jarrow brought matters to a head. Locally there was a profound disappointment with and mistrust of all central government interventions in the town's affairs, which we have noted in chapters 4-5. The reaction was a profound local expression of collective action in the 1936 Jarrow Crusade, while at the same time proposals for an ambitious local industrial development policy were launched (*Newcastle Evening Chronicle*, 25.9.36). The minority report of the Royal Commission on Local Government on Tyneside also advocated municipal powers to start new industries (1937, pp90-1). However the proposals were scaled down into land development and promotion powers on the Liverpool model as the draft bill was formulated in late 1938 (PRO BT 104/11). The £10 millions loan referred to in late 1936 became a borrowing limit of £100,000. Nevertheless it drew a negative reaction from the Ministry of Labour and the Special Areas Office. By early 1939 the full implications of local and central initiative in industrial development were being acknowledged and a more firmly anti- local policy was being defined. However in the absence of a clear central commitment to a national industrial location policy it was politically difficult to refuse limited local powers, especially to Jarrow which had acquired such a special place in national consciousness. Jarrow got its local act, in 1939, but by that stage commitment to a national policy for industrial location had widened considerably. The main focus of these concerns had by then become the Royal Commission on the Distribution of the Industrial Population, the Barlow Commission, appointed in July 1937.

Barlow and the political economy of industrial location policy

The appointment of the Barlow Commission was a direct response to Stewart's last report (1936, p9). In this he called for an embargo on new factory development in Greater London. His other recommendations were incorporated in the 1937 Act, but the government was unwilling to act immediately on this proposal which raised very much wider and more difficult issues. Thus for all their qualitative innovation in state intervention, the Special Areas were quite small areas of the country far away from London, and were quantitatively insignificant. However curbing the normal processes of capitalist development elsewhere in the country, particularly in London, would represent a more profound intervention within the wider economic strategy of a market-led solution to the problem of unemployment. Accordingly Parsons has argued that the Commission was essentially a mechanism to disengage government from this difficult question, appearing to do something while in fact doing nothing (1986, p23).

Certainly dominating figures in the government like Neville Chamberlain (from May 1937 Prime Minister) and Walter Runciman (President of the Board of Trade to 1937) had throughout conceived the Special Area initiatives as essentially political gestures which ran counter to their own orthodox economic beliefs. Clearly they had no desire to see them transmuted into real action, and in that sense Parsons is probably correct. Against this though the mounting sympathy within the Ministry of Labour and increasingly within the service ministries for some more effective policy involving blocks on south eastern development was increasingly challenging these traditional orthodoxies, permitting a less cynical interpretation of state action (A.A. Lonie and H.M. Begg 1979). The evidence submitted by government departments to the Commission rather bears this out. Thus the Board of Trade argued against any industrial location controls on economic grounds, and warned against over emphasising social and strategic arguments (Minutes of Evidence, Days 3-4, especially p93). The Ministries of Health, Agriculture and Transport largely avoided the key question of industrial location, but presented evidence that in aggregate were arguments for more state planning of spatial development that would be likely to require some greater supervision, if not control, of industrial development (Days 1, 7-8). The Ministry of Labour presented the social arguments for intervention but stopped short of a clear recommendation for a full industrial location policy, which it looked to the Commission to decide (Day 10). The evidence of the Committee of Imperial Defence was never published, but seems to have been consistent with their increasing concerns about the strategic vulnerability of the south east and east coast areas. Overall therefore only one government ministry submitting evidence was explicitly opposed to any industrial location policy; the attitude of the rest was increasingly sympathetic agnosticism.

However such debates were not entirely contained within the managerial processes of state policy formulation. They had wider and deeper links. In particular the increasing doubts about conventional wisdoms within the state directly paralleled and were partly animated by those within capital. The 1930s, especially 1935 onwards, saw a serious questioning of laissez-faire ideologies within important sections of capital. Generally the shifts were more pronounced within large scale capitalist enterprise than elsewhere. Thus by the end of the decade we can identify a widening group of big businessmen who were prominently and publicly urging more state intervention and planning, including, inter alia, spatial planning. They included representatives of old and new industries. Thus Lionel Hichens, Chairman of Cammell Laird shipbuilders, was quite forthright in calling for spatial planning of industry, including the power to prohibit development in particular areas in his evidence to the Commission (of which his wife was a member) (Days 25-6, pp871-3). Within the Special Areas we have already noted how the captains of regional industries were recruited into the developing corporate apparatus of state policy. Such figures (like Viscount Ridley and Colonel Appleyard on the north east coast) were increasingly inclined to challenge the anti-interventionist orthodoxies of London-based banking capital and the Treasury. They wanted to see substantial state intervention to sustain capitalist development in outer Britain and saw an effective industrial location policy as part of such a strategy. From the 'newer' industries we can point to Sir Malcolm Stewart as the loudest business voice in favour of industrial location. But Lord Nuffield's involvement was also significant, as was that of Israel Sieff of Marks and Spencer (Rees, p102). He was one of the most earnest advocates of enlightened capitalist planning. Significantly Stewart wanted to involve him closely in the Special Areas (PRO BT 104/30, especially letters 7.1.36 and 10.1.36). He was very sympathetic but work pressures prevented his direct involvement.

There was still a good deal of business scepticism. The Federation of British Industries generally adopted the same line as the Board of Trade. Only social or strategic arguments were conceded and any state action beyond advice and information was emphatically rejected (Day 17, pp502-15). Businessmen of all kinds could still feel threatened by moves to curb their freedom of action in locational matters. The spectre of being forced to move or prohibited expansion in preferred locations continued to make many businessmen very suspicious. The west midlands seems to have been an area where such feelings ran particularly high, perhaps because of the acute awareness that its recent prosperity had depended on unrestricted manufacturing growth. It was a concern that also spilled over into anti-restrictionist municipal views in Birmingham in a way that was not apparent for London (Days 13-14; Day 22, especially p714).

Though the pattern was confused, much resistance seems to have been from single location organisations which, generally speaking, were more likely to be smaller. Larger multi-locational firms were in general more sympathetic. Such sympathy was motivated partly by social concerns, sometimes manifest in a genuine humanitarianism, but underpinned by fears about the harmful effects of prolonged and spatially concentrated unemployment on the long term reproduction of capitalist relations of production. At the individual level the failure to find employment seriously challenged the maintenance of the work ethic amongst the young. Collectively it provided ammunition for anti-capitalist ideologies. In such circumstances limited state intervention justified on social and humanitarian grounds in conjunction with enlightened capitalism could defuse this potential crisis of legitimisation. However more specifically economic arguments for regional policies were also becoming increasingly apparent to big business. Thus the persistence of high regional unemployment was effectively a brake on national economic growth, particularly in the newer industries which relied on mass consumption. In this context unemployment meant underconsumption. Such economic ideas about demand management were only just beginning to be formally articulated, notably after the publication of J.M. Keynes 'General Theory of Employment, Interest and Money' in 1936. They were not properly integrated into regional debates until the 1940s, but some businessmen at least were already beginning to grasp the point intuitively.

Supply side arguments for regional policies were also strengthened by the rearmament fuelled boom conditions of 1937-9 as labour shortages and inflationary pressures were being experienced in inner Britain, reinforcing the strategic arguments for fully reintegrating the depressed areas into the productive economy (Lonie and Begg). As noted in chapter 4, larger firms increasingly sought extra capacity in depressed area branch plants. Clearly firms could and did act individually but some state policy shifts were necessary to provide a framework for such actions. At the very least an end to transference and some substantial state commitment to encouraging industrial development in such areas was needed to create the confidence in which significant numbers of individual firms would act.

Overall therefore it is possible to explain the inconclusive state of regional policy at the outbreak of war largely in terms of this partial shift within British capitalism. As a complete explanation however this capital-logic interpretation is a little too crude. Pressure and interest groups of various kinds played a part in underpinning and informing the debate. The net effect of municipal evidence, for example, was to reinforce the case for some national approach. More importantly the labour movement's evidence presented by the TUC was clear in its call for national industrial location controls and policy (Day 27). The geography of the labour movement was of course heavily weighted towards outer Britain in the very areas most seriously affected by depression and the costs of unemployment were directly experienced by the working class so that such a concern was not surprising. Moreover in contrast to the 1920s, Labour favoured somewhat less challenging and more corporate mixed economy strategies by the later 1930s (Cole pp335-46). Locational controls on capitalist development rather than radical transformation of capitalism were more in keeping with such a climate of opinion. In that sense therefore a new middle ground was beginning to be created with both capital and labour moving towards strategies of state managed capitalism. The role of the labour movement in determining the boundaries of this middle ground became rather stronger in the 1940s as its leaders became more directly involved in policy making (Parsons, pp73-134). But in the 1930s Labour remained a significant minor rather than a major influence. The important shifts of the late 1930s were those that occurred within the state as civil servants influenced by Keynesian and planning ideas, and the more immediate priorities of air vulnerability began to question familiar orthodoxies and, even more importantly, within capital itself. And while a simple capital-logic explanation of the inconclusive fluidity apparent in state spatial policy in the late 1930s may be too crude, it remains the principal element in a more balanced explanation.

Conclusions

We have shown in some detail how the unevenness within the interwar space economy came to be explicitly acknowledged as a problem by central government from 1934 onwards. Gradually, and with great reluctance, the National Governments of the period made remarkable qualitative innovations in state intervention, in many respects laying the basis of post-1945 regional policy. Such interventions were increasingly centralist; the continuing dynamism of local initiative which Stewart had originally tried to harness had become an embarrassment by 1939. One reason for this local activity was the quantitative insignificance of central initiatives. The prevailing central orthodoxy of the interwar period was that capitalist development relatively untrammelled by state intervention would ultimately solve the spatial problem of unemployment. Seen in this context, the Special Areas initiatives were 'a political gesture devoid of economic faith' (Glynn and Booth 1983, p342). By the end of the decade however a new orthodoxy was being made, reflecting a shift occurring within capital, especially large scale finance capital, within the managerial processes of the state and, to a lesser extent, within the labour movement. The shift was still a partial one when war was declared on September 3rd 1939; the focus of late 1930s thinking, the Barlow Commission, was still unpublished. Events after that date were to greatly accelerate it and change some of its internal priorities before a more permanent framework of postwar regional policy appeared in 1944-5.

10

Conclusions

State intervention and uneven development: a summary

The central concern of this book has been the geography of state intervention. Its most important finding has been that state actions tended to exaggerate the uneven development of the interwar space economy, particularly before about 1937. While we have not in general been able to quantify their exact spatial impact, it is an effect we have identified across a wide range of state activity:

1. **Monetary and Trade Policies (Chapter 2)**
   Before its 1931 abandonment the gold standard overvalued the pound and thus damaged the export oriented regional economies of outer Britain. By contrast the home market oriented industries largely concentrated in inner Britain were relatively unaffected. Several of these already enjoyed tariff protection against cheaper imports before free trade was abandoned more generally. Even after 1931, as managed currency and managed trading relations were developed, the immediate impact on depressed outer Britain was very limited. Thus import duties only benefited a few depressed industries. Most suffered more damage from what was effectively encouragement to other countries to further restrict imports. Though some export industries secured overseas markets by negotiated trade agreements, others suffered by the lack of relevant agreements. And, perhaps most important, financial orthodoxy continued to dominate central state budgets until the late 1930s, denying outer Britain a level of state spending sufficient to revive its depressed regions.

Within these key central policies, specific fields of intervention had more specific spatial effects:

2. **Defence Spending (Chapter 4)**
   The spatial allocation of naval contracts reinforced the problems

of the private shipbuilding areas of the north and Scotland. In contrast, the Royal Dockyards of the south were protected and their building profiles peaked in the worst depression years. With rearmament the balance shifted back to the private yards of outer Britain, but only after major long term damage had been done. The newer defence industry of aircraft was largely located in inner Britain anyway, together with the only Royal Ordnance Factories to survive post world war I restructuring. However the labour shortages and fears of air vulnerability that accompanied rearmament brought decentralised multi-plant production in these industries, increasingly in outer Britain. While this reduced a traditional pattern of uneveness manifest in unemployment, it laid the basis for a new hierarchical uneveness between subordinate branch plant economies in outer Britain and a headquarters/research and development economy in inner Britain.

3. **Industrial Rationalisation (Chapter 5)**

There was a marked contrast between industrial capital's functional requirements for state assisted restructuring of very fragmented and inefficient older industries and the continuing ideological adherence to laissez-faire. In steel the state largely intervened in an 'arm's length' way, via intermediaries. Initially it promoted banking capital's project of structural and spatial rationalisation, involving closures in outer Britain and new developments in the east midlands. However state allegiances shifted with the abandonment of free trade. From the mid-1930s the state was endorsing the stabilisation plans of the industry itself advanced via BISF.

In a new industry like electricity, capital's functional requirements for restructuring were greater and, because the state was already involved in the industry, ideological objections were weaker. Accordingly more decisive rationalisation was possible which made the industry particularly effective in servicing the emergent manufacturing economy of inner Britain.

4. **Labour and Unemployment (Chapter 6)**

The state played an important role in containing organised labour in the 1919-26 period, permitting what were perceived as the preconditions of successful capital accumulation on the pre-1914 model. Spatially this was important because organised labour had its main power bases in outer Britain and because the containment of organised labour thwarted the only real interwar challenge to the capitalist development process. After 1926 the state's labour policies were focussed mainly on unemployment. The principal instrument of state policy was unemployment maintenance pay. To offset fears that it inhibited labour mobility, however, transference and retraining were used in conjunction with benefit testing procedures to encourage movement from declining areas and sectors. Overall such policies intensified uneveness by removing the most able and active populations from declining areas and creating a high degree of direct personal dependence on the state in outer Britain.

5. **The Local State (Chapters 7-8)**

Underlying central state financial orthodoxy was a spatial orthodoxy that encouraged local state spending in areas of growth and inhibited it in areas of decline. Such system constraints had marked effects on the geography of local state capital spending on urban development, though local demand and political factors were also important. Broadly local state urban development spending was highest in 'inner outer Britain' (i.e. the buoyant parts of the north) and 'outer inner Britain' (the midlands, east Anglia and the outer south). It was lower in the inner south where infrastructure and amenity spending was high but, because of the buoyancy of private housebuilding, state housing expenditure was limited. And it was lower in depressed outer Britain where local financial weakness and weak demand combined with system constraints to inhibit municipal spending, even where needs were acute. From the mid-1930s such areas were increasingly assisted by central state actions, often involving delocalisation of important local state responsibilities.

6. **Regional Policies (Chapter 9)**

Although there were earlier local state initiatives to promote economic development, central state intervention to encourage development in particular geographical areas began only in the later 1930s. In quantitative terms the Special Areas policies achieved little, reflecting their origins in the 'gesture politics' of the 1930s National Governments. However they were associated with a remarkable series of qualitative innovations that were of long term significance. By 1939 the extent of state intervention in this aspect of the capitalist development process was still an unresolved question. But it was firmly on the political agenda.

Interpreting State Actions

In chapter 3 we identified three alternative interpretations of state action: capital-logic, class conflict and managerialist. While we have not formally tested the validity of any of these, they have provided many useful insights into the aspects of state intervention we have discussed in the empirical chapters. Consistently the most relevant of these interpretations has been the first. Thus, despite mass democracy and the rise of Labour as a political force, state policy between the wars appears, above all else, to have been an expression of the ideological and self defined functional requirements of capital. Such priorities were advanced in a variety of ways. Thus instrumentalist tendencies were still clearly apparent in financial and industrial policies and locally. However there was a gradual and pervasive shift to structural and hegemonic mechanisms within the developing institutional frameworks of state action and more widely within the new mass media.

Having said this though, we must immediately insert some important qualifications. Firstly the logic of capital was no simple, single thing. In practical terms, industry and banking, while sharing a general commitment to capitalist economic and social relations, frequently wanted different state policies. For much of the period, the priorities of banking capital were dominant and it was only at the very beginning and later part of the period that industrial capital assumed a stronger general position in state intervention. In sectors where the unification of banking and industry into monopoly finance capital advanced significantly, some very close linkages with state policy were apparent. However, since such shifts only occurred to a rather limited extent, these sources of influence on state policy, although out of proportion to their real importance within the economy, were also rather limited. Thus the 'rational' state assisted restructuring which might have accompanied a more strongly unified monopoly capitalism was not evident in interwar Britain. The state usually found itself supporting the projects of one fraction of capital against the interests of another. The tentative Keynesianism of the late 1930s began to paper over some of the cracks but did not alter the structure of capital.

A second important point is that the dominance of capital, albeit a fragmented capital, within interwar Britain reflected the outcome of the heightened class conflict of the early 1920s. The result was a successful containment of the labour movement. This prevented any serious socialist challenge to a state supported capitalist development process. Its particular significance is that the dominance of capitalist interests in interwar state actions may well have reflected the prevalent balance of class forces, rather than some automatic supremacy of capital within the state. Certainly state action in the immediate post-world war I period and, to a lesser extent, immediately before world war II reflected the heightened bargaining power of labour. And even contained labour in the later 1920s and 1930s was a considerable force that had to be appeased by the state. Thus, while we have detected no facet of interwar state policy which can be primarily explained in terms of working class action, few areas of state intervention were entirely without concessions to labour, even during the depression years when it was weakest. Thus, for all its links with the dominant orthodoxies of capitalism, even the dole was also a manifestation of the relative strength of labour in interwar Britain.

Thirdly we must admit that the state itself did exhibit a high degree of autonomy in some fields of its activity. Of the areas of intervention we have examined, this was most pronounced in naval spending. The Admiralty resisted the pressures of banking capital and the Treasury, and pursued narrowly defined naval objectives with some success. It was less apparent in the industrial field (like iron and steel) where the persistent unwillingness of governments to closely involve the state in restructuring limited the development of autonomous managerialist tendencies. However there were important exceptions and electricity supply particularly was widely regarded as a model of the rational managerialist state. Similar tendencies were apparent, albeit in a muted form, in other fields. Thus financial orthodoxy and, more especially, its spatial equivalent clearly showed the instrumental and structural impact of banking capital on state intervention. However the process by which such capital priorities were internalised and translated into state forms and practices added managerial elements that cannot be simply or directly derived from what bankers actually wanted. Thus civil servants in close consultation with the Bank of England extended the logic of banking capital into Treasury policies. These were then used by another set of civil servants, more insulated from contact with the City of London, as a basis for further extension into local loan sanction blacklists and labour transference policies. Thus the logic of capital was structurally present within the state, but modified by autonomous managerial elements derived from existing state forms and practices.

Overall though and despite these important qualifications, it remains the case that we can best understand interwar state actions in terms of the priorities of capital. This dominant linkage was reproduced spatially as state reinforcement of the uneven capitalist development process. The translation of the geography of capitalist development into that of state intervention was not perfect, largely because capitalist interests were neither unified nor unchanging and did not ever achieve complete dominance over state actions. But we must not make the mistake of overemphasising the exceptions. Above all else the interwar British state was a capitalist state and its actions in geographical space reflected that central characteristic.

Past and present: an agenda for future work

These conclusions on the state and the geography of interwar Britain are specific as to time and place. They constitute no eternal verities. Yet they are not without a rather pointed relevance for the 1980s. The mounting crisis of capitalism of the 1970s and 1980s has reproduced conditions remarkably similar in some important respects to those of the interwar depression. State policy has again come to reflect the priorities of banking capital (modified by delusions of world power grandeur that at least had some material basis in the interwar period). Old orthodoxies based on notions of international financial confidence have re-emerged. State spending has been cut. The frontiers of the state have been rolled back and the wider ideological legitimacy of capitalism, unfettered by state control, has been reasserted with a vengeance. Real unemployment has risen virtually to interwar levels, well beyond anything that has formerly been regarded as acceptable in the post-1945 period. Organised labour has been pushed on to the defensive. Geographically this has brought an intensifying unevenness between the south and outer Britain, reinforced by state actions. The regional policy goal of reducing spatial unevenness has been relegated to the gesture politics out of which it emerged at the end of the 1930s. Overall though we must not exaggerate the parallels. There are some important differences, not least in Britain's real world position. But the 1980s do seem frighteningly like a sumptuous remake of an old film. The actors and sets are different. The story has been updated to a modern setting. New scenes and characters have been inserted and the story may end differently. But the scenes, the themes and many elements of the scripting and characterisation are strangely familiar.

The point of all this is that it gives a particular relevance to geographical and other research on the interwar period, which in many ways prefigured the problems, spatial and otherwise, of 1980s Britain. No answers to today's concerns can be expected. The main factor in the resolution of the apparently intractable unemployment and spatial problems of the 1930s, war, is hardly to be recommended. But what research on the period can give is insights on the interrelationship between capitalist crisis, state action, and geographical space that enlarge understanding and provide a basis for sounder conceptualisation and theorisation about the nature and origins of the present crisis and the state's responses.

Much about the interwar period remains to be investigated. Few fields of state intervention remain entirely untouched, but few would not benefit by some explicitly geographical work. A few trails have already been blazed most notably on rural and natural resource issues (by Sheail 1981) and by non-geographers on housing (e.g. M.J. Daunton (ed) 1984). This book has hopefully opened up other fields for further exploration. But much remains to be done, for example on health, education, public transport, public utilities and many individual industries. The other agendas of modern geography could also be usefully applied to the interwar period. Thus it would be very useful to know more about the actions in space of specific organisations such as particular manufacturing firms, financial institutions like banks or building societies, or service sector firms like retailing chains. On the other side of industry more work on the geography of the labour movement and labour militancy is desirable and general understanding of an important phenomenon like the 1926 general strike would benefit greatly by the systematic spatial perspective of the geographer. In addition more coherent approaches to understanding places would be valuable. Thus the contemporary geographical interests in locality, which is proving valuable in comprehending the real experience of economic restructuring, could be usefully applied to the interwar period (which leaves an extremely rich legacy of local studies of various kinds). At the regional level there is scope for close co-operation with the work of economic historians, an increasing number of whom are showing sensitivity to spatial issues. The scope for theoretically informed quantitative work attempting the extremely difficult task of assessing the actual material impacts of state and private expenditure on regional and subregional economies is considerable.

We could go on with this list. Generally the interwar period warrants rather more attention from geography and related disciplines whatever the specific research focus. If properly conceived such work could built a real bridge of theoretical approach and subject matter between historical geography and the concerns of contemporary geography. History, as E.H. Carr remarked, is 'an unending dialogue between the present and the past', and we might reasonably claim this as also valid for historical geography. Hopefully this book has advanced that dialogue and encouraged others to participate.

Bibliography: List of Works Cited

This is a select list comprising only those works actually cited in the text. Both here and in the text I have tried to give clear information so that readers may, if they wish, refer to the same sources. However to avoid an unduly long list, primary sources, such as Public Record Office files, are not itemised separately here. Readers can find the exact files I used by following the detailed references in the text. Any reader wishing further information on this or any other matter is welcome to contact the author.

Abrams, M. 1945 *The Condition of the British People 1911- 45*, Gollancz: London

Adams, T. 1932 *Recent Advances in Town Planning*, Churchill: London

Aldcroft, D.H. 1968 *British Railways in Transition*, Macmillan: London

Andrews, P.W.S. and Brunner, E. 1951 *Capital Development in Steel*, Blackwell: Oxford

Andrews, P.W.S. and Brunner, E. 1955 *The Life of Lord Nuffield*, Blackwell: Oxford

Arnot, R.P. 1953 *The Miners: Years of Struggle*, Allen & Unwin: London

Ashworth, W. 1953 *Contracts and Finance*, HMSO/Longmans Green: London

Balfour Report, 1928 (Committee on Industry and Trade, Survey of Industries IV: The Metal Industries) HMSO: London

Balfour Report, 1929 (Final Report) Cmd 3282, HMSO: London

Barlow Report, 1940 (Royal Commission on the Distribution of the Industrial Population), Cmd 6153, HMSO: London

Barlow Report, 1938 Minutes of Evidence (to the above Royal Commission), HMSO: London

Beloff, M. 1975, The Whitehall Factor: The Role of the Higher Civil Service 1919-39, in Peele, G. and Cook, C. (eds), 1975, pp209- 31

Belshaw, D.G.R. 1955 *The Changing Geography of the Merthyr Valley*, Merthyr Tydfil Corporation, Merthyr Tydfil

Benham, F.C. 1941, *Great Britain Under Protection*, Macmillan: New York

Benjamin, D.K. and Kochin, L.A. 1979, Searching for an Explanation of Unemployment in Interwar Britain, *Journal of Political Economy* 87, No 3, pp441-78

Benjamin, D.K. and Kochin, L.A. 1982, Unemployment and Unemployment Benefits in Twentieth Century Britain: A Reply to our Critics, *Journal of Political Economy* 90, No 2, pp410- 36

Bennett, R.J. 1980, *The Geography of Public Finance*, Methuen: London

Bennett, W. 1951, *The History of Burnley: IV*, Lancashire, County Council: Burnley

Berwick-Sayers, W.C. 1938, *The Parks and Pleasure Grounds of Croydon*, Croydon Corporation: Croydon

Bevan, A. 1952 *In Place of Fear*, Heinemann: London

Bialer, U. 1975, The Danger of Bombardment from the Air and the Making of British Air Disarmament Policy 1932-4, in Bond, B. and Roy, I. (eds), pp202-15

Block, F. 1980, Beyond Relative Autonomy: State Managers as Historical

Subjects, in Miliband, R. and Saville, J. (eds), pp227- 42
Bloomfield, G. 1978, *The World Automotive Industry*, David and Charles: Newton Abbott
Bond, B. and Roy, I. (eds) 1975 *War and Society*, Croom Helm: London
Booth, A.E. 1978, An Administrative Experiment in Unemployment Policy in the Thirties, *Public Administration* 56, Summer, pp139-57
Booth, A.E. and Glynn, S. 1975, Unemployment in the Interwar Period: a Multiple Problem, *Journal of Contemporary History* 10, No 4, pp611-36
Bournville Village Trust 1941 *When We Build Again*, Allen & Unwin: London
Bowley, M. 1945 *Housing and the State 1919-44*, Allen & Unwin: London
Branson, N. 1979 *Poplarism 1919-25*, Lawrence and Wishart: London
Branson, N. and Heinemann, M. 1971 *Britain in the Nineteen Thirties*, Weidenfeld and Nicolson: London
Bretherton, R.F., Burchardt, F.A. and Rutherford, R.S.G. 1941 *Public Investment and the Trade Cycle in Great Britain*, Clarendon Press: Oxford
Brierley, W. 1981 (reissue) *Means Test Man*, Spokesman: Nottingham
Briggs, A. 1985 *The BBC: The First Fifty Years*, University Press: Oxford
Briggs, A. and Saville, J. (eds) 1977 *Essays in Labour History 1918-39*, Croom Helm: London
Briggs, E. and Deacon, A. 1973, The Creation of the Unemployment Assistance Board, *Policy and Politics* 2, No 1, September, pp43-62
Buchanan, C.M. 1970 *London Road Plans 1900-1970*, Greater London Research Report No 11, Greater London Council Intelligence Unit: London
Burgess, K. 1980 *The Challenge of Labour*, Croom Helm: London
Burn, D.L. 1961 (reissue) *The Economic History of Steel Making 1867-1939*, University Press: Cambridge
Burnham, J. 1941 *The Managerial Revolution*, John Day: New York
Burnley, County Borough of 1929 *Burnley: The Official Handbook*, CB Burnley: Burnley
Burnley, County Borough of, Improvement Department 1927, *Programme and Souvenir of Official Opening of Yorkshire Street Aqueduct*, CB Burnley: Burnley
Burnley Express and Advertiser, dates as cited in text
Burton, J.H. 1934 *The Finance of Local Government Authorities*, Griffin: London
Butler, D. 1963 *The Electoral System in Britain Since 1918*, Clarendon Press: Oxford
Buxton, N.K. 1979a, Introduction, in Buxton, N.K. and Aldcroft, D.H. (eds), pp9-23
Buxton, N.K. 1979b, Coal Mining, in Buxton, N.K. and Aldcroft, D.H. (eds), pp48-78
Buxton, N.K. and Aldcroft, D.H. (eds) 1979, *British Industry Between the Wars*, Scolar: London
Byatt, I.C.R. 1979 *The British Electrical Industry 1875-1914*, Clarendon Press: Oxford
Byrne, D. 1982a, Class and the Local State, *International Journal of Urban and Regional Research* 6, No 1, pp61-92
Byrne, D. 1982b, Class and the Local State: A Rejoinder to a Reply, *International Journal of Urban and Regional Research* 6, No 4, pp577-83
Calcott, M. 1980, The Nature and Extent of Political Change in the Interwar Years: the Example of County Durham, *Northern History* XVI, pp215-37

Campbell, R.H. 1979, The Scottish Office and the Special Areas in the 1930s, *Historical Journal*, 22, No 1, pp167-83
Capie, F. and Rodrik-Bali, G. 1982, Concentration in British Banking 1870-1920, *Business History* IV, No 3, November, pp280-92
Carr, J.C. and Taplin, W. 1962 *History of the British Steel Industry*, Blackwell: Oxford
Carter, G.F. 1925, Croydon Town Planning Schemes, *Journal of the Town Planning Institute*, XI, No 8, June, pp179-93
Castells, M. 1977, *The Urban Question*, Arnold: London
Census 1921. 1925a, *General Tables*, HMSO: London
Census 1921. 1925b, *Workplaces*, HMSO: London
Census 1921. 1927, *General Report*, HMSO: London
Census 1931. 1934, *Occupations*, HMSO: London
Census 1931. 1935, *Housing Report*, HMSO: London
Census of Production 1934 *Final Report of 4th Census of production 1930*, II, HMSO: London
Census of Production 1939 *Final Report of 5th Census of production 1935*, II, HMSO: London
Checkland, S. 1983 *British Public Policy 1776-1939*, University Press: Cambridge
Chester, D.N. (ed) 1957 *The Organisation of British Central Government 1914-1956*, Allen & Unwin: London
Chisholm, C. (ed) 1937 *Marketing Survey of the United Kingdom*, 2nd edition, Business Publications Ltd: London
Clegg, H. A. 1985 *A History of British Trade Unions since 1889: II: 1911-1933*, University Press: Oxford
Cole, G.D.H. 1948 *A History of the Labour Party from 1914*, Routledge and Kegan Paul
Collier, B. 1957 *The Defence of the United Kingdom*, HMSO: London
Collins, M. 1982, Unemployment in Interwar Britain: Still Searching for an Explanation, *Journal of Political Economy*, 90, No 2, pp369-79
CDP (Community Development Project) 1976 *Whatever Happened to Council Housing?*, Community Development Project Information and Intelligence Unit: London
CDP (Community Development Project) 1978 *Private Housing and the Working Class*, Benwell Community Development Project: Newcastle
Craig, P. 1986, The House that Jerry Built? Building Societies, the State and the Politics of Owner Occupation, *Housing Studies*, 1, No 2, April, pp87-108
Cross, R. 1982, How Much Voluntary Unemployment in Interwar Britain?, *Journal of Political Economy*, 90, No 2, pp380- 5
Crouch, C. (ed) 1979 *State and Economy in Contemporary Capitalism*, Croom Helm: London
Croydon Advertiser, dates as cited in text
CCM (Croydon Council Minutes) 1918-1939, *XVII-LVII, Parts I and II*, as cited in text
Croydon, County Borough of 1951, *Croydon Development Plan: Report of Survey and Written Analysis*, CB Croydon: Croydon
Croydon Times, dates as cited in text
Daly, M. and Atkinson, E. 1940, A Regional Analysis of Strikes 1921-36, *Sociological Review*, XII, pp216-23

Daniel, G.H. 1939, Labour Migration and Fertility, *Sociological Review, XI, pp370-400*

Daunton, M. J. 1977 *Coal Metropolis*, University Press: Leicester

Daunton, M.J. 1983, *House and Home in the Victorian City*, Arnold: London

Daunton, M.J. (ed) 1984 *Councillors and Tenants: Local Authority Housing in English Cities 1919-39*, University Press: Leicester

Davison, R.C. 1938 *British Unemployment Policy*, Longmans Green: London

Daysh, G.H.J. (ed) 1949 *Studies in Regional Planning*, Philip: London

Deacon, A. 1976, *In Search of the Scrounger*, Occasional Papers in Social Administration No 60, Bell: London

Deacon, A. 1977, Concession and Coercion: the Politics of Unemployment Insurance in the Twenties, in Briggs, A. and Saville, J. (eds), pp9-35

Dennison, S.R. 1939 *The Location of Industry and the Depressed Areas*, University Press: Oxford

Desmarais, R.H. 1971, The British Government's Strikebreaking Organisation and Black Friday, *Journal of Contemporary History*, 6, No 2, pp112-27

Desmarais, R.H. 1973, Strikebreaking and the Labour Government of 1924, *Journal of Contemporary History*, 8, No 4, pp165-75

Docherty, C. 1983 *Steel and Steel Workers: The Sons of Vulcan*, Heinemann: London

Dyos, H.J. and Aldcroft, D.H. 1974 *British Transport: An Economic Survey*, Penguin: Harmondsworth

Edgerton, D.E.H. 1984, Technical Innovation, Industrial Capacity and Efficiency: Public Ownership and the British Military Aircraft Industry, *Business History*, VI, No 3, November, pp247- 79

Edwards, K.C. 1949 *The East Midlands*, in Daysh, G.H.J. (ed), pp135-68

Elbaum, B. and Lazonick, W. (eds) 1986 *The Decline of the British Economy*, Clarendon Press: Oxford

Employment and Productivity, Department of 1971 *British Labour Statistics: Historical Abstract 1886-1968*, HMSO: London

Exell, A. 1981 *The Politics of the Production Line: Autobiography of an Oxford Car Worker*, History Workshop Journal: Oxford

Farnie, J.A. 1979 *The British Cotton Industry and the World Economy 1815-1896*, Clarendon Press: Oxford

Fearon, P. 1974, The British Airframe Industry and the State 1918-1935, *Economic History Review*, 2nd series, XVII, No 2, pp236-35

Fearon, P. 1979, Aircraft Manufacturing, in Buxton, N.K. and Aldcroft, D.H. (eds), pp216-40

Financial News, dates as cited in text

Finer, H. 1941 *Municipal Trading*, Allen & Unwin: London

Finer, H. 1950 *English Local Government*, 4th edition, Methuen: London

Fogarty, M.P. 1945 *Prospects of the Industrial Areas of Great Britain*, Methuen: London

Fogarty, M.P. 1947 *Plan Your Own Industries*, Blackwell: Oxford

Foreman-Peck, J.S. 1985, Seedcorn or Chaff? New Firm Foundation and the Performance of the Interwar Economy, *Economic History Review*, 2nd series, XVIII, No 3, pp402-22

Foster, J. 1976, British Imperialism and the Labour Aristocracy, in Shelley, J. (ed), pp3-57

Garrett, G. 1982 *Out of Liverpool: Stories of Sea and Land*, Merseyside Writers' Committee: Liverpool

GCM (Gateshead Council Minutes) 1918-30, 69-84

GCM (Gateshead Council Minutes) 1930-39, New Series, 1-9

Gateshead, County Borough of 1920-36 *Annual Reports of Medical Officer of Health and Chief Sanitary Officer 1919-35*, CB Gateshead: Gateshead

Gateshead, County Borough of 1937-40 *Public Health Department Reports 1936-9*, CB Gateshead: Gateshead

Gateshead Weekly Pictorial Post 1939, dates as cited in text

George, A.D. undated (c. 1982) *Aircraft Builders Around Manchester: the Industrial Archaeology of the Aircraft Factory*, Manchester Polytechnic Occasional Paper: Manchester

Gent, J.B. (ed) 1977 *Croydon: The Story of a Hundred Years*, 4th edition, Croydon Natural History and Scientific Society: Croydon

Gilbert, B.B. 1970 *British Social Policy 1914-1939*, Batsford:London

Gilbert, M. 1976 *Winston S. Churchill, V: 1922-39*, Heinemann: London

Gittins, D. 1982 *Fair Sex: Family Size and Structure 1900-1939*, Hutchinson: London

Glynn, S. and Booth, A. 1983, Unemployment in Interwar Britain: A Case for Re-learning the Lessons of the 1930s?, *Economic History Review*, 2nd series, XVI, No 3, pp329-48

Glynn, S. and Oxborrow, J. 1976 *Interwar Britain: A Social and Economic History*, Allen & Unwin: London

Glynn, S. and Shaw, S. 1981, Wage Bargaining and Unemployment, *Political Quarterly* 52, pp115-26

Gough, I. 1979 *The Political Economy of the Welfare State*, Macmillan: London

Greenleaf, W.H. 1983 *The British Political Tradition, I: The Ideological Inheritance*, Methuen: London

Greenwood, W. 1933 *Love on the Dole*, Cape: London

Grieco, M.S. 1985, Corby New Town: Planning and Imbalanced Development, *Regional Studies* 19, pp9-18

Hallsworth, H.M. 1935, The Shipbuilding Industry, in Research Committee of Economic Science and Statistics Section of British Association, pp247-57

Hallsworth, H.M. 1938, The Shipbuilding Industry, in Research Committee of Economic Science and Statistics Section of British Association, pp342-59

Hannah, L. 1979 *Electricity Before Nationalisation*, Macmillan: London

Hannah, L. 1983 *The Rise of the Corporate Economy*, 2nd edition, Methuen: London

Hannington, W. 1936 *Unemployed Struggles 1919-1936*, Lawrence and Wishart: London

Hannington, W. 1937, *The Problem of the Distressed Areas*, Gollancz: London

Harris, G.M. 1939, *Municipal Self-Government in Britain*, King: London

Hawson, H.K. 1968, *Sheffield: The Growth of a City*, Northend: Sheffield

Haxey, S. 1939 *Tory MP*, Gollancz: London

Health, Ministry of, 1921-39 *Local Taxation Returns/Local Government Financial Statistics 1919-1937*, HMSO: London

Health, Ministry of, 1936 *Report of the Overcrowding Survey in England and Wales 1936*, HMSO: London

Heim, C.E. 1983, Industrial Organisation and Regional Development in Interwar Britain, *Journal of Economic History*, XLIII, No 4, pp931-52

Heim, C.E. 1984, Limits to Intervention: the Bank of England and Industrial Diversification in the Depressed Areas, *Economic History Review*, 2nd series, XXXVII, No 4, pp533-50

Hennock, E.P. 1982, Central/Local Relations in England: an outline 1800-1950, *Urban History Yearbook*, University Press: Leicester, pp38-49

Hicks, U.K. 1970 *The Finance of the British Government 1920-36,* 2nd edition, Clarendon Press: Oxford

Higham, R. 1962 *Armed Forces in Peacetime: Britain 1918-1939, 1939*, Foulis: Henley

Higham, R. 1965, Government, Companies and National Defense: British Aeronautical Experience 1918-1945 as the Basis for a Broad Hypothesis, *Business History Review*, XXXIX, No 3, pp323- 47

Hobson, O.R. 1953 *A Hundred Years of the Halifax*, Batsford: London

Hoggart, K. 1984, Political Parties and Local Authority Capital Investment in English Cities 1966-1971, *Political Geography Quarterly*, 3, No 1,pp5-32

Holman Gregory Commission (Royal Commission on Unemployment Insurance) 1931, *1st (Interim) Report*, Cmd 3872, HMSO: London

Holman Gregory Commission (Royal Commission on Unemployment Insurance) 1932, *Final Report*, Cmd 4185, HMSO: London

Hornby, W. 1958 *Factories and Plant*, HMSO/Longmans Green: London

HC Deb 5s (House of Commons Debates 5th Series) Volumes and columns as cited in text

Howkins, A. and Lowerson, J. 1979 *Trends in Leisure 1919- 1939*, Sports Council and Social Science Research Council: London

Hume, J.R. and Moss, M.S. 1979 *Beardmore: the History of a Scottish Industrial Giant*, Heinemann: London

Hume, L.J. 1970, The Gold Standard and Deflation: Issues and Attitudes in the 1920s, in Pollard, S. (ed), pp122-45

IDAC (Import Duties Advisory Committee) 1937, *Report on the Present Position and Future Development of the Iron and Steel Industry*, Cmd 5507, HMSO: London

ITB (Industrial Transference Board) 1928 *Report*, Cmd 3156, HMSO: London

Industrial Unrest Commission 1917 *Report of the Commissioner for Scotland*, Cd 8669, HMSO: London

Ingot (pseud.) 1936 *The Socialisation of Iron and Steel*, Gollancz: London

Inman, P. 1957 *Labour in the Munitions Industries*, HMSO/Longmans Green: London

Jackson, A.A. 1973 *Semi Detached London*, Allen and Unwin: London

Jeffery, K. 1981, The British Army and Internal Security 1919-39, *Historical Journal*, 24, No 2, pp377-97

Jeffery, K. and Hennessey, P. 1983 *States of Emergency*, Routledge and Kegan Paul: London

Jefferys, J.B. 1954 *Retail Trading in Britain 1850-1950*, National Institute of Economic and Social Research Economic and Social Studies No 13, University Press: Cambridge

Jessop, B. 1982 *The Capitalist State*, Martin Robertson: Oxford

Jones, G. 1984 The 'Old Aunts': Governments, Politicians and the Oil Business, in Turner, J. (ed), pp146-62

Jones, L. 1957 *Shipbuilding in Britain: Mainly Between the Two World Wars*, University Press: Cardiff

Jones, M.E.F. 1985, The Regional Impact of an Overvalued Pound in the 1920s, *Economic History Review*, 2nd series, XXXVIII, No 3, pp 393-401

Kingsford, P. 1982 *The Hunger Marchers in Britain 1920-1939*, Lawrence and Wishart: London

Kirby, M.W. 1973, Government Intervention in Industrial Organisation: Coalmining in the 1930s, *Business History*, XV, No 2, pp160-73

Kirby, M.W. 1974, The Lancashire Cotton Industry in the Interwar Years: A Study in Organisational Change, *Business History*, XVI, No 2, pp145-59

Kirby, M.W. 1977, *The British Coalmining Industry 1870-1946*, Macmillan: London

Kirby, M.W. 1979, The Politics of State Coercion in Interwar Britain: The Mines Department of the Board of Trade 1920-1942, *Historical Journal*, 22, No 2, pp373-96

Klugmann, J. 1976, Marxism, Reformism and the General Strike in Shelley, J. (ed), pp58-107

Labour, Ministry of 1925- *Annual Reports 1923-*, (Command Publications), HMSO: London

Labour, Ministry of 1934 *Reports of Investigations into the Industrial Conditions in Certain Depressed Areas*, Cmd 4728, HMSO: London

Langan, M. and Schwarz, B. (eds) 1985 *Crises in the British State 1880-1930*, Hutchinson: London

Law, C.M. 1981 *British Regional Development Since World War I*, Methuen: London

Lazonick, W. 1986, The Cotton Industry, in Elbaum, B. and Lazonick, W. (eds), pp18-50

Lee, C.H. 1981, Regional Growth and Structural Change in Victorian Britain, *Economic History Review*, 2nd series, XXXIV, No 3, pp438-52

Lee, J.M. 1963 *Social Leaders and Public Persons*, Clarendon Press: Oxford

Lenman, B. 1977 *An Economic History of Modern Scotland*, Batsford: London

Liepmann, K.K. 1944 *The Journey to Work*, Kegan Paul, Trench, Trubner: London

Lloyd, I. 1978 *Rolls Royce: The Years of Endeavour*, Macmillan: London

Local Government in the Tyneside Area, Royal Commission on, 1937 *Report*, Cmd 5402, HMSO: London

Longstreth, F. 1979, The City, Industry and the State, in Crouch, C. (ed), pp157-90

Lonie, A.A. and Begg, H.M. 1979, Comment: Further Evidence of the Quest for an Effective Regional Policy, *Regional Studies*, 13, pp497-500

Lowe, R. 1978, The Failure of Consensus in Britain: the National Industrial Conference 1919-1921, *Historical Journal*, 21, No 3, pp649-75

Mair, D. 1986, Industrial Derating: Panacea or Palliative?, *Scottish Journal of Political Economy*, 33, No 2, pp159- 70

Manders, F.W.D. 1973 *A History of Gateshead*, Gateshead Corporation: Gateshead

Martin, J.E. 1966 *Greater London: An Industrial Geography*, Bell: London

Marwick, A. 1964, Middle Opinion in the Thirties: Planning, Progress and Political Agreement, *English Historical Review*, LXXIX, No 311, pp285-98

Marwick, A. 1967 *The Deluge*, Penguin: Harmondsworth
Marx, K. and Engels, F. 1967 (reissue) *The Communist Manifesto*, Penguin: Harmondsworth
May Committee (Committee on National Expenditure) 1931 *Report*, Cmd 3920, HMSO: London
McCord, N. 1979 *North East England*, Batsford: London
Melling, J. (ed) 1980 *Housing, Social Policy and the State*, Croom Helm: London
Mess, H.A. 1928 *Industrial Tyneside*, Benn: London
Metcalf, D., Nickell, S.J. and Floros, N. 1982, Still Searching for an Explanation of Unemployment in Interwar Britain, *Journal of Political Economy*, 90, No 2, pp386-99
M'Gonigle, G.C.M. and Kirby, J. 1936 *Poverty and Public Health*, Gollancz: London
Middleton, R. 1983, The Treasury and Public Investment: A Perspective on Interwar Economic Management, *Public Administration*, 61, pp351-70
Middleton, R. 1985, *Towards the Managed Economy*, Methuen: London
Miliband, R. 1969 *The State in Capitalist Society*, Weidenfeld and Nicolson: London
Miliband, R. and Saville, J. (eds) 1980 *The Socialist Register*, Merlin: London
Miller, F.M. 1974, National Assistance or Unemployment Assistance: the British Cabinet and Relief Policy 1932-3, *Journal of Contemporary History*, 9, No 2, pp163-84
Miller, F.M. 1976, The Unemployment Policy of the National Government 1931-6, *Historical Journal*, 19, No 2, pp453- 76
Miller, F.M. 1979, The British Unemployment Assistance Crisis of 1935, *Journal of Contemporary History*, 14, No 2, pp329- 52
Miller, M. and Church, R.A. 1979, Motor Manufacturing, in Buxton, N.K. and Aldcroft, D.H. (eds), pp179-215
Millett, J.D. 1940 *The Unemployment Assistance Board*, Allen and Unwin: London
Mitchell, B.R. and Deane, P. 1962 *Abstract of British Historical Statistics*, University Press: Cambridge
Mitchell, B.R. and Jones, H.G. 1971 *Second Abstract of British Historical Statistics*, University Press: Cambridge
Mitchell, M. 1985, The Effects of Unemployment on the Social Condition of Women and Children in the 1930s, *History Workshop Journal*, Issue 19, pp105-27
Moggridge, D.E. 1969 *The Return to Gold*, University Press: Cambridge
Morris, M. 1976 *The General Strike*, Penguin: Harmondsworth
Moser, C.A. and Scott, W. 1961 *British Towns*, Oliver and Boyd: Edinburgh
Mowat, C.L. 1955 *Britain Between the Wars 1918-1940*, Methuen: London
NHTPC (National Housing and Town Planning Council) 1910 *Report on Housing and Sanitary Conditions of Burnley*, NHTPC: Rochdale
Navy Estimates 1919-1939 (Command Publications), HMSO: London
Nevin, E. 1970, The Origins of Cheap Money 1931-2, in Pollard, S. (ed), pp67-84
Newcastle Evening Chronicle, dates as cited in text
Nockolds, H. 1978 *Lucas: The First Hundred Years II: The Successors*, David and Charles: Newton Abbott

North East Lancashire Joint Town Planning Advisory Committee 1929 *Regional Planning Report*, NE Lancashire Jt. TP Ctte: Burnley
O'Connor, J. 1973 *The Fiscal Crisis of the State*, St Martins: New York
Orbach, L.F. 1977 *Homes for Heroes*, Seeley Service: London
Ormerod, P.A. and Worswick, G.D.N. 1982, Unemployment in Interwar Britain, *Journal of Political Economy*, 90, No 2, pp400- 9
Owen, A.D.K. 1937, The Social Consequences of Industrial Transference, *Sociological Review*, XXIX, pp331-54
Page, E.C. 1985 *Political Power and Bureaucratic Power*, Wheatsheaf: Brighton
Parkinson, J.R. 1960 *The Economics of Shipbuilding*, University Press: Cambridge
Parkinson, J. R. 1979, Shipbuilding in Buxton, N. K. and Aldcroft, D. H. (eds), pp79-102
Parsons, D.W. 1986 *The Political Economy of British Regional Policy*, Croom Helm: London
Payne, P.L. 1979 *Colvilles and the Scottish Steel Industry*, Clarendon Press: Oxford
Peacock, A.T. and Wiseman, J. 1967 *The Growth of Public Expenditure in the United Kingdom*, 2nd edition, Allen & Unwin: London
Peele, G. and Cook, C. (eds) 1975 *The Politics of Reappraisal 1918-1939*, Macmillan: London
Peden, G.C. 1983, The Treasury as the Central Department of the Government 1919-1939, *Public Administration* 61, pp371- 85
Peden, G.C. 1984a, The Treasury View on Public Works and Unemployment in the Interwar Period, *Economic History Review*, 2nd series, XXXVII, No 2, pp167-81
Peden, G.C. 1984b, Arms, Government and Businessmen 1935-45, in Turner, J. (ed) pp130-45
Pembroke and Rosyth Dockyards 1925: Savings to be Effected by Reduction to a Care and Maintenance Basis, Cmd 2554, HMSO: London
Pepler, G.L. 1923, Open Spaces, *Town Planning Review*, X, pp11-24
Phillips, G.A. 1976 *The General Strike*, Weidenfeld and Nicolson: London
Pickard, T. 1982 *Jarrow March*, Alison and Busby: London
Pilgrim Trust 1938 *Men Without Work*, University Press: Cambridge
Pinder, J. (ed) 1981 *Fifty Years of Political and Economic Planning: Looking Forward 1931-81*, Heinemann: London
Pitfield, D.E. 1973 *Labour Migration and the Regional Problem 1920-1939*, unpublished PhD Thesis: University of Stirling
Pitfield, D.E. 1974, Regional Economic Policy and the Long Run: Innovation and Location in the Iron and Steel Industry, *Business History*, XVI, No 2, pp160-74
Pitfield, D.E. 1978, The Quest for an Effective Regional Policy 1934-7, *Regional Studies*, 12, pp429-43
Plowden, W. 1973 *The Motor Car and Politics in Britain*, Penguin: Harmondsworth
PEP (Political and Economic Planning) 1936 *Report on the Supply of Electricity in Great Britain*, PEP: London
PEP (Political and Economic Planning) 1937 *Report on the British Social Services*, PEP: London

PEP (Political and Economic Planning) 1939 *Report on the Location of Industry*, PEP: London

Pollard, S. 1962 *The Development of the British Economy 1914-50*, Arnold: London

Pollard, S. 1970 *The Gold Standard and Employment Policies Between the Wars*, Methuen: London

Postgate, R.W., Wilkinson, E. and Horrabin, J.F. 1927 *A Worker's History of the General Strike*, Plebs League: London

Powell, W.R. (ed) 1973 *Victoria County History of Essex*, VI, University Press: Oxford

Priestley, J.B. 1934 *English Journey*, Heinemann/Gollancz: London

Pronay, N. 1982, The Political Censorship of Films in Britain Between the Wars, in Pronay, N. and Spring, D.W. (eds), pp98- 125

Pronay, N. and Spring, D.W. (eds) *Propaganda, Politics and Film 1918-1945*, Macmillan: London

PRO (Public Records Office, Kew), Files as cited in text

Pugh, M. 1982 *The Making of Modern British Politics 1869- 1939*, Blackwell: Oxford

Ramsden, J.A. 1982, Baldwin and Film, in Pronay, N. and Spring, D.W. (eds), pp126-43

Read, D. 1972 *Edwardian England*, Harrap: London

Reader, W.J. 1968 *Architect of Air Power*, Collins: London

Reader, W.J. 1975 *Imperial Chemical Industries: A History II: The First Quarter Century*, University Press: Oxford

Rees, G. 1969, *St Michael*, Weidenfeld and Nicolson: London

Research Committee of Economic Science and Statistics Section of the British Association 1935 *Britain in Depression*, Pitman: London

Research Committee of Economic Science and Statistics Section of the British Association 1938 *Britain in Recovery*, Pitman: London

Richards, J. 1984 *The Age of the Dream Palace*, Routledge and Kegan Paul: London

Richardson, H.W. and Aldcroft, D.H. 1967 *Building in the British Economy Between the Wars*, Allen & Unwin: London

Richardson, K. 1972 *Twentieth Century Coventry*, Macmillan: London

Robson, W.A. 1939 *The Government and Misgovernment of London*, Allen & Unwin: London

Roskill, S. 1968 *Naval Policy Between the Wars I: 1920-29*, Collins: London

Rowntree, B.S. 1941 *Poverty and Progress*, Longmans Green: London

Royal Institute of British Architects Art Standing Committee et al (20 organisations listed) 1923 *Destroying an English Work of Art: the Case for the Preservation of the Historical and Beautiful Building, the Whitgift Hospital, Croydon*, RIBA etc.: London

Ryan, P. 1976, The Poor Law in 1926, in Morris, M. pp358- 78

Ryder, R. 1984, Council Housing in County Durham 1900-1939: The Local Implementation of National Policy, in Daunton, M. (ed) pp39- 100

Schwarz, B. 1985, The Corporate Economy 1890-1929, in Langan, M. and Schwarz, B. (eds) pp80-103

Scopes, F. 1968 *The Development of Corby Works*, Stewarts and Lloyds: no place of publication cited; London?

Scott, J. and Griff, C. 1984 *Directors of Industry*, Polity: Cambridge

Scott, J.D. 1962 *Vickers: A History*, Weidenfeld and Nicolson: London
Select Committee on Estimates 1932 *Minutes of Evidence*, HMSO: London
Seymour-Ure, C. 1975, The Press and the Party System Between the Wars, in Peele, G. and Cook, C. (eds), pp232-57
Sharpe, L.J. and Newton, K. 1984 *Does Politics Matter?*, Clarendon Press: Oxford
Sheail, J. 1981 *Rural Conservation in Interwar Britain*, Clarendon Press: Oxford
Sheail, J. 1983, Deserts of the Moon: The Mineral Workings Act and the Restoration of Ironstone Workings in Northamptonshire 1936-1951, *Town Planning Review* 54, pp405-24
Skidelsky, R. 1967 *Politicians and the Slump*, Macmillan: London
Slaven, A. 1977, A Shipyard in Depression: John Browns of Clydebank 1919-1938, *Business History*, XIX, No 2, pp192-217
Smith, R. 1974, Multi-Dwelling Building in Scotland 1750-1970: A Study Based on Housing in the Clyde Valley, in Sutcliffe, A. (ed), pp207-43
Smith, W. 1949 *An Economic Geography of Great Britain*, Methuen: London
Smithies, E.D. 1974 *The Contrast Between North and South in England 1918-1939: A Study of Economic, Social and Political Problems with Particular Reference to the Experience of Burnley, Halifax, Ipswich and Luton*, unpublished PhD Thesis, University of Leeds
South Tyneside Regional Planning Scheme 1928 *Report of the Joint Committee*, South Tyneside Regional Joint Town Planning Committee: Gateshead
Southall, H. 1986, Regional Unemployment Patterns Amongst Skilled Engineers in Britain 1851-1914, *Journal of Historical Geography* 12, No 3, pp268-86
Special Areas (England and Wales), Commissioner for 1935-8, *Reports* Command Publications, HMSO: London
Special Areas (Scotland), Commissioner for 1936-8, *Reports*, Command Publications, HMSO: Edinburgh
Stevenson, J. 1977 *Social Conditions in Britain between the Wars*, Penguin: Harmondsworth
Strachey, J. 1934 *The Coming Struggle for Power*, Gollancz: London
Sutcliffe, A. (ed) 1974 *Multi-Storey Living*, Croom Helm: London
Swenarton, M. 1981 *Homes Fit For Heroes*, Heinemann: London
Swenarton, M. and Taylor, S. 1985, The Scale and Nature of the Growth of Owner Occupation in Britain between the Wars, *Economic History Review*, 2nd series, XXXVIII, No 3, pp373-92
Sykes, J. 1926 *The Amalgamation Movement in English Banking 1825-1924*, King: London
Taylor, A.J.P. 1965 *English History 1914-1945*, Clarendon Press: Oxford
Thomas, M. 1983, Rearmament and Economic Recovery in the late 1930s, *Economic History Review*, 2nd series, XXXVI, No 4, pp552-73
Tolliday, S. 1984, Tariffs and Steel 1916-1934: The Politics of Industrial Decline, in Turner, J. (ed), pp50-75
Tolliday, S. 1986, Steel and Rationalisation Policies 1918-1950, in Elbaum, B. and Lazonick, W. (eds9, pp82-108
Tout, H. 1938 *The Standard of Living in Bristol*, Arrowsmith: Bristol
Transport, Ministry of 1926 *Report of the Committee to Review the National Problem of the Supply of Electrical Energy*, HMSO: London

Transport, Ministry of 1930 *Census of Mechanically Propelled Road Vehicles 1929*, HMSO: London
Turner, J. 1984a, The Politics of Business, in Turner, J. (ed), pp1-19
Turner, J. 1984b, The Politics of Organised Business in the First World War, in Turner, J. (ed), pp33-49
Turner, J. (ed) 1984, *Businessmen and Politics*, Heinemann: London
UAB (Unemployment Assistance Board) 1936- *Annual Reports 1935-* (Command Publications), HMSO: London
Vaizey, J. 1974 *The History of British Steel*, Weidenfeld and Nicolson: London
Vinson, A. J. 1980, Poor relief, public assistance and the maintenance of the unemployed in Southampton between the wars, *Southern History*, 2, pp179-225
Wakefield, City of 1920-1940 *Report on Public Health and Sanitary State of City of Wakefield 1919-1939*, CB Wakefield: Wakefield
Wakefield, City of 1932 *Wakefield Commercially Considered*, CB Wakefield: Wakefield
Wakefield, City of undated (c1950) *City of Wakefield: Number of Homes Erected During Years 1878-1950*, typescript, Wakefield Reference Library
Wakefield Express, dates as cited in text
Ward, S.V. 1982a, Interwar Britain: A Study of Government Spending, Planning and Uneven Economic Development, *Built Environment*, 7, No 2, pp96-108
Ward, S.V. 1982b, Class and the Local State: A Reply, *International Journal of Urban and Regional Research* 6, No 4, pp567-76
Ward, S.V. 1983 *Approaches to Public Intervention in Shaping the Urban Environment 1919-1939*, unpublished PhD Thesis, University of Birmingham
Ward, S.V. 1984a, List Q: A Missing Link in Interwar Public Investment, *Public Administration* 62, pp348-58
Ward, S.V. 1984b, Local Authorities and Industrial Promotion 1900-1939: Rediscovering a Lost Tradition, in Ward, S.V. (ed) pp25- 49
Ward, S.V. 1984 (ed) *Planning and Economic Change: An Historical Perspective*, Oxford Polytechnic, Department of Town Planning Working Paper No 78: Oxford
Ward, S.V. 1985, British Boosterism: An Area of Interest for Planning Historians, *Planning History Bulletin* 7, No 2, pp30- 8
Ward, S.V. 1986, Implementation Versus Planmaking: The Example of List Q and the Depressed Areas 1922-1939, *Planning Perspectives* 1, No 1, pp3-26
Warren, K. 1970 *The British Iron and Steel Sheet Industry Since 1840*, Bell: London
Warren, K. 1979, Iron and Steel, in Buxton, N.K. and Aldcroft, D.H. (eds) pp103-28
Waters, M. 1984, Dockyard and Parliament: A Study of Unskilled Workers in Chatham Yard 1860-1900, *Southern History* 6, pp123- 38
Webster, C. 1982, Healthy or Hungry Thirties? *History Workshop Journal* 13, pp110-29
Weightman, G. and Humphries, S. 1984 *The Making of Modern London 1914-1939*, Sidgwick and Jackson: London
Wigham, E. 1982 *Strikes and the Government 1893- 1981*, Macmillan: London
Wilkinson, E. 1939 *The Town That Was Murdered*, Gollancz: London

Williamson, P. 1984, Financiers, the Gold Standard and British Politics 1925-31, in Turner, J. (ed) pp105-29
Winch, D. 1969 *Economics and Policy: A Historical Study*, Hodder and Stoughton: London

INDEX